The Dalit Movement in India

This book analyses new 'practices' and discussions among Dalit
activists since the 1990s and shows how these practices have
both shaped and changed social relations. It is an attempt
to reach behind the surface of the contemporary
Dalit movement.

The discussion moves beyond the borders of India to take into
account broader geographical and theoretical contexts.
The author follows Dalit activists in various networks
and explores their linkages—from Buddha *viharas* in
India and Britain, to local practices in the city of
Lucknow, and further to the international arena
and the global justice movement.

The book presents its arguments through various concepts
like network, power, and public sphere. Based on extensive
fieldwork, the study also contributes to the debate on
how a transnational movement may be understood in
anthropological terms.

The Dalit Movement in India
Local Practices, Global Connections

Eva-Maria Hardtmann

OXFORD

UNIVERSITY PRESS

OXFORD
UNIVERSITY PRESS

Oxford University Press is a department of the University of Oxford.
It furthers the University's objective of excellence in research, scholarship,
and education by publishing worldwide. Oxford is a registered trademark of
Oxford University Press in the UK and in certain other countries

Published in India by
Oxford University Press
22 Workspace, 2nd Floor, 1/22 Asaf Ali Road, New Delhi 110002, India
© Oxford University Press 2009

First Edition published in 2009
Oxford India Paperbacks 2010
25th impression 2022

ISBN-13: 978-0-19-806548-7
ISBN-10: 0-19-806548-5

Typeset in NewBrunswick 10/12
by Excellent Laser Typesetters, Pitampura, Delhi 110 034
Printed in India by Manipal Technologies Limited, Manipal

Contents

Acknowledgements

This volume is the outcome of long-term anthropological field-work among Dalit activists. It is carried out in periods since the beginning of the 1990s, up to the more recent World Social Forum-process in 2008. It is a partly reworked and updated version of my thesis *'Our Fury is Burning'—Local Practice and Global Connections in the Dalit Movement* (Department of Social Anthropology, Stockholm University, 2003). I collected new material during my more recent projects on Dalit activists in relation to United Nations and also as part of the global justice movement, which has now been incorporated. An extended discussion on Dalit feminism and gender relations has further been included.

I thank Stockholm Anthropological Research on India (SARI) and my colleagues in the Department of Social Anthropology in Stockholm University for providing a stimulating environment for research on India, globalization, and gender-issue. During my time of initiation to the movement in India I was affiliated to the Centre for the Study of Regional Development, School of Social Sciences in Jawaharlal Nehru University, which facilitated my learning about the movement. Thanks also to the Dalit Research Institutes and Dalit Centers in different parts of India, where valuable work related to scheduled castes and Dalits are carried out.

My greatest gratitude goes naturally to all the Dalit activists, Dalit scholars, Dalit friends, and others in India and Great Britain who have been involved at different stages during my fieldwork. They have tirelessly discussed with me and some of our topics have been dwelt on for days, weeks and even years. I have been invited for dinners, stayed during longer periods in their homes, been taken to offices, teashops, and coffeehouses as well as to speeches, meetings, and celebrations, and I was introduced to their colleagues, relatives, and friends. Many thoughts were shared on the way to places they told me to visit and occasions they suggested me to attend. They have carried me along on foot, on scooters, in trains, buses, cars or rickshaws to villages and suburbs, into the fields, and up to the hills. This is just another way to say that without their company and guidance this book would have never been written. Everybody may not agree on all points in this volume, but they have all in different ways generously shared their experiences with me, debated, constructively criticized, and encouraged me. The volume is dedicated to you, who all took out your time to guide me during fieldwork.

My husband and colleague, Per Ståhlberg as well as our daughters Saga Li and Henny have shared it all with me. I owe them more than thanks!

I would like to thank the editors in Oxford University Press, New Delhi who took the manuscript through the different stages and meticulously read and commented on it in the most professional way. Thanks also to the Department of Research Co-operation (SAREC) within the Swedish International Development Cooperation Agency (SIDA) for extensively financing the work.

Prologue
A Touch of the Dalit Movement

Dalit[1] activists are today visible in a multitude of contexts, from their local networks and practices in India to their global involvements, for instance, at the World Social Forum in Nairobi, Kenya, in 2007. It is almost two decades since I interacted with Dalit activists for the first time. My journey into the movement chanced to begin in Bangalore in South India in 1991. I had arrived there by train from New Delhi and knew about a few Dalit organizations in Bangalore. The day after my arrival I phoned the numbers I had jotted down in my notebook. For a few weeks some Dalit activists living in the city, one woman but otherwise men, would come to take me to their own villages nearby, to show me the situation of their families and friends. Most of these activists were studying in colleges or at the university. Although I had read about the movement and been

[1] Scholars and activists use the term 'Dalit' in more ways than one: according to the criteria of either social status or economic position. A common usage among scholars, activists as well as the public is to mean the so-called untouchables, or those who are officially defined as 'Scheduled Castes' (SCs), a category which was coined in 1935 when backward groups were listed on a schedule to get access to reserved seats. The most common usage among today's scholars and activists seems to be to include all caste groups that were traditionally regarded as 'untouchables', although not all of them are now among the official list of 'SCs'. Sometimes 'Scheduled Tribes' (STs) and even 'Other Backward Classes' (OBCs) are included. The other definition in which an economic criterion is used includes the economically disadvantaged, regardless of caste category. This has been a common usage among Marxist scholars. More recently Dalit activists have come to include other categories outside of India in their definition, like Burakumin in Japan, to mention just one. In this study 'Dalit' will be used as an emic concept, referring to people who use it self-ascribingly.

to Indian villages during earlier travels, this was the first time I interacted with Dalit activists and came in touch with their thoughts and emotions. These activists pointed out that the SCs were still economically exploited and socially discriminated against. They all argued that there was one main reason for this: Hinduism.

Traditionally, the so-called untouchables were seen as unclean in a religious sense, and presumed to defile others by their touch or presence. This meant that they had to live in separate areas, at some distance from others. They were born for the purpose of serving others, it was believed, and for carrying out the occupations dealing with ritually defiled materials. Education, or rather all kinds of reading and writing, was not meant for those who lack a *varna*,[2] the scriptures stated. In 1991, when I visited Bangalore, the Dalit activists took me to their native villages to show me that the SCs still often lived in the same conditions as they had done traditionally. They lived segregated at a distance from the main village in *kaccha* houses, mud huts, easily destroyed by the monsoon and lacking the most basic amenities such as water and electricity. This should be compared with the considerably larger concrete *pakka* houses, in the main village, often with electricity as well as water easily available.

In spite of working full time, seven days a week, as agricultural labourers, the income of the relatives and friends of these activists was minimal. I was struck by the fact that parents, working at the height of their capacity, *still* did not earn enough to satisfy the most basic needs of their children. In spite of the odds, the Dalit activists whom I met had in one way or another managed to move to the city of Bangalore to get an education. Some of them had found work as government employees due to affirmative action. Their material standards had risen, but they still had a low status in society. Even in an anonymous urban setting their community membership was often easily traced

[2] There are four varnas, according to Hindu scriptures—the Brahmins (priests), Kshatriyas (warriors), Vaishyas (merchants), and Shudras (servants). Below these lacking a varna and outside the varna system, are the so-called untouchables, as a fifth category (see, for example, Dumont 1980[1966]: 65ff).

by their surname, and they now felt discriminated against in more subtle ways.

One evening during my first week in Bangalore, after a day spent in a village, I had an appointment with a Dalit activist, a journalist in his 30s whom I had never met before. In an initial attempt to understand my curiosity for the movement, he began by putting to me the question: 'What do you *feel* when you see the situation of our people?' Overwhelmed by all the impressions during the day I felt very uncomfortable with the question, as I did not really have an answer, but still knew that it was reasonable that I ought to have one.

About a week later another Dalit activist in his 20s, studying sociology in Bangalore, took me to his village an hour's drive away. He had been born and brought up there and his parents and siblings still lived there. They lived at a distance from the main village, in kaccha houses without electricity and running water which had to be fetched from far away. They worked as agricultural labourers at below even the minimum wage. In the late afternoon, after a day in the company of his family and friends, we were sitting outside his parents' hut, drinking a cup of tea. He nodded towards the hut and asked me the same question the journalist had done a week earlier: 'What do you *feel* when you see this?' This time I was more prepared and, if not in a very articulate manner, I could express some of my emotions. To my reply I also added a counter-question: 'What do *you* feel?' His answer came without hesitation: 'You see—our fury is burning.' This was not the last time I was to hear the same words. Dalit activists in villages as well as cities repeated it, across the country. The words may have differed, but I was left in no doubt about the meaning.

What, then, is the meaning of emotions, such as joy and anger, happiness and fury? I will not go into the psychological aspects of this, but agree with Lutz and Abu-Lughod that 'emotion talk must be interpreted as *in* and *about* social life' (1990: 11, italics in original). Talk of happiness and fury does not first of all, or at least not only, refer to an internal and psychological state of the individual. Discourses on emotion are also 'commentaries on the practices essential to social relations' (ibid.: 19, italics in original). Talk of anger (or the discourse of emotion) is, furthermore, a form of social action that creates effects in the

world (Lutz and Abu-Lughod 1990: 12). In the following chapters I shall not deal exclusively or even mainly with emotion talk,
but with practices among Dalit activists, including discourses
in a broader sense. Discourses (and this includes emotion talk)
will thus be seen in a Foucauldian manner, as '...practices
that systematically form the objects of which they speak'
(Foucault 1972: 46). To make myself clear, I shall be occupied
with practices among Dalit activists, including discourses, which
I regard as able to form and change social relations.

Appadurai (1990) has noted the importance of praise in
the 'Hindu world', that is, praise of the divine as well as superiors: 'praise (or, more exactly, flattery) is one of the standard
means not simply to mark hierarchy but to mark dependence'
(ibid.: 97, parenthesis in original). The activists in the Dalit
movement, however, do not want to mark either hierarchy or
dependence in relation to the divine or superiors in the 'Hindu
world'. This study will not therefore be about the expressed
praise or flattery of which Appadurai speaks. On the contrary,
the focus in the following chapters will be on the contempt
and fury expressed among Dalit activists, to signal distance
from the 'Hindu world'—a world they claim as guilty of the
discrimination to which SCs are exposed.

It is not a new phenomenon of the last decade that so-called
untouchables express an identity different from that of the
Hindus. Many of the Dalit activists who figure in this study
were born into the category of Chamars,[3] traditionally leather
workers and regarded as 'untouchables'. In a classic book about
the Chamars, Briggs (1995 [1920]) observed already early in
the twentieth century the difference between a self-ascribed
identity and an identity ascribed by others.[4] Although the
Chamar does not meet any of the determining tests of Hinduism, he is [classified in the census as] a Hindu, Briggs wrote.[5]

[3] They are the most numerous among the SCs in North India today.
[4] Carroll (1978) has discussed in an interesting way how the colonial
census reports strengthened and even created hierarchical categori-
zations of caste groups in India. The census reports were attempts by
the British to come to grips with the complex Indian society.
[5] The Chamars were categorized as Hindus in the 1911 census report
in the United Provinces (today's Uttar Pradesh) (Briggs 1995[1920]:
121f).

He also commented in a note that the Chamar does not usually call himself a Hindu (ibid.: 19).

Half a century later, in the 1970s, Juergensmeyer, who carried out fieldwork among activists involved in movements against untouchability, had a street-side conversation with some SC sweepers and municipal employees in New Delhi. Discussing social change and religion with them he concludes: '...they were emphatic about one point: they were not Hindus' (Juergensmeyer 1982: 1).

The Dalit movement has grown tremendously all over India since the beginning of the 1990s. Today, its networks are spread across the globe, including Dalit activists in the diaspora as well as non-Indian sympathizers. Outside of India some people may have received their first glimpse of this movement in the media, reporting from the United Nations World Conference against Racism, Racial Discrimination, Xenophobia and Related Intolerance in Durban, South Africa, in 2001 which focused on racism and related issues. Dalit activists have also, since its inception in 2001, attended the World Social Forums in Porto Alegre, Brazil, Mumbai, India, and in Nairobi, Kenya. It was, however, in 2004 when the Forum was arranged in Mumbai that Dalit activists had the possibility to attend en masse. In international media and over the Internet one could see Dalit activists demonstrating against caste discrimination; Dalit dance and music troupes were also seen performing.

A closer look at the Dalit activists in Durban or Mumbai revealed that many of them wore a small badge which, if one zoomed in on it, had a picture of B.R. Ambedkar (1891–1956), the most important personage within the movement. He was born a so-called untouchable, received higher education, and became the first Law Minister in independent India. He is also known for his denunciation of Hinduism that culminated in a mass conversion to Buddhism which he led in 1956.

Outside of India M.K. Gandhi (1869–1948) is probably the name most closely associated with the struggle of the so-called untouchables. But among the Dalit activists he is condemned and the respectful title 'Mahatma', the Great Soul, is never added to his name. The criticism against him is not because of his *satyagraha*s, the method of non-violent resistance, often used by Dalit activists themselves to achieve different goals. The reason for their disapproval is that he wanted to include the so-called untouchables among the Hindus. Most of us have been taught that the so-called untouchables are part of the Hindu caste system and traditionally placed at the bottom of the caste hierarchy. To M.K. Gandhi it was self-evident that they were Hindus, and his life mission was to include them on a premise of equality among the Hindus. In the following chapters, I shall discuss how Dalit activists identify and present themselves in a different manner. Whether so-called untouchables are Hindus or not is more than ever a contested issue. In the contemporary Dalit movement, the activists have become even more explicit and elaborate on the point that they are not Hindus.

1

Introduction

A social movement may attract you or put you off. Movements differ from one another, and you may sympathize with or condemn the activists. They may be in favour of global justice, demonstrate support of religious fundamentalism, turn inwards to sect-like hidden networks or against politicians at summit meetings. The activists may be engaged in non-violent debates or in violence like throwing stones. Some people are involved, partly or wholeheartedly, in a movement; others are silently sympathizing with or condemning one or the other issue of a movement. For some people activism may be a matter of survival, while for others it is an activity on the side regarding some minor issue in their lives. Seldom, however, do movement activists leave other people totally indifferent. Their ideas and activities are often reported in the media, and people discuss them and have opinions about them. In that sense social movements are familiar to all of us.

On the other hand, for those who are not the insiders in a movement, the logic of the activists may be difficult to grasp. At times arguments and activities may appear contradictory or even totally incomprehensible. One reason may be that if we are not personally engaged in a movement, we just catch glimpses of it—from demonstration placards or brief interviews with activists, for example. To the activists involved in a movement, it is altogether a different story. They belong within a common framework within which they work and understand each other. The tacit knowledge which they come to share over time makes them part of one and the same cultural discourse and they often understand each other's actions without words. When it comes to grasping this knowledge in a social movement, anthropologists may be well suited for the task. It is through fieldwork that I believe anthropologists could give some new and complementary insights to theories about social movements, still a relatively new domain within the anthropological discipline. Chapter 2 will for this reason be devoted to relating the method of anthropological fieldwork to theories about social movements.

INTRAPUBLIC VERSUS INTERPUBLIC RELATIONS

This study is an anthropological network-ethnography of the Dalit movement, which is in the process of becoming globalized. The movement will be portrayed as a network of various internal networks, reaching out transnationally beyond the border of the Indian nation-state. It will also be shown as a part of global networks, a network within networks in a broader sense.[1] This is to emphasize that the Dalit movement is part of, and belongs within, something wider. The meanings produced in the Dalit networks occur within a broader global field, structured by power relations. In the vein of Fraser (1992), Alvarez (2000), and Randeria (2007) among others, I take a theoretical stand that emphasizes that the social fields where the movement activists produce meaning, from the local to the global contexts are structured by different power relations.

The flow of meanings produced by the Dalit activists has historically been constrained by the broader networks, which they were part of or were related to but where they were silent or muted, such as those in Indian civil society. The exclusion over the years of Dalit activists from the public sphere led to the formation of an alternative counterpublic from the 1920s onwards. Although their flow of meaning has increasingly trickled out to the Indian public during the twentieth century, and to a greater extent during the recent past, its reach in the public sphere is still to only a very limited degree.[2]

[1] Hannerz has discussed these kinds of complex networks in terms of a 'global ecumene' (1989, 1992b). This was a way of getting away from the simplistic image of the world as a mosaic of separate, geographically localized cultures.

[2] For example, this is evident from the writings by Zelliot (1992) and Omvedt (1994a).

I find it analytically fruitful to differentiate between the Indian public sphere and the Dalit counterpublic. This will be to better illustrate, in the vein of Fraser (1992), how the 'intrapublic' (within a public) and 'interpublic' (between publics) relations in the movement differ in an important and qualitative way.[3] Intrapublic relations (within the Dalit counterpublic sphere) are inclusive in the sense that differences are expressed and debated. Interpublic relations, on the other hand, are built on the premises that the Dalit activists are excluded from the debates in the public sphere, that they are silenced in a unilateral way and for that reason have formed their own public. The same tendencies to form their own counterpublic will be seen among the Dalit feminists *within* the broader Dalit movement; since the 1980s they have formed their own arenas, separate from the Dalit men in order to be able to express their opinions.

What has characterized the interpublic relations—between the Indian public sphere and the counterpublic of the Dalit movement as a whole, women and men—is that there have been neither dialogues nor tense debates, but rather a forced one-way communication. Jeffrey (2000: 160, note 80) comments, for example, that during his ten-year study of the Indian-language press, in which he visited twenty towns and interviewed more than 250 journalists, he never came across a Dalit journalist working for a mainstream publication. Ståhlberg (2002a: 137–42) confirms the almost total absence of 'scheduled caste' (SC) journalists in Lucknow, the capital of the state of Uttar Pradesh. The lack of SC journalists working for mainstream publications or SC authors publishing in mainstream publishing houses seems to be one reason for the non-visibility of the message of Dalit activists in the public sphere.

The Dalit activists have instead formed their own spaces over the decades. They have communicated in their own arenas, published a huge number of magazines, books, and booklets from their own publishing houses, and interacted within their own networks. The massive media coverage of the Bahujan Samaj Party (BSP) leader, Mayawati and former leader Kanshi Ram since the middle of the 1990s was a break from an earlier pattern. With international media coverage of first, the World Conference

[3] 'Interpublic' and 'intrapublic' are taken from Fraser (1992: 121 ff).

against Racism and related issues in Durban in 2001 and later of the World Social Forum in Mumbai in 2004, a Dalit discourse reached out worldwide. During the World Social Forum in Nairobi, in 2007, Dalit activists interacted and confirmed their new global relations and strengthened their ties with activists within the global justice movement.

Parts of the messages of the activists conveyed within the Dalit counterpublic, such as an anti-Gandhi stand, has now reached the general public, although in a fragmented and incoherent way. In this book I will present the complexes of ideas within the Dalit discourses. By putting them in historical, as well as religious and political contexts, I hope to bring some clarity to the issue.

TENSIONS WITHIN THE DALIT MOVEMENT

The Dalit movement, and its counterpublic, is not a homogenous field; on the contrary, it is highly diversified. The Dalit movement—like the feminist movement in Latin America, as described by Alvarez—seems to be filled with 'tensions and contradictions in an expansive heterogeneous social movement field' (1998: 311ff). Focusing on heterogeneity and variations within the movement, I find myself close not only to the theory of Alvarez, but also to Gerlach and Hine (1970a). I will look more closely, not only at heterogeneity, but also at the tensions within the movement. The organizational aspect, which will be described in Chapter 4, is closely related to the cultural flow of meaning that takes place within the movement.[4] It will be argued that the internal tensions and debates in the Dalit movement have a major significance in moulding, refining, and strengthening a tacit knowledge about Hindu values as well as about a Dalit identity. The intrapublic tensions among Dalit activists with different movement perspectives differ, I will show, in a significant way from the interpublic perspectival clash taking place when the activists in the Dalit alternative counterpublic express themselves in relation to the public sphere.[5]

[4] For more about cultural flow within movements and a discussion about movements as part of a cultural totality, see Hannerz (1992a: 46ff).

[5] 'Perspectival clash' is taken from Hannerz (ibid.: 129 ff), using it mainly in relation to the individual, confronted with different perspectives.

My main argument is that the Dalit activists involved thus value conflicts differently and contextually. They distinguish between the perspectives of their 'main opponents', who circulate their messages in the public sphere, and of their Dalit opponents, who circulate theirs within the common alternative counterpublic. Conflicts are given different values, depending on whether they are interpublic or intrapublic. In an attempt to understand how conflicts are valued in relation to each other, account must be taken of the fact that the activists interact or communicate within a historically formed counterpublic, which will be shown, where some tacit knowledge has been at work for decades.

DALIT ACTIVISTS IN NATIONAL, INTERNATIONAL, AND GLOBAL CONTEXTS

Durban became a turning point for the Dalit movement. The United Nations World Conference against Racism, Racial Discrimination, Xenophobia and Related Intolerance was held in the South African city in 2001. Efforts had been made earlier to raise the issue about caste discrimination in international contexts, but it had never been done on such a massive scale. Dalit activists participated in large numbers, and according to many reporters the group was among the best represented and most visible at the conference:

The Dalit caucus arrived in Durban with a formidable publicity army of more than 200 representatives. (The more typical NGOs sent five to 10). By the time the official conference opened, NGO delegates and journalists from all over the world were sporting vests, shirts, stickers, and buttons with the slogan: 'Include Caste in WCAR'. (Polakow-Suransky, 2002)

The 'World Conference Against Racism's (WCAR)' NGO Forum was held from 28 August to 1 September, prior to and overlapping with the intergovernmental conference. Dalit activists attracted the attention of the media in many ways. They were not only seen distributing stickers, buttons, etc., but also playing drums and singing. Dalit women initiated a hunger strike to put caste discrimination on the agenda, and Dalit activists were reported to be demonstrating and marching together with NGOs working for human rights from all over the world.[6] Dalit activists presented themselves, en masse, to the international media and made the issue of caste discrimination known internationally. A Dalit woman activist I met in New Delhi commented on the large presence of the Dalit activists in Durban: 'You see, instead of buying one expensive ticket, we bought two cheap ones. That's why so many of us could go.'

THE INDIAN GOVERNMENT

The intergovernmental conference in Durban began as the NGO Forum came to an end, from 31 August to 8 September. Omar Abdullah, the Indian Minister of State for External Affairs made a short statement at the conference—as one in the long line of government ministers, many of them claiming compensation for poverty and underdevelopment stemming in part from slavery and colonialism. Abdullah, however, made a statement in which he condemned the activities preceding the inter-governmental conference, focusing on caste discrimination. In the first part of his speech he referred to Mahatma Gandhi's opposition to apartheid in South Africa, and commented that 'India was the first country to raise its voice against apartheid at the United Nations' (UN RD/942, 4 September 2001). He condemned racism and racial discrimination, and referred to Gandhi as the main inspiration for the Indian constitution, which prohibits 'discrimination on any grounds, including race' (ibid.).[7] Furthermore, he declared that the issue of caste-based discrimination did not belong within the Durban conference:

In the run-up to the World Conference, there has been propaganda, highly exaggerated and misleading, often based on anecdotal evidence, regarding caste-based discrimination in India. India has faced that evil squarely' (ibid.).

In the next passage Abdullah made clear the stance of the Indian government that caste discrimination should not be a matter for the UN:

[6] For articles about the Dalits in Durban, see, for example, 'publications' at www.dalitusa.org.

[7] Referring to Gandhi as the main inspirer of the Indian Constitution provoked many Dalit activists for whom Ambedkar is the 'Father of the Constitution' as well as father of the Dalit movement.

We are here to ensure that States do not condone or encourage regres-sive social attitude. We are not here to engage in social engineering within Member States. It is neither legitimate nor feasible nor practical for this Conference, or, for that matter, even the United Nations to legislate, let alone police, individual behaviour in our societies. The battle has to be fought within our respective societies to change thoughts, processes and attitudes. This is the task that we pledge ourselves to remain engaged in (ibid.).

There were two different positions at play before, during, and even after the Durban conference. The governmental stand was to keep the issue of caste discrimination out of the Durban conference, arguing that it was an internal matter and not an issue for the United Nations. The activists in the National Campaign on Dalit Human Rights (NCDHR) were of the opinion that caste discrimination was still, fifty years after constitutional safeguards were established, a problem that ought to be brought to the attention of the world community.

In Chapter 7, I shall show how Dalit activists created a space for themselves through a national network and how, having conquered a national platform, they worked their way to the international arena. The Dalit discourses about caste discrimination, which I will portray in Chapters 3 to 6, took a new turn as the activists moved into this new context. The main attempt will be to discern the character of Dalit discourse in an international context and to show why, for different reasons, it took on a new shape in the international arena. What happens to the Dalit discourse about caste discrimination when it intersects with the structure and discourse of the UN and also with the representatives of the Indian government and representatives of other states, in an international context?

Being able to put caste discrimination on the agenda in the World Conference in Durban involved a lot of negotiations. In Chapter 7, I shall give an overview of the discussions that took place in the meetings preceding Durban, as experienced by the activists representing the NCDHR. The material is taken from email reports, sent successively to the Dalit network, from different meetings as the World Conference approached, and also from my personal communication with activists. What kind of negotiations did they take part in? Whom did they negotiate with?

What were the negotiations all about? The Durban conference itself and its outcome are also discussed.

THE ACADEMIC DISCUSSION IN INDIA

Let me briefly summarize the debate in the Indian media among academics such as André Béteille, Gail Omvedt, and Dipankar Gupta regarding caste vis-à-vis the race issue in relation to the participation of the Dalit activists in Durban.[8] André Béteille criticizes the UN in an article titled 'Race and Caste' in *The Hindu* of 10 March 2001 for reviving and expanding the idea of race, which is a concept which has been scientifically criticized for a long time: 'The Scheduled Castes of India taken together are no more a race than are the Brahmins taken together. Every social group cannot be regarded as a race simply because we want to protect it against prejudice and discrimination.'

As I will show in Chapter 7, nobody ever argued that SCs should be regarded as a race. Of course, if somebody had argued along these lines, Béteille's comment would have been relevant. Gail Omvedt responds to his argument in the following way:

As Mr Béteille has argued, 'race' in terms of naturally different species does not exist among human beings. The science of genetics is now strikingly clear on this—there are no significant genetic differences among socially identifiable groups of people. The genetic variation among individuals is by far greater than among any society groups. But, this is only to say that 'racism' as a social phenomenon is based on a lie; it does not provide us an analysis of why that lie has come to exist (Omvedt, 'The UN, Racism and Caste' *The Hindu*, 10 April 2001).

Béteille is right in his criticism of the UN where the concept of race is still used in spite of it having been rejected for decades by researchers. Nevertheless, as Omvedt comments, racism as a social phenomenon still exists, although it is based on a lie. The point I want to make in Chapter 7, however, is that, although the concept of race is still used within the UN, it is not expanded within the UN framework to be applied to the SCs. Béteille's criticism may be directed against the UN in general, but it is not valid regarding the attitude within the UN towards

[8] For a collection of articles related to the debate see Thorat and Umakant (eds) 2004.

SCs, as I will show. Béteille's argument as to why Dalits should not take part in the Durban conference falls along the line of the Indian government: caste is not race.

After the Durban conference the Indian magazine *Seminar*, which often invites scholars and others to comment on topical questions, brought out an issue dealing with 'caste, race and the dalit question' (*Seminar*, 508, December 2001). Dipankar Gupta writes in the introductory paragraphs of his article in this issue:

Though, on occasion, the professional academic might get a sense of *deja vu* while going through this paper, the fact that the parallelism between caste and race are still compelling enough for many political activists demonstrates that something was obviously missing in previous presentations (2001).

His argument reaches the same conclusion as the Indian government, simply that caste is not race and for that reason the question of caste discrimination does not belong in Durban. It is notable that Gupta, contrary to the wishes of representatives of the SCs, still uses the concept of Harijan instead of SCs or Dalits.[9] In this usage he seems to be quite alone nowadays.

To argue that caste discrimination does not equal racism is a waste of time, as I will show, because there is consensus between the Dalit activists, the UN, and the Indian government. The Dalit activists were of the opinion that caste discrimination belonged in the Durban conference in spite of not being akin to racism. The Indian government found caste discrimination to be an internal question and not a matter for the UN, and argued for this reason that caste is not race. A UN report (of Goonesekere)[10] clearly stated that caste discrimination is not the same as racism, but still falls within the ambit of the Committee on the Elimination of Racial Discrimination (CERD). Why Béteille and Gupta, two of India's most famous academics, were engaged in this debate and argued that caste discrimination is not the same as racism is not easily explained. Within another

---

[9] Gupta avoids the concept of Dalit and talks about 'Harijans' or 'political activists' (2001). Also, throughout his book on caste in India (2000), the usage of 'Harijans' for SCs is prevalent.

[10] See chapter 7, note 13.

context it might be seen as a question of scientific principles: scientifically caste discrimination should not be confused with racism. There is no argument about that. But why they took part in the debate about the Dalits in Durban, in this highly politically sensitive context, on the wrong premises, I will leave as an open question.

THE UN DISCOURSE

The opposition, however, came in the end not mainly from Indian academics, who essentially tried to understand and analyse the issue in a serious way, but from the government representatives from across the world involved in the negotiations prior to and during the conference.

In the preparatory meetings preceding the conference, the space for the activists was exceedingly limited. I will show that the discursive field was clearly structured by power relations regarding the messages that were allowed to be displayed. The representatives of the different governments were in a strong position to decide the agenda for the conference, in relation to the Dalit activists. The discourse within the Dalit counterpublic, in terms of caste discrimination, was, during the time-span of about 20 months negotiations, emptied of all religious and political content.

When the Dalit discourse intersected with an international cultural discourse in the UN, it was forcibly twisted in such a way as to become unrecognizable. In the final documents from Durban, even remnants of their message were not found. They were thus silenced by government representatives from across the world and could not put forward their message. In this official international context, the Dalit activists lacked a discursive space, which is reminiscent of their exclusion historically from the public sphere in the Indian context.

The UN 'Sub-Commission on the Promotion and Protection of Human Rights' report by Goonesekere, presented prior to the Durban conference, was, on the other hand, a break with this pattern of exclusion. The report made a connection with the Dalit discourse about caste discrimination as related to Hinduism, and also to the dispute between B.R. Ambedkar and M.K. Gandhi, religiously and politically important to the Dalit activists.

The same kind of exclusion of issues related to caste-discrimination in the international context resurfaced six years later in 2007. The UN went through an organizational restructuring and the Sub-Commission, in which two special rapporteurs had during three years developed principles and guidelines for the elimination of 'discrimination based on work and descent' (understood to include caste-discrimination), ceased to exist. The UN restructuring made it unclear what kind of mechanisms there were for retaining the report, either by transferring it to the Human Rights Commission (HRC) or to its Advisory Committee (HRCAC), which replaced the Sub-Commission (See also Ch. 7, pp. 190–207).

THE GLOBAL JUSTICE MOVEMENT

In Durban—outside the formal negotiations—the Dalit activists voluntarily redesigned their message to make it more general, so as to be able to relate it to a global movement discourse prevalent among other activists. Caste discrimination was related to a neoliberal world order. The Dalit activists were drawn into new kinds of social relations, and demonstrated on common issues, together with Palestinians and African Americans among others. Journalists and photographers from across the world, who were reporting from Durban, often included a passage or photographs of Dalit activists in their accounts. Human rights activists reported to their organizations about Dalits in India. To elaborate on Fraser's (1992) concept of counterpublic, the Dalit activists became part of something that may be seen as a global counterpublic[11] and along with their sympathizers, they acted on a global scale. Their message was spread across the world.

Dalit activists have recently become connected in a more direct way with what is known as the global justice movement—the network of heterogeneous organizations and movements across the world—that was born in demonstrations in Seattle in 1999. This has, for example, entailed participation in the WSFs in Mumbai 2004, in Porto Alegre, Brazil 2003 and 2005, as well as in Nairobi, Kenya 2007. Dalit activists are now interrelated on a more regular basis with movement activists outside India,

[11] Activists from various counterpublics—historically formed in different settings—relating to each other and taking part in the same alternative world cultural discourse.

who express similar experiences, demands, and emotions as they do. Let me just present a glimpse from the WSF in Nairobi in 2007, where I carried out fieldwork, to give an idea of the global context for their involvement.

The inaugural ceremony for WSF, 20–25 January 2007, was held in Uhuru Park in the centre of Nairobi. Among the speakers was the front figure for WSF, the liberation theologian Chico Whitaker from Brazil, who was awarded the Right Livelihood Award ('Alternative Nobel Prize') in 2006. 'We know the world we want', he told the audience, and made it clear that this should be a world of mutual respect and not one dominated by the West. The Kenyan dailies reported from the occasion, and news of a Dalit drum team covered the front page in *Daily Nation* (22 January 2007). The show of the same Dalit drummers also appeared twice in Kenyan national television.[12]

'Cast out Caste' and 'Enough is Enough' were slogans raised by Dalit participants when the drummers, in red and black, caught the attention of the media entering the main gate to the Moi International Sports Centre, in the north-eastern outskirts of the city where the WSF was held. With sharp and steadfast drumming, the Dalit activists slowly marched around the arena with their banderols and slogans about solidarity not just with minorities in India and Asia, but also across continents.

In WSF, Mumbai 2004, Dalit activists got recognition across the world because of their number and visibility. Also in Nairobi Dalit activists could be spotted all over. The blue headbands with 'Cast out Caste' were generously distributed and also in demand, even among people from other countries. It was quite clear during the Forum that caste discrimination is not something which is limited to India. Activists from, for example, Senegal, Kenya, Japan, Nepal, and Sri Lanka described vividly how caste discrimination is part of their own history and experiences in their respective countries.

In the last day of WSF 2007 environmentalist Wangari Maathai, the first African woman to win the Nobel Peace Prize in 2004, reminded everyone of the strength of the WSF: 'You meet others who face the same challenge as you do, and you get to know that you are not alone.'

[12] Channel NTV, 22 January and Channel KTN, 24 January 2007.

It was an expressive and colourful ending of the Forum with music, dance and songs—performed on stage as well as among the audience—which blended with brief statements from the proposals worked out during the preceding days. Let me take a few quotations read out by Sonia, who entered the scene in Uhuru Park on the last day of the Forum and introduced herself with the following words: 'Hello Africa. I am Sonia from Brazil. We have chosen some favourite lines from the proposals, which came out of our working groups these days, and we will read them here and now.

- 'Long live struggle of workers, women, minorities!'
- 'US troops out of Iraq! Go back to your home!'
- 'Viva, viva Palestina!'
- 'We need to live and love together!'
- 'Down, down with homophobia! Down down with homophobia!'

Dalit activists have now reached beyond the Dalit counter-public; in Chapter 9, I will return to their involvement in the global justice movement and for what historical reasons they are now well prepared to interrelate with activists from other parts of the world.

OVERVIEW OF THE STUDY

The study is an anthropological attempt to reach behind the surface of the contemporary Dalit movement. My aim, more generally, is to give as varied a picture as possible of this multi-faceted social movement, to better understand processes related to identity-formation. To this end I initially put some questions that I found central: what kind of discourses are to be found among Dalit activists? What is the organizational structure of the movement? What kind of local practices take place among activists? How are discourses transmitted and transformed between different contexts? In the following chapters I shall present Dalit activists in a multitude of contexts, ranging from the local/regional (Chapter 5) to the translocal[13] (Chapter 4)

[13] In a multilocal study the interconnections or linkages between sites need not always be in focus or even relevant, although the study

and transnational[14] (Chapter 6) and further to the state-related, international[15] (Chapter 7) and global[16] (Chapter 9). Questions related to gender issues on the different levels are dealt with in a separate chapter (Chapter 8).

Classic studies about the caste system have most often been confined to the Indian context as the caste system has been seen as culturally specific and not possible to compare with any other phenomenon in the world. The Dalit movement has opened up the possibility for studies to take broader geographical and theoretical contexts into account. Discussing the Dalit movement in the framework of social movements makes it possible for me to tie the issue of caste to more general theoretical discussions, both in terms of organizational structure and cultural discourse.

In Chapter 2, 'Follow the Field' I shall relate the image of the classic anthropological fieldwork—'one year in one place'—to a geographically dispersed field such as a social movement. How could the knowledge about social movements developed in sociology, and more recently in social anthropology, be combined with the anthropological method of fieldwork? In what way could the more recent theoretical stances in social anthropology dealing with geographically dispersed fields be useful when

---

has been carried out in multiple localities. In this study the concept of 'translocal' is used to emphasize the interconnections *between* localities or sites (Hannerz 1998). The translocal context is in this study further limited to connoting only contexts within the borders of the same state, compared to the broader use by Hannerz, in order to be able to differentiate the context from the 'transnational' context.

[14] 'Transnational' context is used here to denote interconnections across state borders. In this study it is further intended to draw attention specifically to interactions, connections, and networks among movement activists across state borders. For a comment on the tendency to conflate nation and state in this context, see Hannerz (ibid.).

[15] The 'international' context refers to contexts in which Dalit activists and representatives of different governments, among others, interact with each other.

[16] The 'global' context in this study attempts to draw attention to the involvement of Dalit activists with networks and webs with a transcontinental scope.

approaching a social movement? The concept of network will be central throughout the book, and I shall discuss how it has been used in sociology, social anthropology, and also in some classic theories about Indian society. The chapter will end with a detailed description of the way I went about anthropological fieldwork within the Dalit movement and of the methods I found suitable for the purpose.

Chapter 3, 'Traditions of Protest', will offer a historical context as a prerequisite to understanding processes in the contemporary Dalit movement. It will be shown that activists who similarly protest against the caste hierarchy nevertheless belong in two different traditions. I shall make clear the religious and political reasons that have caused activists in these two traditions of protest, one represented by B.R. Ambedkar and the other by M.K. Gandhi, to stand in opposition to each other. It will implicitly be shown how an alternative counterpublic among the so-called untouchables has been taking shape at least since the 1920s.

In Chapter 4, 'Movement Perspectives: Dalit Discourses Across the Country', I shall focus on the heterogeneity and the geographical spread of the contemporary Dalit movement. I have chosen to present what I find to be three influential Dalit discourses, with the help of movement literature and written materials of importance to the Dalit activists. I shall also give some examples of how these texts are used among the activists. The first perspective to be presented is Dalit Buddhism, the second Dalit Christian theology, and the third a Dalit political perspective, with the Bahujan Samaj Party (BSP) as an example. The picture of three clearly separable perspectives will be complicated, however, and the organizational structure of the movement will be discussed. Different Dalit perspectives will be related to each other, first in the sense of being expressed among networks in the same alternative counterpublic, and second by having a few anti-stances as common points of reference. The importance of these anti-stances for the movement will be discussed.

Chapter 5, 'Dalit Activities in Lucknow: Buddhism and Party Politics in Local Practice' will portray some local practices within the movement in the city of Lucknow in Uttar Pradesh. In this chapter I aim to show how different networks can be highly fused in practice. It will also be seen how Dalit activists have created some alternative spaces for themselves. Ethnography from a local Buddhist *vihara* (temple) and also from the revival meetings of a political party will be presented. The life histories of three Dalit activists will also be delineated to show how Buddhist and political perspectives are experienced as combined on an individual level. Kinship and friendship will be seen to have important roles to play among networks within the movement.

Chapter 6, 'A Transnational Dalit Counterpublic: The Example of Ambedkarites in Britain', deals with the transnational aspect of the Dalit movement. I shall look at processes where transnational connections are created and recreated between India and Britain. The chapter aims to show how messages and organizational structures may be conveyed transnationally. It will be seen how Ambedkarites (Dalit activists) in *viharas* in Birmingham and Wolverhampton are interrelated to Dalit activists in northern India. The fused Buddhist and political networks in India and Britain will be seen to belong to the same movement, closely bound together by networks of kinship, friendship, and community membership.

In Chapter 7, 'Translating "Caste Discrimination" into an International Discourse', I attempt to show what happens when the Dalit activists enter the international arena. The NCDHR, formed in 1998, will be discussed. The negotiations, in which the Dalit activists in this campaign took part, prior to the UN Conference on racism and related issues in Durban 2001, will be presented from the activists' own point of view. My argument is that the internationalization of Dalit issues strengthened the position of Dalit women and made them much more visible than before. In the public sphere they have been largely invisible and when they have been portrayed by the media, it has been in a negative way. In Durban, however, they approached media on their own terms. In the long run, however, Dalit feminists who have tried to collaborate with Dalit men in international contexts have, on the one hand, found new channels and contexts to raise their voices, but, on the other hand, have not been able to represent themselves in some important roles, such as being elected to international committees or taking part in financial decisions.

In Chapter 8, 'Dalit Feminism in a Neoliberal World' I begin by discussing Dalit feminism and gender issues within the framework of a neoliberal economy. Next I look at Dalit women historically. They have faced problems in getting their voices heard, not only in society at large, but also within the Dalit movement, as well as within the broader women's movement in India. Yet, in the last few decades they have organized in networks separately from both the Dalit men and also the general women's movement. At the end of the chapter, I will illustrate how cultural recognition and economic position may be entangled and undermined for Dalit women and men, at a point in history when Dalit activists are about to deconstruct an image of their material bodies as impure, and reconstruct them as human.

Finally, in Chapter 9, 'Dynamics of Diversity', I shall summarize and discuss the organizational structure of the Dalit movement, as well as the relationship between the different movement perspectives. I shall argue that tensions within a social movement do not necessarily cause disintegration, a common view among scholars as well as movement activists. Under specific circumstances, as in the Dalit movement, tensions may on the contrary contribute to the growth of the movement, and a strengthened cultural identity. When Dalit women were excluded or muted by Dalit men, on the other hand, we find the tendencies of fission—a Dalit feminist counterpublic is growing from within the broader Dalit counterpublic. I shall also sketch out how the message of the movement takes different shapes, depending on which organizational level it is expressed at, and to whom it is addressed. At the end of the chapter I will discuss the more recent involvement of the Dalit activists, in WSFs and the global justice movement. What circumstances have made Dalit activists prepared to be active in these new alternative networks? Or, in other words, why are Indian Dalits suddenly everywhere?

2

Follow the Field
Fieldwork Methods in a Social Movement

WHERE IS THE FIELD?

Bronislaw Malinowski (1987[1922]) has become legendary for his classic fieldwork in the western Pacific. A great deal of fieldwork came to be modelled on his way of carrying it out—in one geographical setting for an unbroken period of time. He projected his fieldwork as an activity demarcated in time and space, and also as different from and in contrast to our normal doings, both physically and mentally. It was carried out under circumstances of hardship far from his home and he was furthermore all alone among the 'natives', whose language he did not know when he arrived. It is too easy, and it may be premature, to see the image of classical fieldwork as a caricature that everyone knows but nobody really takes seriously any more, write Gupta and Ferguson (1997: 11). They further point out the difficulties one needs to be aware of to understand the influence archetypes may have:

After all, archetypes function not by claiming to be accurate, literal descriptions of things as they are, but by offering a compelling glimpse of things as they should be, at their purest and most essential. Such archetypes operate ideologically in a way that is peculiarly hard to pin down; their effects are simultaneously ineffable and pervasive (ibid.).

I agree that it is 'peculiarly hard to pin down' how the archetype of the Malinowskian type of fieldwork operated, but there is no doubt that it played some role for me. My interest lay, as already mentioned, on the Dalit movement in India and this was a great challenge. How was I to do fieldwork on a social movement which was geographically dispersed all over India and even abroad? Where was my field? My solution to the problem was to postpone a decision about where to carry it out.

After many trips and about one year spent in India I had finally, in 1995, come to choose Lucknow, the capital of Uttar Pradesh as the place where my fieldwork should be carried out. At that time I already knew quite a lot of Dalit activists and their families and the Dalit counterpublic, in terms of groups, magazines, conferences, etc., mainly in northern India, was familiar to me. Stationed in Lucknow, though, the field did not 'behave'. There is a famous quotation by Malinowski (1987[1922]), cited more than once in the anthropological literature—seriously, ironically or jokingly—which many anthropologists know now by heart. Not surprisingly it came to my mind: 'Imagine yourself suddenly set down surrounded by all your gear, alone on a tropical beach close to a native village, while the launch or dinghy which has brought you sails away out of sight' (ibid.: 4). To me there was one overwhelming problem—the people in the 'field' ran away from the geographical location where they were supposed to be. During my time in Lucknow the Buddhist monk in the vihara where the Dalit activists used to gather, left for Birmingham in Britain. One of the two most important Dalit politicians, Mayawati, went off on an election tour. Dalit activists from Lucknow went to New Delhi for conferences or rallies, and activists from other places turned up for a day or two, only to leave again. Let me paraphrase Malinowski: 'Imagine yourself suddenly set down, alone on a tropical beach, while the natives sail away out of sight'.

The story of my fieldwork came to be in many ways a balancing act, at first not by choice, but as the only solution to a problematic situation. I was interested in a dispersed contemporary social movement but still wanted to carry out anthropological fieldwork. Escobar (1992) questioned why there was a lack of social movement studies in social anthropology, and at least I knew that I was not alone with my problems regarding field-method.[1]

---

[1] For more general discussions about field-methods in a translocal field, see, for example, Garsten (1994) and Hannerz (2001, 2003).

The anthropological self-reflexivity literature of the 1980s put the concept of culture under scrutiny, and discussed how to write ethnography and how to relate to people in the field. Curiously enough, 'the field' itself was left out of the discussion, as Gupta and Ferguson commented as late as 1997. The concept of the 'field' belonged to a common-sense knowledge, they noted, and was simultaneously a taken-for-granted and mysterious space, beyond and below the threshold of reflexivity, where fieldwork could be done (ibid.: 2).

THE HISTORICAL IMPORTANCE OF A DEMARCATED FIELD

Natural science with the methods of comparison, classification, and systematization was long seen as an ideal model also for social scientists. Social anthropologists were no exceptions. They used the methods of natural science also in relation to fieldwork, keen to be accepted as legitimate and mature scientists. The demarcated field was a prerequisite to being able to compare and build evolutionary schemes of societies. Later on, demarcation and comparison became important for classification in another sense, without the aim of ranking societies as higher or lower in an evolutionary scheme. Now it was important to demarcate and decide the unit, because our first task as social anthropologists (within a science that had comparison of human societies as its subject) was to learn as much as we could about the varieties, or diversities, of structural systems through field research (Radcliffe-Brown 1952[1940]: 193). Radcliffe-Brown argued that 'we must aim at building up some sort of classification of types of structural systems' (ibid.: 194f). In this context we can better understand the need to delimit and create units out of complex situations.

The demarcated field also became important as a mirror for self-reflection. A classic example is Louis Dumont's *Homo Hierarchicus* (1980[1966]). The units Dumont compared were nothing less than 'India' and the 'West'. His point was that the hierarchical values, which are the ideal in India, could also be found in 'western' societies, but on a hidden level and expressed, for example, in the form of racism. When we compare other societies with our own we thus gain insights about hidden levels in our own society. The field as a unit made it possible to compare, not mainly, or at least not only, for the purpose of achieving a systematic classification of societies, but as a way of leaving ethnocentrism behind and getting critical insights about cultural values in our own society. This kind of comparison, in the form of juxtapositions (Marcus and Fischer 1999 [1986]), was built on the image in social anthropology of distinct geocultural regions, juxtaposed to each other, each with certain practices embedded in particular cultural, linguistic, and social systems (Marcus 2002: 195).

Self-reflexivity was in the 1960s built on the idea that you have to leave your home to be able to look at yourself from a new angle. When the 'field' came closer, in terms of fieldwork 'at home', or multilocal studies in which part of the fieldwork was sometimes carried out in the neighbourhood, the geographical border between home and 'field' was blurred. It became a difficult task to clearly demarcate the 'field'. Most important to note in this context is that self-reflexivity (regarding one's own cultural values) was built on the premise that the 'field' could be geographically demarcated and separated from 'home'. The 'field' was a non-familiar place that could be set up as a contrasting mirror against the familiar and unreflected values in our own society. To get a clear picture, the mirror should not be held too close. What could be seen in a mirror touching the tip of one's nose?

Today there is an acceptance of multisited, translocal, and transnational fields, and juxtaposition has also kept a prominent position when it comes to designing these fields. What, then, are the implications of having juxtaposition or comparison, reflectively or non-reflectively, as a landmark when designing the field? First, it may confirm the image of 'cultures' as a mosaic of separate comparable units (although interconnected, intertwined, overlapping or however one formulates this interdependence). Second, it restricts our flexibility and ability to move in *any* direction of importance. I want to focus on how Marcus (1995) brings the concept of comparison with him into the new realm of multisited ethnography. According to Marcus:

Comparison reenters the very act of ethnographic specification by a research design of juxtapositions in which the global is collapsed into and made an integral part of parallel, related local situations rather than something monolithic or external to them. This move toward comparison embedded in the multisited ethnography stimulates accounts of cultures composed in a landscape for which there is as yet no developed theoretical conception or descriptive model (ibid.: 102).

I want to dwell on this quotation for more than one reason. First, I want to put the focus on how Marcus has uniquely formulated a way to study the global, not only theoretically, but also with fieldwork methods in mind. By studying parallel and related local situations, we implicitly study the global, which is not something external to these relations. The research is described by Marcus as being designed around chains, paths, threads, conjunctions, or juxtapositions (ibid.: 105), and the strategies as following connections, associations, and putative relationships (ibid.: 97). The second reason why I find the above quotation interesting is because of the prominent position Marcus has given in this context to comparison, in spite of pointing out that this activity should not decide the field design.

He writes that what is essential to multisited research is the function of translation from one cultural idiom or language to another, adding 'although this is not practised in a dualistic "them-us" frame' (Marcus 1995: 100). One important aspect of the anthropological discipline has been to translate between two (or more) localized cultures. The new type of multisited ethnography is about making 'connections through translations and tracings among distinctive discourses from site to site' (ibid.: 101), he writes. It is easy to agree with Marcus that what one is to a large extent preoccupied with in multi- or translocal fieldwork is to trace and connect. But why is it important in this context to preserve the concept of comparison? The reason why the concept of 'comparison' and also 'translation' enters into the discussion about multisited ethnography seems not to be because they are of particular analytical value in this context. Let me suggest that it is rather because they, legitimize a new necessary field design as a natural extension of the traditional anthropological fieldwork. Comparison and juxtaposition (together with translation) may have their values and be ingredients in many studies, mine included.[2] My point is that it

---

[2] For a related discussions, see Gingrich and Fox (2002).

is unfortunate if these concepts determine the field design, and make us deductively point out a specific amount of demarcated juxtaposed localities or sites for fieldwork.[3]

The 'field' will probably play an important part within anthropology, and be our 'trademark' at least for the near future, and there is every reason not to abandon it, as Gupta and Ferguson (1997) comment. It should, however, be redefined and thought of in a new way. It is well worth remembering that it was A.C. Haddon, a former zoologist, who introduced the concept of fieldwork in anthropology. His first fieldwork was carried out within natural science, 'to study the fauna, the structure and the mode of formation of coral reefs' (Gupta and Ferguson 1997: 6, references to Stocking 1992). The well-known fact that the concept of the field was historically constructed should be emphasized in this context, because what was historically constructed gives the possibility of reconstructing according to the new needs of the day. [4]

The localities or sites between which relations are to be discovered and examined could be the core when a field is designed. But there is also another possibility, namely of not

[3] Scientific problems are not formulated in a vacuum, or within a closed scientific world ruled by its own discourse, but in negotiation with the surrounding society and also in an exchange with the discourses in the public and in the media, for example. But making comparison and translation the core of social anthropology does not only have a negative effect on the field-design, it may also express an attitude to science as unique in relation to other forms of knowledge. It is a stand that is not easy to defend, when 'society has become "scientized" and science "socialized"', as expressed by Delanty (1997: 140). The idea of the anthropologist as being in possession of unique knowledge based on his or her ability to compare is problematic. 'It must be recognized', Delanty writes, 'that the social situation of science today is one in which science has, on all fronts, lost its claim to uniqueness'. (ibid.: 139). He suggests that social science is seen in a broader context, as a discursive practice among others. Cf. Fuchs (2000b: 72f), who in the context of social movements comments that the analyst would have to be more 'a listener to ideas and imaginations which crop up in the ongoing negotiation of sociality (social relationships).'

[4] For a detailed account of the history of the concept see, for example, Stocking (1992), Kuklick (1997), Vincent (1990), referred in Gupta and Ferguson (1997: 6).

choosing a predestined number of sites, but giving the inter-relations priority and incorporating new localities in the fieldwork process, when they are discovered and found to be relevant to the research project formulated.

DESIGNING THE FIELD AROUND INTERRELATIONS

Geographic locality, whether it is single-sited, multi- or translocal, whether it is far from home or in a demarcated area just across the threshold, is no longer the only way to define the field. I define my field, in accordance with Olwig and Hastrup (1997: 8, with reference to Barth 1992), 'not primarily in terms of locality, but as the field of relations which are of significance to the people involved in the study'. Further, I see the fieldwork as processual, in the sense that new localities have been incor-porated into the research as I have become aware of their relevance to the Dalit activists (ibid.). In this way, the locations have been of subordinate importance to the interrelations in the formation of the field. Most fields today may be seen as interrelational in one or the other sense, but it could be a point to reserve 'interrelational field' for those kinds of fields in which geographical locality has been subordinated to interrelations in the field design. The concept signals that the field is dispersed and mutually connected, but not designed around predestined sites or localities, as is most often the case and also hinted at in the second part of concepts such as 'multisited', 'multilocal' or 'translocal' fields. In the interrelational field, the sites are instead included in the fieldwork process.

It may be seen as a question of nuance, and of less importance, whether it is the interrelations or the geographic locations that are the core around which the field is designed, but I find it to be central to this discussion. If the field is designed around two or more predestined locations, you will have a multi- or translocal field and an extension of the 'traditional' field. But if you put the interrelations at the centre, there will be a new form of field and fieldwork, where not comparison but following will be the key word. When the multi- or translocal fieldworks are seen as extensions of the 'traditional' single-sited fieldwork, the criticism about lack of depth, etc. will be understandable. It is easily calculated among the sceptics that two localities will give half the depth of a traditional single-sited fieldwork if you do not compensate in time, three localities will give a third of the depth, and so on, leading up to, say, twenty localities that will give hardly any depth at all. You could, of course, compensate for some of the losses with the new type of knowledge you have gained, the sceptics ponder, but it may be difficult to reach the same, preferable, depth as in a single-sited field-work.

To clarify the point, geographic localities with their own specific histories will have an importance in forming different messages or strategies within the Dalit movement, but they are not the criteria by which I define my field or my unit of analysis. The processual approach to the field was in the beginning not a conscious decision or according to some well considered theoretical or methodological ideas, but simply the only possibility to obtain any knowledge about the activists in the movement that had caught my interest. It was only, as already mentioned, in the later phases of my fieldwork I found this way of designing the field as legitimate and consciously incorporated new sites.[5]

For me as for many others, the fieldwork to be meaningful came to a point of no return—after my experiences in Lucknow—when I had to go along with the interrelations and not regard one, two, three or even ten geographically demarcated locations as my field.[6] The simple reason was that what constituted my field in terms of a geographical locality one week could have lost most of its relevance to my project the following week. The Dalit activists are to a high degree flexible, moving between

---

[5] I returned to Delhi, which I now had come to recognize as part of my field. Retrospectively I included localities, such as Bangalore, Chennai, and Patna, for example, where I had interacted with Dalit activists. But it was not until my Lucknow experience that I more consciously incorporated new localities, such as Birmingham, Wolverhampton, and London in Britain or Jullundur in Punjab, to mention a few.

[6] The argument is not that the 'interrelational' field necessarily involves more sites than a 'multi-' or 'translocal' field, but that the sites involved are not predestined. This means that a multilocal study may involve three sites, while the interrelational may involve only two. The criterion is whether the localities or sites were decided before the fieldwork began, or whether they are the outcome of fieldwork practice.

locations. In a contemporary social movement it is a matter of 'ongoing interconnectedness, interaction, exchange or mobility' and the studies dealing with social movements are not by definition comparative, as expressed by Hannerz (1998: 237), speaking about transnational studies more generally.

In the interrelational field 'comparison' and 'translation' will be played down and exchanged for the activities of tracing and mapping. Tracing paths of mobility, finding interconnections, and pointing out relations are instead what has become important. There will be an inherent demand for pointing out relations for an understanding, and the mapped or visualized interrelations and connections provide the depth for the interrelational field. It has then become a question, not only theoretically but also methodologically, of following paths of relevance with an open mind, rather than staying in predestined sites. In this alternative field design 'comparison has got out of control', in the words of Marcus (2002: 195), but I would argue that this does not actually matter.

NETWORKS AND CONTEMPORARY SOCIAL MOVEMENTS

My attempt is neither to go through the full history of how the concept of network[7] has been used, nor to explore the wide range of social movement theories that has developed in different disciplines. Rather, I shall in a few pages give something of a context to situate my own study in a broad and complex field of theories. Since the late 1970s the interest in contemporary social movements grew steadily in disciplines like sociology, political science, and history, but anthropologists were largely absent from this extremely active and engaging trend, as Escobar wrote at the beginning of the 1990s. He asked why anthropologists had not shown any interest in contemporary social movements. What does this lack of studies of contemporary social movements in anthropology say about the discipline, he asked (Escobar 1992: 396). The point he made was that the anthropological discipline lacked methods which could deal in

[7] For an overview of network theories in social anthropology, see Hannerz (1980, 1992b).

a satisfactory way with *collective* political actions.[8] One decade later not much had changed in this regard. Alvarez, Dagnino, and Escobar (1998a) were, together with their associates, among those few researchers who more systematically developed a theoretical framework to be able to deal with contemporary social movements in an anthropological way.

One of the main reasons, historically, why social movements have been problematic in social anthropology seems to have been the importance of the demarcated field. Strangely enough, though, the introduction of geographically dispersed multilocal, translocal or transnational fieldworks did not make much of a difference when it came to introducing social movements into the discipline. The reason seems to be that, although the field-work came to be extended geographically to more localities, the numbers of them were limited to two, three or maybe four locations, decided well in advance. The point I made earlier was that when studying a social movement you need to introduce not one, two or even ten localities, but most probably even more. The burden will fall on you to defend the 'loss of depth' as the localities increase if you design your field in a traditional way. It may still be analytically useful for some reasons and for some researchers to demarcate one, two or three chosen locations as their field. But for most of us geographically demarcated localities, connected or not, is probably not the optimal field-design any longer.

My argument was that when interrelations rather than localities are at the core when the field (during the process of the fieldwork) is designed, depth, or rather an understanding of complex matters, would be achieved in a way that differs from the traditional one. Now, depth is no longer a question of staying long enough in one, two or three localities, or travelling between them, but of extensive following in *any* direction of importance to the people in the field. Following what, then? I shall elaborate on this when I deal more directly with research methods. First, though, I shall provide a brief theoretical frame-work that makes it easier to deal methodologically with the

[8] It seems that these difficulties in relation to field-method appeared to the anthropologists in *any* type of collective activities that were not geographically localized to one or a few demarcated settings.

interrelational field. The aim is to make a contemporary social movement, the Dalit movement, available for anthropological fieldwork with methods that correspond to the theories. In so doing I shall place the concept of network in focus.

In the 1950s, 1960s, and 1970s there was some limited interest in millenarian movements, cargo cults, and other religious movements that could be studied with participant observation in narrow settings. Apart from these studies, the interest in social movements among anthropologists was, as already mentioned, almost non-existent until very recently. Gerlach and Hine (1970a; 1970b) were exceptions to the rule, when dealing with contemporary social movements in a broader setting. In their study of the Black Power and Pentecostal movements in the US, they describe the social structure of the movements as segmentary, made up of economically and politically independent groups or cells that divided or united according to different situational demands. The movements were decentralized with a multitude of leaders, and also reticulate, that is, linked through networks that were unbounded and extensively ramified (Gerlach and Hine 1970a: 393). The high degree of fission and fusion and the decentralized character made the movements hard for outsiders to control.

An Italian authority on social movements, Melucci, however, is the one who made the concept of networks popular in social movement theories. It is well worth noting that Melucci (1985) refers to Gerlach and Hine (1970a) when talking about social movements in terms of networks. The concept of networks as well as that of webs, also used by Gerlach and Hine, has now been taken up again by anthropologists and elaborated on in movement theories (Alvarez, Dagnino, and Escobar, 1998a). Melucci (1985), however, came to put the focus on how networks may be embedded in everyday life. This was in contrast to earlier movement theories mainly occupied with the visible aspects of the movement that were easily recognized, such as public meetings, demonstrations, etc.[9]

To look at Indian phenomena in terms of networks is not something new. Already in McKim Marriott's *Village India* (1955),

---

[9] For more about social movement theories and the concept of 'new social movement', see Chapter 5.

Indian society was understood through the concept of network. This study differed from earlier ones in not being a desk-study, but based on fieldwork in Indian villages. The contributors looked at the joint family, caste, and the village not as isolated social units, but interrelated through social networks. This new way of looking at the village in terms of interrelations was the source of inspiration when Redfield and others discussed civilization as a structure of networks and cultural centres in their macro-theories in the following decade.[10] *Structure and Change in Indian Society* (Singer and Cohn 1996 [1968]) was another important volume occupied with interconnections and social networks in the Indian context.[11] Singer and Cohn stated that they differed from their predecessor Radcliffe-Brown, who regarded social relations as being connected by complex networks that he called 'social structure'.[12] They pointed out how they were influenced by the conceptual models of Redfield and Lévi-Strauss, for example. In the 1950s and 1960s, in the

[10] For an overview see Singer and Cohn (1996 [1968]: vi–vii).

[11] The volume was the outcome of a conference held in Chicago in 1965 and included well-known names, such as Marriott, Srinivas, Rowe, Lynch, Galanter, and Gould. In the preface it is said to focus on 'the specific patterns of interconnection which can be traced through empirical studies of particular groups in particular localities, and to the changes in such patterns' (ibid.: viii).

[12] Discussing and explaining what he means by concepts such as networks, social relations, and social structure and what he regards as the relation between them, Radcliffe-Brown writes as follows: '...direct observation does reveal to us that these human beings are connected by a complex network of social relations. I use the term "social structure" to denote this network of actually existing relations' (1952 [1940]: 190). He further makes clear that he does not mean it to be exactly the same thing to study social structures and social relations: 'A particular social relation between two persons (unless they be Adam and Eve in the garden of Eden) exists only as part of a wide network of social relations, involving many other persons, and it is this network which I regard as the object of our investigations' (ibid.: 191). We can make direct observations of actually existing relations, but it is not the unique relations of Tom, Dick and Harry or the behaviour of Jack and Jill which interest us as scientists, according to Radcliffe-Brown. It is the general structural form abstracted from the particular instances, he explains (ibid.: 192).

Indian context, the concept of network was thus used to understand, on the one hand, the micro-level of village, caste, and the joint family and on the other hand, in a macro-anthropology to understand the Indian civilization as a whole. Sometimes it referred to social structural aspects and at other times to more conceptual models.

In Europe, a study by Barnes (1954) in rural Norway is seen as the beginning of a more organized interest in social networks in anthropology (Hannerz 1992b). But it was not until the end of the 1960s and beginning of the 1970s that the concept came to be used more, in the kind of micro-anthropology carried out by, for example, Mitchell (1969; 1973; 1974). These studies, however, looked mainly at face-to-face relations. They were based on observational data and became extremely micro-sociological, as they had to be carried out in small units. When larger units were dealt with, they were impractical and also soon became overloaded with information and impossible to handle. Thus the concept of network as so used soon went out of fashion in social anthropology (Hannerz 1992b). The main reason seems to have been that the concept had to fit into either a face-to-face micro-anthropology with participant observation in a demarcated geographical area, or into the more abstract theoretical macro-discussions about civilizations, for example. Hannerz suggests that the concept of network could be revived in social anthropology, and comments that the concept is still often used in a manner that comes close to the social structural use of Radcliffe-Brown in the 1940s (ibid.: 34). He suggests that it could instead be used in conceptualizing culture and the management of meaning (ibid.: 44).[13]

In macro-theories about globalization, the concept of network had a revival in the 1990s, and *The Rise of the Network Society* by Castells (1996) and Hardt and Negri's (2004) *Multitude* gave it a broader popularity. There are now also a growing number

[13] According to Hannerz, networks could be used '...as a root metaphor when we try to think in a reasonably orderly way (without necessarily aiming at rigour of measurement) about some of the heterogeneous sets of often long-distance relationships which organise culture in the world now—in terms of cumulative change or enduring diversity' (1992a: 51).

of studies focused on how control over globalization, in terms of flows of capital and information, for example, is something which is highly contested. In these studies an alternative globalization or 'transnationalism from below' is also increasingly dealt with in terms of 'networks' (see Smith and Guarnizo; 1999 and Escobar 2001, for example). The massive demonstrations in recent years, organized transnationally by movement activists, in favour of global justice have probably contributed to an increased interest in studying movements in terms of transnational networks. In studies about human rights movements, women's movements, and environmental movements 'advocacy networks' became a popular term to connote those extended networks that activists are connected with (see Keck and Sikkink 1998 and Khagram, Riker, and Sikkink 2002, for example). Global movements and 'globalization from below' are now popular themes among researchers, often including the concept of network (della Porta and Kriese 1999; della Porta *et al*. 2006; Escobar 2001, 2004; McDonald 2006; Smythe and Smith 2002; Tarrow 2005 and Smith *et al*. 2008).

The concept of network has been used in a multitude of ways, as we have seen, to connote everything from face-to-face relations on a local level (Mitchell 1969; 1973; 1974), to more abstract macro-theoretical relations, in discussions about globalization (Castells 1996). It has been used to refer to social structures (Radcliffe-Brown 1952) as well as to cultural aspects (Hannerz 1992a; 1992b; 1998). Networks of movements are complex and multifaceted, and it is difficult to make general statements about them, as Crossley (2002: 97) has commented. The networks of the Dalit movement are no exception in this regard. How, then, is the concept of network most fruitfully used to study a contemporary social movement in an anthropological way?

My own use of the concept will be contextual. The reason is not to avoid the difficulty of defining 'network', but rather a well considered idea that a contextual use of the concept will reveal the complexity of the movement and processes at work *between* different levels. It will show the elasticity, an important idiosyncrasy of networks that is lost when they are defined according to some general formula. The networks in a movement are used in an adaptable manner among activists. This means that the strings of the networks may better be thought of as springs or straps used and activated in an elastic way according to the demands of the situation. They may be stretched out over vast geographical distances, or rapidly reduced for narrower situations.

I shall take the concept of network along as I move between different levels in the movement. It will be used when the networks are activated on a local/regional level as well as on a national and transnational level. Sometimes 'network' will refer to the organizational structures of the movement and at other times to the cultural aspects regarding the meaning held among activists—two closely related aspects. Most often it will be clear from the context how it is used, and in cases where it is not obvious, I shall clarify the situation. For the 'extra-movement linkages' (Gerlach and Hine 1970b: 395f) stretched to people and groups not directly active in the movement, but associated with it and sympathizing in one way or another, I shall use the concept of web (ibid.: 395; Alvarez, Dagnino, and Escobar 1998a: 15f).

RESEARCH METHODS IN THE
INTERRELATIONAL FIELD

THE EXAMPLES OF MALINOWSKI AND ORTNER

Two well-known anthropologists who could serve as examples of how an interrelational field could be designed are Malinowski (1987[1922]) and, closer in time, Sherry Ortner (1997). Although Malinowski is seen as the father of classic fieldwork, I would like to adopt a somewhat different perspective on what he was actually doing. It may be seen as the easiest solution to keep Malinowski as a patriarch to legitimate a new field design. It may be right or wrong or just sentimental, but I shall return to Malinowski's *Argonauts of the Western Pacific*. There are, of course, large differences between Ortner and Malinowski. Ortner (1997) carried out translocal fieldwork among her own school-mates, the high school graduates in Newark, New Jersey, while Malinowski [1987 [1922]) 75 years earlier carried out his fieldwork in the western Pacific. In any case, let me point out some similarities regarding their respective field designs. Ortner's schoolmates were, at the time of her fieldwork, spread across the United States. She drove over several thousand miles of American freeways, and she writes under the subtitle *Fieldwork on the Road and in the Mind:* 'The fieldwork consisted of travelling all over the country and interviewing people wherever they happened to be, at any site of their choosing' (1997: 67).

Compare these words with Malinowski's description of his fieldwork. He is not travelling the freeways of the United States, but the seas of the western Pacific:

Immediately after leaving Sarubwoyna and rounding the promontory of the two rocks, we come in sight of the island of Sanaroa... Sailing further, some fine scenery unfolds itself on our left, where the high mountain range comes nearer to the sea shore...as we sail on, rounding one after the other...(1987 [1922]: 45)....

Leaving the bronzed rocks and the dark jungle of the Amphletts for the present—for we shall have to revisit them in the course of our study . . . we sail North into an entirely different world of flat coral islands (ibid.: 49).

We find him constantly leaving one island and heading for another. Malinowski carried out his fieldwork with the techniques 'follow the thing' and 'follow the people', described by Marcus (1995: 106), who also noted that Malinowski used a methodology suitable for translocal studies. Malinowski explains that the *kula*, which he studied, is a form of exchange of extensive, intertribal character and 'it is carried on by communities inhabiting a wide ring of islands' (1987 [1920]: 81). Probably not everybody will agree that Malinowski was the 'anthropological father of an interrelational field-design', but at least it could be agreed that not even *his* classic fieldwork was carried out in one year in one and the same village. Already for Malinowski, the field appeared gradually and dependently of what he experienced along the route. The unit of analysis was not created beforehand in a deductive manner.[14]

The processual approach has always been a reality to the anthropological fieldworker and not only to Malinowski and Ortner. This approach was, however, easier to legitimize at a time when anthropologists went away to explore the 'white spots'

[14] See also Hannerz 2003: 230f.

on the map, and could not possibly know beforehand what they were going to encounter. There was a consensus on the fact that they could not know what and whom they were going to meet, but they should in the process come to know it. Today it seems more difficult to legitimize a processual approach; nobody will be satisfied with a project plan explaining that I have an interesting theme to explore but it remains to be seen where I am going to end up.

To be able to legitimize and furthermore to know in a more structured way what we are up to in an interrelational field, we need a theoretical framework with pertinent methods for fieldwork. Hannerz (1992b) discusses network analysis without special reference to social movements, but some of his observations seem relevant for movement studies. One advantage with the concept of network is its openness, which means that the unit of analysis will not be restricted to a closed group:

...the concept of social network paves the way to an understanding of the linkage existing between different institutional spheres and between different systems of groups and categories... [the network] ramifies in every direction, and for all practical purposes, stretches out indefinitely... (Srinivas and Béteille 1964: 165–6).

Another advantage which comes with this openness is that local social relations (that are, of course, also of importance) do not overshadow long-distance relationships. Communication and message transmission in contemporary social movements are, as we know, taking place via letters, phone-calls, the Internet, etc., and in this way relationships are maintained over long distances. When we take long-distance relations into consideration, we also do not confine the analysis in space to a specific geographical territory, as discussed above. Social movements are, in most cases, spread over vast geographical areas and to understand the dynamic forces of the movement, the anthropologists will have to adjust to new, unconventional methods to carry out their fieldwork. To take up network analysis in a new form and reflect about fruitful pertinent anthropological field-methods will perhaps be a step towards participating more actively in the discussions about movements going on among sociologists, historians, political scientists, and others.

DESIGNING THE FIELD:
THE PATTERN OF SERENDIPITY

An interrelational field like a social movement may be thought of in terms of 'networks', 'webs', 'threads', 'chains', 'channels', 'paths', 'loops', etc. These concepts have all been used in anthropology. Other ways of thinking about the field could be in terms of its having a fibrous, stringy, rope-like or capillary character.[15] Marcus (1995) has given an idea of what a method could look like that is suitable for this kind of thread-like and open-ended field.[16] The verb 'to follow' may play an important role in multisited fields, he suggests. 'Strategies of quite literally following connections, associations, and putative relationships are thus at the very heart of designing multisited ethnographic research' (ibid.: 97).

Marcus discusses six different modes to construct the multisited space of research (ibid.: 106), or the interrelational[17] field. These are: to follow the people, the thing, the metaphor, the plot (story, or allegory), the life (or biography) or the conflict (ibid.: 110). I shall give examples from my own field; although my own following does not always fit the modes described by Marcus but falls in-between or with two or more of them overlapping, it is still a good way to think about what I have been doing. Although I did not have my own car, but mainly travelled by train, bus, rickshaw, and aeroplane, Ortner's formulation is also illustrative of my own fieldwork, when she explains that she was driving to people 'wherever they happened to be, at any site of their choosing' (1997: 67). I went wherever Dalit activists happened to be.

I shall extend the modes of following described by Marcus, and suggest that the field-pattern of serendipity may also be

[15] These concepts are taken from Latour (1996) when discussing actor-network theory.

[16] Marcus is even talking about an alternative method as 'an alternative paradigm of ethnographic method', to emphasize its radically new character (2002: 198).

[17] I earlier suggested that a distinction could be made between multisited (multilocal or translocal) and interrelational fields to signal a break with the common way of designing the former fields around a predestined number of locations or sites.

helpful in designing the field.[18] Robert Merton (1961 [1949]: 103ff) described serendipity half a century ago, in the context of the relation between empirical research and sociological theory, as the fairly common experience of observing an unanticipated, anomalous, and strategic datum. By this he meant that an observation was a by-product which was unexpected and surprising. Furthermore it provoked curiosity and stimulated one to make sense of the observation to fit it into the broader frame of what was known. The serendipity pattern put pressure on the investigator for a new fruitful direction of inquiry. Most researchers today will probably agree with Merton regarding the importance of serendipity for research in different disciplines. Its importance for anthropological fieldwork has also been acknowledged.[19] My point in this context, however, is that the serendipity pattern may be a helpful tool for designing the interrelational field.

Let me briefly explain what I mean by serendipity in relation to my field. In a site where I am by chance, or because I have followed some thread or path, there may pop up something unexpected, an unknown to me, and as yet unconnected element in the field. The first time the 'surprise' appears (in the form of a person, an association, a thing, etc.) it may be seen as a coincidence, but when it happens again, and maybe over again, it will soon be the starting point in a new sequence of events. In a meeting among Dalit Buddhists there may be a Dalit Christian, or vice versa, who is not expected to be there. He or she may be the starting point for finding out about a new network of which I was unaware. I may switch over to another path for some time, or maybe leave the track I came from, never to return. Simultaneously with my deliberate following, an individual, an association or a thing may pop up, independently of my own ideas about what I am doing in that specific site or locality.

[18] It was Ulf Hannerz who pointed out to me that I could relate my own field-experiences to the concept of serendipity.

[19] Signe Howell arranged, for example, a workshop at the 5th Biennial Conference of the European Association of Social Anthropologists (EASA) in Frankfurt, 4–7 September 1998, on the theme 'Fieldwork: The Value of Serendipity'.

In an interrelational field, elements, people, and ideas are moving in more than one direction. Every situation is a combination of routes or paths, on which practically anybody, anything or any ideas may move and meet. They pass my way and may interact in the site where I happen, or have chosen, to be. When adding the aspect of serendipity, I hope to complicate the picture. What I want to emphasize is that I am always in the midst of different paths and threads, free to make my choice of where to go and what to be alert to. This may also give a better impression of people, ideas, and things, moving simultaneously in different directions, just to cross each other's paths in quite an undetermined fashion, never to be repeated in exactly the same way. They are passing the ways of each other in a specific site, and also my way, but out of my control. It is seldom that things are neatly in agreement with my own purposes or what I am up to for the moment. Instead of seeing the unexpected anomalies that turn up as problematic distractions, which I sometimes had a tendency to, I think they should better be seen as vital toggles, making it possible to attach and switch over to new strands or paths in the field.

When following leads to an 'explosion' of a broad array of unexpected 'pop-ups', known to belong in connected research contexts, a firework display or a phosphorescence, to speak metaphorically, may be seen on site. That may be what Martin has called an 'implosion' in fieldwork. She described this as 'when elements from different research contexts seemed to collapse into one another with great force' (Martin 1994: 91).[20] It is then easily recognized that you are in the right place at the right moment. The same may be said about the opposite situation. It is not difficult to realize when you have completely lost your track. What may be a problem is the zone in between, where nothing is directly and obviously of importance for the study, but is still interesting enough to give some clues to a better understanding of the field.

So long as I have found something of interest in relation to the Dalit movement, I have regarded myself as being in the right place. Whenever I felt myself to be navigating within my

[20] For an example in my ethnography, see the Buddhist conversion in Patna in Chapter 4 note 12.

area of interest, however peripheral it might have seemed, I did not feel lost. DeLillo (1984) describes a similar situation with the poetic expression, to hear a 'white noise'. Whatever the importance of these 'noises' and 'phosphorescences', I shall now leave these diffuse metaphorical descriptions of a method, which most people may find too close to what we call intuition to be of any use. In, it is to be hoped, a more concrete way, I shall instead look at my method with the pattern of serendipity in mind and with the inspiration of the six modes of following suggested by Marcus. To repeat, these modes are: follow the people, the thing, the metaphor, the plot (story, or allegory), the life (or biography), and the conflict (Marcus 1995: 110). They will be slightly modified to fit my own field. I have not regarded them as absolute, but more as a source of inspiration to think about and also describe the method in an interrelational field in a more structured way—without the aim of classifying.

MOVING ALONG FIELD TRACKS—LOOKING FOR FRUITFUL DIRECTIONS

When studying social systems it is advisable to start with social actors and trace their activities and networks—'to follow the loops', Barth (1992: 25) writes, with an expression taken from Bateson (1972). One way to follow the threads between different localities in my field was with the help of individuals, namely the Dalit activists. These individuals I followed, liter- ally, to find out which networks they were a part of, how they moved between different sites and localities, which strategies they used, and how they created new spaces for their activities. Some individuals I followed for just one or a few days, while others became more key informants with continued importance throughout my fieldwork. Many of them I interviewed more formally to get their life histories and to understand how they regarded the movement, their relations with others (within as well as outside the movement), and their own role within it.

Compared with Ortner, who travelled the US highways in her own car to reach the geographically dispersed field-sites, I expe- rienced a closely related, but still very different field situation. In Britain I often travelled *others'* cars—it could be Buddhist monks or Dalit activists. My field was in this sense often in motion. In India I travelled by rickshaw, bus or train, together with activists. These field situations, in motion, were also some of the most relaxed circumstances, when the information came to me without any strain.[21] The reason probably was that all of us experienced the situation as some kind of 'time off', as an 'in-between-the-work-situation'. These situations may be seen not as travelling *in* the field, or *between* field-sites, but as 'travelling *with* the field', in a quite literal sense.[22]

In most cases one thing turned into the next, and one locality often opened up in many directions with many different threads or paths to follow. I found specific sites that I used to return to, where some specific individuals either lived or turned up and left again. Some of these were of a more permanent character, like somebody's home, a Buddhist vihara or an office of a political party. In other cases the sites had more of an occasional character, and I only came for one visit, such as at a crossroads where a demonstration took place or a rented hall where the anniversary of the birth of Ambedkar was celebrated.

I also followed Dalit activists out of India. Activists whom I had met in India I went to see again in Britain. In other instances I only traced their contacts to Britain and went to meet their friends and relatives. During my time in Britain I discovered new transnational networks and when I went back to India later it was with these new networks in mind. This may be seen as 'following the people', the most obvious and conventional mode, as described by Marcus (1995: 106). Still, I think this 'conventional' mode should not be underestimated, as it is a good starting point in a complex field. Everything possible or impossible could be added to this first mode. It was a trustworthy base, for me, in an unpredictable field without any steady demarcations—follow the people, quite simply.

'Follow the thing' in terms of a material object was another mode. In the study of a social movement, symbols are of the

---

[21] It could be compared with the traditional expression of 'gathering information' in the field, which is usually associated with some kind of effort.

[22] For a discussion on travel, translation, and fieldwork, see Clifford (1997).

utmost importance and objects with these symbols can be easily tracked. Often they functioned as reminders or pop-ups, when I thought I had lost my way or when I had deliberately taken a much-needed 'break'. During my fieldwork I tried to be observant or alert when an object with some connection with the movement's role model Ambedkar turned up. It could be a pen or a poster with his face on it, cassettes of his speeches, books, statues in the villages or on the outskirts of the cities, etc. These objects put me into contact with activists whom I did not know before. One of the advantages of this mode was that these contacts did not emerge from prior networks with which I was familiar. My new contacts could be unrelated and even be in conflict with activists in the other networks I knew. The point is that, if all the contacts in the field are created in a process of extending networks from initial contacts, the overwhelming risk is that many parallel networks are lost. Paying attention to the things that turn up unexpectedly is a good way of being introduced to networks which were previously unfamiliar.

Whether an editorial office could be seen as a 'thing' is highly questionable. However, I have followed a Dalit periodical when it changed its editorial office from Bangalore to New Delhi and back again. The same periodical I also followed as a material object in another sense, namely to see who within the movement read it. Maybe I am turning now more to a mode that could be called 'follow the media'. To read periodicals and newspapers was an important part of my fieldwork. The daily newspapers provided a type of information that was important, as a context, to be able to discuss different topics, often related to politics, with Dalit activists. In Dalit periodicals, I got to know about demonstrations, conferences, seminars, etc. to attend. The letters from readers gave information about who knew whom in the movement and what kind of topics were discussed.

Gusterson (1997: 116)[23] suggests that we abandon our, what he calls, 'fetishistic obsession with participant observation',

[23] Gusterson (1996; 1997) has studied the nuclear weapons community in the United States, a community that is dispersed between California, New Mexico, and Washington, DC, which makes his field similar to my own dispersed field, with Dalit groups and activists spread across India and even abroad.

and leave some room for 'polymorphous engagement'. By this expression he means that we should interact with informants across dispersed sites, sometimes in virtual form, as well as using different research techniques, such as formal interviews or readings of newspapers, and with attention to popular culture, for example. Participant observation is a research technique which does not travel well up the social structure, Gusterson argues. His arguments seem to be valid in a more general sense, not just when studying up. We have all got problems, if we try to carry out fieldwork with only participant observation. The method seems not to travel well by itself anywhere—up, down, diagonally or sideways—in today's world (and maybe not even in yesterday's world). I therefore find Gusterson's concept of 'polymorphous engagement' useful, as one solution among others to deal, not least, with the dispersed field.

My own field is a good example of the fact that, without the use of different research techniques, I did not know very much about the Dalit movement. I was forced to make use of various methods including interviews, subscriptions to different Dalit magazines, reading newspapers, following the activities on the Internet, etc. Another type of polymorphous engagement, with special relevance for a dispersed field, has been to make use of the research of others, integrating their findings with my own work (see Hannerz 1992a: 52, 1998). To cover the Dalit movement in Maharashtra (Zelliot 1992) and the south of India (Omvedt 1994a), for example, I have incorporated the knowledge of researchers who have devoted their entire lives to these areas.

Another mode that could be distinguished is 'follow the theme'. A recurrent theme in seminars, periodicals as well as in every-day talk among activists was 'Ambedkar and Gandhi'. I went to seminars where this theme was discussed, read articles about it, and when it was being discussed among activists, I tried to keep my ears open. Closely connected is a mode that I call 'follow the association'. In the Dalit discourses about Ambedkar and Gandhi, for example, I followed closely what kind of ideas Ambedkar and Gandhi respectively gave rise to religiously, politically, etc.

In the Dalit movement, as well as among activists in many other social movements, there are recurrent themes related to origin.[24] Common questions to be answered are: 'Who are we?' 'How, where, and when did it all begin?'. Many Dalit activists are claiming the status of being the original inhabitants of the country and consequently they argue that they are the legitimate owners of the land. Statues of Ambedkar were put up in many villages and even in urban quarters by Dalit activists during the 1990s, to mark plots of land they claimed the SCs were entitled to. In one site a discourse may be focused on Dalits as the original inhabitants of India. The same kind of discourse in another situation may put a much stronger emphasis on the original inhabitants as Buddhists. In a third site it may have turned into an emphasis on the Buddhists' right to land. In a fourth, international context, the theme of Dalits as original inhabitants of India may be focused exclusively on discrimination against minorities in different parts of the world. There are many discourses and also variations on a theme within the movement. The beginning and end were seldom in consonance when I followed some themes or associations. At times it was not even possible to see any correspondence at all, if a few of the associational links were not inserted in-between.

Following the life history may not only be a way of understanding the individual's conception of himself and the world around him. It may also be, as Marcus (1995: 110) suggests, a guide to finding ethno-graphic spaces which are otherwise lost in a system which is shaped by categorical distinctions which hide these (often subaltern) spaces. Another way to express the same thing is to say that life histories may reveal spaces, where alternative counterpublics are formed, which are otherwise hidden by a discourse shaped by the surrounding society. In my own field, spaces occupied by Dalit activists could, in other words, be revealed by looking at novel associations among sites, or social contexts suggested in these life histories. In the life histories of two different Dalit activists, the roof-veranda of a Buddhist vihara occurred. In one of the histories it was the site connecting the vihara with a political party, and in the other instance it connected the vihara with a social organization. When investigated, the political party and the social organization

[24] Marcus talks about something similar as 'follow the plot, story or allegory' (1995: 109).

had earlier both been connected with the vihara and also with each other. These were unknown and unexpected connections to me. It was something that I had not been aware of, despite frequent visits to the vihara, as well as regular discussions with members of both the political party and the social organization for a considerable length of time.

To complicate the picture one mode of following may coincide with another, modes may overlap, and sometimes one mode may turn into another on the way. However, having these kinds of modes as a lodestar may be a way to regain at least some control of the method when you are moving among people, things, and ideas in the interrelational field, exercising 'participant observation', overwhelmed by impressions, and without any obvious way to go. It is further a good way to organize the material later on, and also a way to structure the ethnographical writing.

The mode, which Marcus has spoken about as 'follow the conflict' (1995: 110), may be seen as the main mode in my own field. Conflict has a far too important role to play in many contemporary social movements to give it a similar status to the other modes discussed so far. For me, as for many others with a social movement as a field, each and every following leads to the occurrence of conflict. This may even be seen as a leitmotif that permeates all the other modes discussed so far. The activists in the Dalit movement regard themselves as being in conflict with Hinduism as a religion and with the Hindu community and Hindu nationalism as a political ideology. To follow a Dalit activist is definitely to follow him or her to a context where this conflict is discussed. The same will happen if you follow the thing, the media, a theme, an association, or a life history. The component of conflict, in one or other form, is to be found everywhere.

Evelina Dagnino writes, when discussing Gramsci (1971) and the concept of hegemony, that '[i]f the conception of culture as the attribution of meanings embedded in all social practices has been established in the field of anthropology, what the theory of hegemony brought to light was the fact that this attribution of meanings takes place in a context characterized by conflict and power relations' (1998: 43). The Dalit activists take part in a struggle in civil society and attribute meaning, not least to their own identity, in a context characterized by conflict and power relations. Their interpretations often differ in a significant way from that given by other groups and individuals. Furthermore, Dalit activists have occupied their own spaces, published their own periodicals, arranged their own conferences, and taken part in other events quite separately from others, for a long time. This has some implications for the anthropologist. The field of the Dalit movement, as well as of other social movements, may be easier to design than some other multi-, translocal or interrelational fields where conflict does not have this explicit and significant position. My field thus took shape as I moved along and tracked new paths to follow with the help of people, things, media, themes, associations, and life histories that turned up unexpectedly—all occupied with or permeated by the leitmotif of conflict.

3

Traditions of Protest

I'm burning with a feeling of revolt
*   and I call out to you*
I will write the poems of revolt on your sword
Today I have become a storm—come with me!
I reach out to you—give me your hand!
I have become the sun, my friend—sing with me!
I have become the fire, today I am afire with fire—
*   give voice to the volcano within you!*
I'm out of my senses, out of control
Make me a limitless sky with words
I will hurl myself into the battle
If I should win, shout out my victory!
If I should break, bury me deep!
If I come to your door confused, try to understand me!
If I return bloodied, hold me to your breast!
If I die out there, take my body in your arms!
Someone make me believe I am and will be yours!
Shed a few tears and remember me forever!

                                                  (Manohar 1992: 113)

Civil society is not 'one homogeneous happy family', as Alvarez,
Dagnino, and Escobar (1998b: 17) comment, 'but also a terrain
of struggle mined by sometimes undemocratic power relations
and the enduring problems of racism, hetero/sexism, environmental destruction, and other forms of exclusion.' The so-called
untouchables in India have traditionally been excluded on the
basis of being regarded as unclean in a religious sense. This
background will be an attempt to understand the first more
organized efforts among the so-called untouchables to protest
against the caste system and their own place at the bottom of
this system.

There has been a tendency among researchers to dub the protests against the caste system under the common labels of 'social reform movements', 'protest movements', 'anti-caste movements' or something similar. In this background chapter I shall distinguish between two traditions of protest, and I am making a sharper distinction than many others dealing with the issue. I shall differentiate between, on the one hand, the *Hindu caste-reform tradition* and, on the other, the *autonomous anti-caste tradition*.[1] This is more than a matter of subtle distinctions. Behind the superficial similarities that seem to unite activists in a common opposition against the caste system and in favour of an egalitarian society, there are different complexes of ideas, which, during a large part of the twentieth century, have put activists in conflict with each other.

Simply expressed, the Hindu caste-reform tradition could be seen as integrative in its approach, wanting to integrate 'untouchables' within the religion of Hinduism. Activists in the autonomous anti-caste tradition, on the other hand, find Hinduism to be the base of the caste system and consequently want to separate the 'untouchables' from the Hindu religion and the Hindu community. It is my conviction that a more nuanced understanding of the protests against the caste system may shed some new light on the contemporary Dalit movement.

EARLY PROTESTS IN THE CASTE SABHAS AND SOCIAL REFORM MOVEMENTS

THE TRADITIONAL CASTE HIERARCHY

First, before looking more closely at the protests against the caste system, something more has to be said about the traditional caste system against which the protests were directed. Louis Dumont (1980 [1966]) wrote *Homo Hierarchicus* almost half a century ago; although criticized for his generalizations concerning 'India' and the 'West', he should be given the credit of making

[1] The labels are influenced by Omvedt's discussion (1994a) about Dalits in relation to a reform movement versus an independent anti-caste movement. My approach will to a large extent be influenced by and overlap with the views of Omvedt, but there will also be major differences, which I shall discuss later in this chapter.

relevant observations regarding the religious written ideals about the caste system. The hierarchical interdependence between caste groups is, according to Dumont, one of the main features of the ideal caste system.

Dumont uses hierarchy in different senses. One way in which he found hierarchy to be the guiding value was in the interrelation between castes. The different caste groups are interrelated in a hierarchical and metonymical way based on the religious values of purity and pollution, with purity on the top and pollution at the bottom. The system as a whole (accompanied by interdependence) is valued more highly in India than in the West, he argued, and each caste group is part of the whole. In the West the individual and individualism are the prime values at the expense of interdependence between groups and individuals. It should be added that the ideal interdependence described by Dumont is contained in the religious scriptures, accompanied by descriptions of the types of ostracism, to be implemented from the top down when someone has not been following his/her own *dharma*[2] (religious duty). That is, the ideal varna system in the Laws of Manu[3] include laws about penalties to be carried out when the prescribed social, political, and economic duties have not been fulfilled by the different categories (see Thorat and Hardtmann 2003).

Another related way in which Dumont talked about hierarchy was with regard to religion being superior to and encompassing politics and economics in a metonymic way, that is, the political and economic spheres (and also power) are seen as subordinated to, but part and parcel of and directed by, the Hindu religion. An example of this is how the king (Kshatriya) and his worldly power ideally should be subordinated to the Hindu priest (the Brahmin) and his religious status.

One of the main points made by Dumont was that those hierarchical values seen as ideal in India were also to be found

[2] Dharma can be translated as 'religion', 'duty', 'law', 'right', 'justice', 'practice' and 'principle' (Doniger and Smith 1991).

[3] The Laws of Manu, Manusmriti, is the Hindu text, which prescribes the rules for varna relations. It is usually dated to AD 200 and consists originally of 2,685 verses (2,694 stanzas in 12 chapters) dealing with a range of themes; family life, caste relations, relations to money and material possessions, politics, ritual, etc. (Buhler 2004).

in western societies, in spite of the West's explicit dissociation from them in favour of equality. They worked on a 'subconscious' level and made their appearance in a different form—racism.[4] In the same way egalitarian values could be found in India on a different level. The moral of *Homo Hierarchicus* was, from a 'western' point of view, that trying to understand India from within not only gives a better non-ethnocentric understanding of India's culture, but it also gives the 'West' a better under-standing of its own culture and hidden hierarchical values.

Marriage relations and eating and drinking relations, but also occupations, for example, were seen in the light of these religious values. In the 1950s and 1960s, simultaneously with the writings of Dumont, social anthropologists were also making the first attempts to understand the caste system at a grassroots level (Marriott 1955, for example). They came now to speak not so much about the four varnas in the religious scriptures, as about the multitude of different *jatis* (caste groups) they paid attention to during their fieldwork in the Indian villages.[5] Similarly to the relations described between the varnas in the religious scriptures, however, they found the relations between the jatis in the villages to be structured, to a high degree, by the religious values of purity and pollution. The human bodies, materials, occupations, marriage relations, eating and drinking relations, etc., were all seen in relation to these religious values. The so-called untouchables constituted different jatis but stood outside and below the four varnas,

[4] This did not mean for Dumont that the hierarchical caste system was the same as racism. On the contrary, he meant that caste should not be confused with race. One of the differences was, according to Dumont, that the caste system is a coherent system based on the religious principle and ideals of inequality, while racism is based on colour and, as a kind of disease, is seen to contradict the ideal values of an egalitarian system within which it occurs (see further Dumont 1980 [1966]: 255).

[5] The relation between jatis and varnas, that is the categorization of each jati into one of the four varnas or below them, seems to have been, if not a total construction of the British during the colonial period (with censuses every 10 years from 1901 onwards), at least a major factor in formalizing hierarchical relations on a village level that were often quite diffuse before the intervention of the British (see Carroll 1978).

and were consequently seen as the most polluted, with major consequences for their social relations—they were excluded from many activities and places in Indian society.

The so-called untouchables did not have access to the main village but lived outside it. People regarded as being of higher status were supposed to keep them at a distance. The 'untouchables' were not allowed to take water from the village well; their touch was seen as polluting to the extent that if an 'untouchable' had been in contact with the well it had to be ritually cleansed before it could be used again. The Hindu temples were closed to the so-called untouchables and they were not allowed to read the religious scriptures. If the 'untouchables' were at any time allowed into the village it had to be at high noon, when the shadow is at its smallest for even the shadow was regarded as polluting (Zelliot 1992: 315, note 20).

They were not allowed to read or get any education. The occupations which the so-called untouchables were allowed to practise were those connected with material that was seen as religiously defiled, such as excrement (latrine cleaners) or dead animals (the work of taking dead animals out of the village), for example.

CASTE ASSOCIATIONS

During the nineteenth and twentieth centuries the practice of untouchability was contested and the so-called untouchables came to mobilize themselves on the basis of a common exclusion. There was not *one* reform movement during this time, but many independent groups protesting against untouchability and its practice (Heimsath 1978). The caste *sabhas*[6] were the first more conscious efforts to mobilize around a caste identity. Low caste associations were formed across India to work for the uplift of the so-called untouchables from the end of the nineteenth century, but it was at the beginning of the twentieth century that they became more common.[7] Many of the leaders

[6] Sabha means 'assembly', 'association', 'meeting' or 'society'.
[7] The caste associations and caste federations were not restricted to the low castes, though, but could also be found among caste categories higher up the hierarchy. Among these the caste sabhas were often directed more to other activities than social reform and were more reminiscent of business networks, for example.

in the caste associations had been active in reform movements like the Arya Samaj, a Hindu reform movement founded in 1875. Others were inspired by the Hindu *bhakti* movement, a devotional movement denouncing hierarchy between men and emphasizing a personal relationship with god (Zaehner 1984; Brockington 1985; Lorenzen 1995).[8]

The caste sabha differs from caste group (jati) in the traditional caste system in which belonging is ascribed, that is, you are born into a specific group or category. It also differs from associations or organizations in which, for example, one has to earn one's membership. In the caste sabha, both these circumstances are required; you must be born into the relevant caste category and also have actively gained your membership, for example, by paying a membership fee, giving financial support or taking part in meetings.

We can also see another organizational form in which caste played a role in the Indian village, namely, the caste *panchayat* which could be translated as 'caste council'. As Simmons has noted, the caste panchayat is in charge of 'regulating caste behaviour' (1971: 86), and although it could be seen as organized on a caste base, it differs from the caste sabha in protecting caste behaviour and traditional caste relations. Caste panchayats, however, do not belong within either of the two traditions of protest that interest us here. However, let me say a few more words about the caste panchayat in comparison with the caste sabha, mainly to better understand the latter.

Simmons writes about the result of the census in 1911:

The Census found two basically different institutions of caste government: the caste panchayat and the caste association, or the caste sabha. The caste panchayat is the traditional counsel of caste elders in charge of regulating caste behaviour. The caste association on the other hand is of recent origin. It dates back to the end of the last [19th] century, has witnessed considerable growth during the

---

[8] The conditions which made it possible for the caste sabhas to be formed, their aims, strategies, and organizational forms have been dealt with at length by researchers in the 1960s, 1970s, and 1980s (see, for example, Srinivas 1962; Rudolphs and Rudolph 1967; Fox 1967,1970; Rowe 1968; Washbrook 1975; Heimsath 1978; Molund 1988 and Zelliot 1992: 86–125).

following decades, and is a rather wide-spread institution in modern India (ibid.: 86f).

The caste sabha has a regional influence aiming to be national, while the caste panchayat has local influence. The former is a formal organization in which the leader is elected and decisions are taken according to written rules. In the caste panchayat, on the other hand, leadership is informal and is either inherited or depends on age or some other kind of influence. Decisions are taken according to narrated local tradition (Simmons 1971).

In the caste panchayat the status quo is defended, in contrast to the caste sabha where the members see themselves as representatives for change. The differences are obvious, and I would say that it can be easily concluded from these differences that the caste sabha is a forerunner of the Dalit movement, just because it is a new organizational form based on caste, and in favour of change and caste reform. This is also the way the caste sabhas are often treated in the literature: as part of a social reform tradition or anti-caste tradition in India, of which the contemporary Dalit movement is just the latest expression. But this is something that should not be taken for granted.

Heimsath writes about the caste associations:

Since the turn of the [20th] century caste associations have superseded general religious and social reform movements and the great national personal law reform crusades and have carried the main weight of *the Hindu social reform movement*. Created to enhance the social prestige and economic welfare of certain castes, all caste associations of which I am aware instructed their members in reforms of personal behaviour, marriage practices, religious or secular rituals, and urged and actively arranged educational opportunities for the community (Heimsath 1978: 23, emphasis added).

The caste sabhas were of great importance in religious and social reform work, and they were by and large working within the Hindu caste-reform tradition that I have distinguished from the autonomous anti-caste tradition. Social reforms within the Hindu caste-reform tradition were often a way for so-called untouchables to reach a higher status within the caste hierarchy. Sanskritization was the concept used by Srinivas (1952) for the attempts among low castes to leave what were considered as polluting activities and occupations to reach a higher status within the existing hierarchy. The leaders of the caste sabhas told their members not only to leave 'polluting' activities, but to also take on some habits of the higher castes. One example of this was how they started to wear the 'sacred thread', which was a sign of belonging to the three highest varna categories, that is Brahmins, Kshatriyas, and Vaishyas.[9]

CASTE FEDERATIONS

Kothari and Maru (1970) differentiate between two forms of caste sabhas, one the caste association which I have just dealt with, and the other an organizational form which they call a caste federation. There is a qualitative difference between the caste association and the caste federation. The caste federation is broader in two senses. First, it has a wider geographical spread. Second, it is often formed around a varna identity instead of a jati identity. According to Kothari and Maru, the caste federations often reach across the ascribed identity of jatis (the more narrow concept of endogamous caste groups). They write as follows:

The caste federation is thus no more agency of an endogamous group or groups set up for undertaking a specific task. Rather, it represents a new notion of caste organization, is based on real or supposed sharing of interests and status attributes, and gives rise to its own symbolism. [...]
A caste federation is, therefore, to be distinguished from a caste association both because of the range of social reality that it covers, and because of its search for an inclusive rather than 'functional' identity (ibid.: 72).

Galanter describes the caste federation in the following way, this time comparing it with the caste panchayat:

Caste organization brought with it two important and related changes in the nature of caste. The salient groups grew in size from the endogamous jatis into region-wide alliances. Concomitantly,

---

[9] Traditionally Brahmins, Kshatriyas and Vaishyas go through the 'sacred-thread-economy', for Brahmins it should take place in their childhood and for Kshatriyas and Vaishyas when they are teenagers. Through the ritual they are considered to be 'twice-born'.

the traditional patterns of organisation and leadership in the village setting were displaced by voluntary associations with officials whose delimited authority derived from elections (Galanter 1991: 23).

The caste associations and caste federations were not necessarily a matter of replacement, but more a parallel form of organization to the caste panchayat.

The caste federation was no longer made up only of the members from one endogamous caste group, and it was clearly 'a new notion of caste organisation', as Kothari and Maru and Galanter point out. The caste federation has the organizational structure of a 'network of networks', although more formalized than in social movements, for example. The network of members in a caste association (drawn from one endogamous jati) form, together with networks of members in other caste associations (each one similarly drawn from one endogamous jati), a geographically broader caste federation, also with a broader identity. It is based more on a 'supposed sharing of interests and status attributes' than the endogamous caste association, and it 'gives rise to its own symbolism' (Kothari and Maru 1970: 72).

Caste federations were formed among different caste categories and my interest here is in those formed among the so-called untouchables. Whereas the federations among the so-called untouchables lacked a notion of a common, often local, endogamous identity among their members, what brought them together seems to a greater extent to have been their common experiences of exclusion. Their discourses and symbols were consequently often built around these common experiences. An identity came to be formed around the common experience of non-belonging.

Caste Associations, Caste Federations, and the Dalit Movement

It is not in the local caste associations, mobilized on the basis of one endogamous jati, but in the geographically and also identity-wise broader caste federations, mainly mobilized around the experience of exclusion, that we can find resemblance to the Dalit movement. Regarding organizational form, the caste federation could be seen as the forerunner to the Dalit movement, although the members did not aspire to make it a nation-wide or 'all-India' movement, as was later the case among the members in the depressed classes organizations in the 1930s, to which I shall return. When it comes to content, on the other hand, the caste associations as well as the caste federations, in general, among the so-called untouchables, differed from the Dalit movement that was to come. They were often focused on attaining a higher status for the so-called untouchables through their attempts at leaving despised practices or taking on practices admired within the framework of the existing caste system. It should be emphasized that in this sense they belonged within a Hindu caste-reform tradition and not in the autonomous anti-caste tradition, where we find the Dalit movement later on.

THE ADI MOVEMENTS: EARLY FORMULATIONS OF AN AUTONOMOUS IDENTITY

The forerunner to the Dalit movement in organizational struc-ture *and* content is to be found in the Adi movements of the 1920s. These movements, found across the country, were the first major attempts among the 'untouchables', with a geographi-cal spread, to break with Hinduism. The activists in the Adi movements claimed to be the original inhabitants of India and their status in the hierarchy was explained in racial terms. The Aryans were supposed to have invaded the country from the north-west and they were met by the original inhabitants of India (Dravidians in many presentations). According to the activists in these movements, the so-called untouchables were the descendants of the defeated original inhabitants. The Adi movements broke the bonds with the Hindus and they did it on racial grounds, as the original inhabitants, claiming to be the rightful owners of the Indian soil.

According to Juergensmeyer (1982), the Adi Dravida move-ment in the south seems to be the first movement in the country to have formulated these ideas (ibid.: 25), although Ad Dharm in Punjab, in the north, claimed to be the first to use the concept of 'Adi'.[10] The ideas seem to have been taken up by the Ad Dharm

[10] 'Ad' or 'adi' means ancient or original. Jotiba Phule (1826–90) was a forerunner and an inspiration to many of the organizations criticizing contemporary Hinduism. He criticized Brahminism and even .

in Punjab as well as by the Adi Hindu movement in today's Uttar Pradesh. But it is not documented whether, or to what extent, there was communication between the movements in the north and south. It is clear, however, that there were contacts between Ad Dharm and the Adi Hindu movement in the north (Juergensmeyer 1982: 25). In 1926 there was a meeting in Delhi arranged by Swami Achchutananda, the leader of the Adi Hindu movement.[11] The purpose seems to have been to create a unity among SC activists in Delhi, Punjab, and Uttar Pradesh (ibid.).

The 1920s, when the autonomous anti-caste tradition began to take shape, was a time of change. The Indian National Congress was on the rise across the country, not least because of Gandhi. Hindu and Muslim identities were formulated in opposition to each other and Hindu nationalism was on the ascendant (Omvedt 1994a: 106).[12] In this atmosphere of change there were thus also attempts across India to form political organizations which reflected the autonomy of the SCs, or 'depressed classes' at that time (Juergensmeyer 1982: 24).

It did not automatically follow from the argument that the 'untouchables' were Adi Hindus that they existed prior to, and separate from, the Hindus. It could, albeit exceptionally, mean that the Adi Hindus, were the very first and the 'true' Hindus (Omvedt 1994a: 122).[13] Although the Adi movements were most often formulating a separate identity from the Hindus, there was thus not always an agreement about where they belonged, as can be seen in the case of the Ad Dharm movement.

Hinduism and formulated theories that the Brahmins were Aryans who conquered the original inhabitants, who belonged to another race. Phule was partly influenced by European theories about the Aryan race (Omvedt 1994a: 240ff). He also emphasized the importance of education and scientific knowledge (ibid.: 97–104). E.V. Ramasami 'Periyar' (1879–1973), agitating for atheism was, together with Phule, one of those who early on rejected Hinduism.

[11] For a biographical account and the ideology of Achchutananda (based on an account of Jigyasu), in the context of contemporary Lucknow Chamars, see Khare (1984: 81–92).

[12] In the north, Hindu Mahasabha was formed in 1915 and Rashtriya Swayamsevak Sangh (RSS) in 1925 (Omvedt 1994a: 106).

[13] The example Omvedt gives is the 'Hyderabad controversy' (1994a: 122).

Regarding Ad Dharm in Punjab in the 1920s, for example, the activists were originally formulating a clear message that they were not Hindus, although they took their inspiration in poetry from a Hindu tradition. They are not easily categorized either into an autonomous anti-caste tradition or a Hindu caste-reform tradition. This is something that I shall return to in Chapter 6, when looking more closely at the contemporary Ambedkarites in Britain and their ambivalent relation to Ravidasis.

THE EXAMPLE OF AD DHARM

Ad Dharm was an organization founded in 1925 in Punjab among Chamars, traditionally leather-workers and seen as 'untouchables'. A sixteenth century bhakti poet called Ravi Das became the foremost guru and thus the members came to be called Ravidasis. The bhakti tradition criticized the caste system and its ritual hierarchy, and was a source of inspiration for many of the low caste associations which were formed at the beginning of the twentieth century to work for a change in Indian society.[14] Within Hinduism, the religious scriptures written in Sanskrit were not available to the majority of the people, but through the spread of religious texts and poetry in the spoken local languages, the bhakti movement threatened caste hierarchy. The discontent with the caste system can be found also in the *Bhagavata Purana*, which is one of the most important texts within the bhakti tradition.

Ravi Das falls within this bhakti tradition, and was seen as a *sant*.[15] The fact that he himself was a Chamar made him an

---

[14] The bhakti movement was a devotional movement which could be traced back to the seventh century, with its roots about two centuries earlier (Brockington 1985: 130). It had two strands, one which focused on Siva and the other on Vishnu, both gods within the Hindu pantheon. The bhakti movement evolved in South India and spread to the north. The movement, according to Brockington, passed into the hands of lower caste preachers and poets, such as Namdev (c. 1270–1350), Eknath (1533–99), and Tukaram in the first half of the seventeenth century (ibid.: 152). For more about bhakti religion in North India, see Lorenzen (1995).

[15] Sant means, literally, good or saintly; in this context it refers to one of a group of medieval religious poet-saints (Juergensmeyer 1982: 319; Schaller 1995). The Vaisnava bhakti movement came under

attractive choice as a guru for the Chamars. Within the bhakti tradition devotional love, song and meditation were seen as ways to reach communion with god. With his poetry Ravi Das challenged the caste hierarchy and turned it upside-down:

> And I, born to be a carrier or carrion, am now
>   the lowly one to whom the Brahmans come
> And lowly bow. They seek
>   the shelter of my name, Servant of the Sun
> Whose service is the service of the Lord.

(Juergensmeyer 1982: 86)

Within Ad Dharm, not only did poetry by Ravi Das spread, but also new texts and myths. A poster giving information about the first Ad Dharm conference in 1927 read:

We are the original people of this country, and our religion is Ad Dharm. The hindu qaum came from outside and enslaved us. When the original sound from the counch was sounded, all the brothers came together—chamar, chuhra, sainsi, bhanrje, bhil, all the Untouchables—to make their problems known. Brothers, there are seventy million of us listed as Hindus, separate us and make us free. We trusted the Hindus, but they turned out to be traitors. Brothers, the time has come: wake up, the government is listening to our cries. Centuries have passed, but we were asleep, brothers. Look at the lines that Manu has written, but he is a murderer. There was a time when we ruled India, brothers, and the land used to be ours. The Hindus came from Iran and destroyed our qaum. They became the owners, and then called us foreigners, disinheriting seventy million people. They turned us into nomads. They destroyed our history, brothers. There is hope from God (bhagwan) and help from the king. Send members to the council and start the qaum anew, brothers. Come together to form a better life. (Juergensmeyer 1982: 46, translated from Punjabi).

---

influences of the Nath cult and Islam in its Sufi form. This came to be called the 'sant tradition' and the holy men—individuals, not an organized group or sect—were mainly from the lower castes and some from Muslim backgrounds. Namdev is sometimes seen as a sant and Kabir (1440, or as early as 1398 according to some accounts—1518) is a sant within this tradition. Nanak (1469–1539) was the first Sikh guru and shared the sant background with Kabir (Brockington 1985: 156f).

This text emphasizes that the 'untouchables' are a *qaum*, which is Urdu and can be translated as 'a nation', but primarily means 'a people' or 'a community' (ibid.: 45, note 1). In the poster it is claimed that 'untouchables' form a community that has existed during all times. They are 'a people' in the same way as Hindus, Muslims, and Sikhs. Ad Dharm is the religion which belongs to the original inhabitants of the country who were discriminated against by the Hindus from outside. Different caste groups and caste categories are reminded of their common past as original inhabitants. The traditional status hierarchy is turned upside-down to provide a new identity for those who are at the bottom of the caste hierarchy.

To summarize, the first organizational attempts to unite among the so-called untouchables could be seen in the caste federations at the beginning of the twentieth century. But it was among the Adi movements, from the 1920s onwards, that a separate identity in relation to the Hindu community was formulated across the country. We have also seen that sometimes there was an ambivalent stance in these movements as to whether they belonged within Hinduism or were separate from it. Ad Dharm was taken as an example to demonstrate this two-sided stance regarding the Hindu tradition. They take their inspiration from the bhakti movement and Ravi Das, which clearly belong within a Hindu tradition. But in their rhetoric they dissociate themselves from the Hindu religion and Hindu community.

By the end of the 1920s, however, the so-called untouchables had found an established organizational form in the caste federations. Regarding content, an autonomous identity, separate from the Hindus, had been elaborated on for about a decade in the Adi movements.

THE AUTONOMOUS ANTI-CASTE STAND CRYSTALLIZES IN THE 1930s

AMBEDKAR AND GANDHI

During the 1930s the autonomous anti-caste stance would come to crystallize more explicitly in opposition to the Hindu caste-reformers. The social organization within the autonomous anti-caste tradition was now linked to the Independent Labour Party on a national level, while the social organization of the Hindu caste-reformers was linked to the Congress Party. The controversies between B.R. Ambedkar (1891–1956) and M.K. Gandhi (1869–1948) were crucial in the formation of the autonomous anti-caste position. The idea that 'Depressed Classes'[16] were to be separated from Hinduism and the Hindu community was represented by B.R. Ambedkar. In the opposite camp, M.K. Gandhi argued in favour of the inclusion of the 'Depressed Classes' among the Hindus and caste reforms.

Some biographical data about Ambedkar and Gandhi seem to be relevant for the context. Ambedkar was born a so-called untouchable Mahar, a caste group which traditionally worked as 'village servants' in Maharasthra. Gandhi was also born in western India, but in the state of Gujarat. He belonged to the caste group Bania,[17] who were traditionally merchants. Ambedkar received a Ph.D. in economics at Columbia University, New York, highly unusual for a so-called untouchable. He continued his studies, now in law, and was called to the bar at Gray's Inn in London and received a D.Sc. in economics at the London School of Economics and Political Science. Gandhi was similarly educated in London. Both became barristers and both were also equally engaged in the struggle against untouchability, although they differed as to how the changes should be accomplished. Ambedkar was of the opinion that the so-called untouchables had to change their circumstances by their own efforts, while Gandhi argued for a change of heart among the caste Hindus. These opinions could well have gone hand in hand had it not been for the different political and religious opinions that put them in opposite camps.[18]

---

[16] Before 1935 the government used the concept of 'Depressed Classes'. In 1935 the Government of India Act introduced the category 'Scheduled Castes'.

[17] Banias belong to the third varna, Vaishya.

[18] Zelliot (1992: 150–83) gives more biographical details of Ambedkar and Gandhi. She also compares and analyses their roles as leaders. For an exhaustive Ambedkar biography, see Keer 1990 [1954]. For a more recent book on Ambedkar, see for example Jaffrelot 2004.

Gandhi came to be known as 'Mahatma', 'the Great Soul'. He is known as the 'Father of the Nation' for his non-violent struggles, or satyagrahas, against the British colonial power, which finally led to India's independence in 1947. Non-violence, search for the Truth, self-control, and a simple life are some of the notions often associated with Gandhi. Ambedkar became known as 'Babasaheb' Ambedkar, 'the Great Man'. He is probably best known as 'The Father of the Constitution', because he was the first Minister of Law in independent India and chairman of the committee that drafted the Indian Constitution. Compared to Gandhi, Ambedkar has been quite unknown outside India until recently. It is only with the intensified activities of the Dalit movement in the 1990s, and its global spread, that his name has become somewhat better known. Ambedkar is often associated with his slogan: educate, agitate, and organize.[19]

Let me now make clear how the social organizations occupied with caste issues of the time differed from each other and belonged to different political folds, before turning to the differences between Ambedkar and Gandhi, which resulted in a final political and religious break between them.

DEPRESSED CLASSES FEDERATION AND ITS WEBs

Omvedt (1994a) summarizes a few things that she finds characteristic of what she calls the Dalit movement as a whole in the 1930s.[20] This movement took shape as a political force at the same time as the non-Brahmin movement, the working class, and the peasantry formed their organizations. The Dalit movement, however, differed from the others by remaining unabsorbed by the Congress. I cite Omvedt:

This process [being absorbed into Congress and part of an 'anti-imperialist united front', not only in rhetoric but also in practice] happened with the non-Brahman movement in spite of the historic

[19] This slogan was promulgated by Ambedkar in July 1924, when his first organization Society for the Welfare of the Excluded (Bahishkrit Hitkarini Sabha) was establised (Juergensmeyer 1982: 168, note 17).

[20] I shall discuss Omvedt's usage of the concept 'Dalit' and what she means by 'the Dalit movement' later.

opposition to and distrust of the Congress by Phule, in spite of efforts of Periyar to prevent it; it happened with the working class and peasantry in spite of continual tensions and betrayals of their interest by the bourgeois-dominated Congress, and largely because of the political decision of the communists to work within the Congress as an 'anti-imperialist united front'. *That this did not happen with the Dalit movement is almost solely due to Ambedkar.* Here we can see the role of the individual in history (1994a: 166, italics in original).

The non-Brahmin movement as well as the communist movement, by and large, were working within the Congress party at this time, but the Dalit movement differed in this respect.[21] Whether this was 'almost solely due to Ambedkar' or not is not my concern here, but rather the fact that a movement among the 'Depressed Classes' crystallized and remained outside the Congress fold. In this movement there was an explicit opposition to the Congress regarding its policies in relation to the 'Depressed Classes'.[22]

On an organizational level, it was not until the 1930s that three 'pan India' organizations had emerged which dealt with caste issues (Omvedt 1994a).[23] These early social organizations attempting to be 'all-Indian' were, however, not formally organized on such a level. But they were *linked* to political parties on an all-India level and through networks or webs, to follow Alvarez (1998), they reached and represented three different directions in all-Indian politics. These social organizations

[21] During 1937–40, the communists who could have been a possible alliance partner for Ambedkar, who was a socialist, joined the Congress fold. The Communist Party, militant in its anti-imperialist struggle, existed as an underground party. Instead, the communists worked within the Congress and used the Congress Socialist Party (CSP, formed in 1934) as a vehicle for organizing the masses (ibid.: 186). This meant that they also withdrew from political forces that stood in opposition to the Congress. Hence, the non-co-operation between Ambedkar's Independent Labour Party and the Communists in the 1930s.

[22] Periyar and his Self-Respect movement simultaneously stood outside of, and in opposition to, the Congress Party.

[23] Although they pretended to be 'all-Indian', it was not until the Scheduled Caste Federation, formed by Ambedkar in 1942, that we can find an organization which functioned on this level (Omvedt 1994a).

should not be confused with each other, as their webs reached out in completely different directions: (*a*) *The Depressed Classes Federation* was Ambedkarite and connected with Ambedkar's Independent Labour Party; (*b*) *The Depressed Classes League* (or the 'Harijan' League) was Gandhian and connected with the Congress Party (ibid.: 181); and (*c*) *The Depressed Classes Association* was linked to the Hindu fundamentalists in Hindu Mahasabha (Omvedt 1994a).[24]

These organizations, equally interested in caste issues (and with names confusingly similar), belonged, and this is my point, within different traditions of protest. The Depressed Classes Federation stretched its webs in an Ambedkarite direction at a national level to the Independent Labour Party.[25] This is the only 'all-India' organization during the 1930s that can be regarded as belonging within the autonomous anti-caste tradition, working for an autonomous status for the 'Depressed Classes'. The other two, the Depressed Classes League (connected to the Congress Party) and the Depressed Classes Association (with links to the Hindu Mahasabha) were instead working for caste reforms within Hinduism and integration of the 'Depressed Classes' among the Hindus. They belonged within the Hindu caste-reform tradition.

The Depressed Classes Federation could be compared to the earlier caste federations in its organizational form. As already shown, the caste federations were networks of the geographically more local caste associations (Kothari 1970: 21). However, the earlier caste federation belonged, as shown, within the Hindu

[24] The Depressed Classes Federation was founded in 1930 by Ambedkar. This federation developed into the 'Scheduled Castes Federation' from 1942 onwards (Omvedt 1994a: 181). The Communists (and other leftists within the Congress) did not have any links to social organizations focusing on caste issues, although at a local level communist cadres were involved in anti-untouchability campaigns (ibid.).

[25] The Independent Labour Party (ILP) was founded in 1936 by Ambedkar and was succeeded by Ambedkar's Scheduled Castes Federation in 1942 and Republican Party in 1956. For more about Independent Labour Party and Scheduled Castes Federation, see, for example, Omvedt (1994a: 190–222). For more about Ambedkar as a radical economic and political leader, especially after 1936 when the ILP was formed, see also Thorat (1998, 2000).

caste-reform tradition with the exception of the Adi movements in the 1920s, emphasizing their autonomy in relation to the Hindus. The Depressed Classes Federation followed thus in this tradition of the Adi Movements, similar in organizationally form and similarly formulating an autonomous identity. Here we have traced the earliest forrunners of today's Dalit movement.

AMBEDKAR VERSUS GANDHI (I)—THE POLITICAL BREAK

The differences between Hindu caste-reformers and activists within the autonomous anti-caste tradition were not about minor issues. They should rather be seen as core issues, fundamental for their total work and direction with political and religious implications even worth dying for. This can be seen in the two major controversies between Ambedkar and Gandhi in the 1930s: one regarding politics and the other regarding religion. Questions of politics and religion were intricately interwoven into the debates, and Ambedkar and Gandhi confronted each other in both these fields. I shall describe two of the most important disputes between them; the first one, more political, regarding the Poona Pact and the second, more religious, in relation to the publication of Ambedkar's *The Annihilation of Caste* (1979 [1936]). These controversies are of significance for an understanding of today's Dalit movement because Dalit activists in their discourses now constantly refer to this historical period.

In 1932 a political break took place between Ambedkar and Gandhi, resulting in the so-called Poona Pact. The British government held three round table conferences in London, with the purpose of finding out Indian opinion regarding reforms for the proposed new constitution of India which resulted in the 'Government of India Act 1935'. The second of these was held September to December 1931, and both Ambedkar and Gandhi were present. This meeting developed into an outright confrontation between these two historical figures, both claiming to represent the 'Depressed Classes'. In connection with this conference, the so-called Communal Award was announced, according to which, the 'Depressed Classes' were given electoral benefits in relation to the rest of society.[26] With these benefits

[26] At the first conference November 1930 to January 1931, Ambedkar, but not Gandhi, attended. During this conference the responsibilities

they were supposed, over time, to gain a political strength which they did not have. The Communal Award generously announced that the category of 'Depressed Classes' should be given the benefit of two votes in elections.[27]

The privilege of two votes each for persons belonging to the category of 'Depressed Classes' is specifically noteworthy. The 'Depressed Classes' were to remain part of the Hindu community and be able to vote on an equal footing because, *in addition* to one vote in a separate electorate, they would also have a second vote in the general electorate in a limited number of reserved (dual member) constituencies. This meant that since they had the right to vote for the general candidate in reserved constituencies, as well as the right to vote in a large number of non-reserved (general) constituencies, they were still to be regarded as part of the Hindu community. They could also, at least theoretically, stand for the general constituencies. The arrangement of the double vote for the 'Depressed Classes' was to be valid for 20 years, after which they were expected to be on par with the rest of society regarding political representation.

Ambedkar expressed his satisfaction with the arrangement as follows: 'The second vote given by the Communal Award was a priceless privilege. Its value as a political weapon was beyond reckoning' (1991a [1945]: 90). Gandhi, on the other hand, began 'a fast unto death', on 20 September 1932, to have the Communal Award withdrawn. The British Prime Minister Ramsay MacDonald assumed that Gandhi had misunderstood the content of the Communal Award, giving two votes to the 'Depressed Classes' when he opposed it. In his reply Gandhi explained why he could not accept it: 'The mere fact of "Depressed Classes" having double votes does not protect them or Hindu society in general from being disrupted. In establishment of a separate

---

were delegated to nine committees, one of them the Minorities Committee, which was to find a solution to the communal question. Prime Minister Ramsay MacDonald himself was chairman of the committee (Keer 1990; see also Ambedkar 1991a: 41).

[27] This was, according to Ambedkar, partly in response to Gandhi who did not want separate electorates because he was afraid this arrangement would divide the Hindu community.

electorate at all for "Depressed Classes" I sense the injection of poison that is calculated to destroy Hinduism and do no good whatsoever to "Depressed Classes"' (Gandhi 1972[1932]: 31; see also Ambedkar 1991a[1945]: 87).

In his reply Gandhi repeated his opposition to the Communal Award and explained that he was afraid that double votes for 'Depressed Classes' implied a risk. Ambedkar comments on Gandhi's fast in his book *What Congress and Gandhi Have Done to the Untouchables* as follows: 'There was nothing noble in the fast. It was a foul and filthy act. The fast was not for the benefit of the Untouchables.... How can the Untouchables regard such a man as honest and sincere?' (1991a [1945]: 259).

The end of the controversy was, however, the withdrawal of the Communal Award in an agreement between Ambedkar and Gandhi. About the negotiation Ambedkar writes:

As to myself it is no exaggeration to say that no man was placed in a greater and graver dilemma than I was then. It was a baffling situation. I had to make a choice between two different alternatives. There was before me the duty, which I owed as a part of common humanity, to save Gandhi from sure death. There was before me the problem of saving for the Untouchables the political rights which the Prime Minister had given them. I responded to the call of humanity and saved the life of Mr Gandhi by agreeing to alter the Communal Award in a manner satisfactory to Mr Gandhi. This agreement is known as the Poona Pact (Ambedkar 1991a [1945: 88]).

Gandhi was able to break his fast and the Poona Pact was signed, increasing the reserved seats for the 'Depressed Classes' from 78 to 148 out of a total of 780 (Gore 1993: 138). But this could in no way compensate for the loss of the double vote and the separate electorate, according to Ambedkar (1991a [1945]: 90).[28] He found that the problem with the voting system was that the 'Depressed Classes' were in a minority in the general constituency. Without a separate electorate there was an overwhelming

[28] Reading Ambedkar it is clear that he was in no way satisfied with the outcome resulting in the Poona Pact. He was strongly and explicitly against it. Reading Omvedt (1994a: 174) regarding this issue one may be misled into thinking that Ambedkar was satisfied with the Poona Pact.

risk that the Hindu majority would come to choose the representatives among the 'Depressed Classes' who were seen to be most loyal to their own interests and not to the interests of the 'Depressed Classes'. [29]

AMBEDKAR VERSUS GANDHI (II)— THE RELIGIOUS BREAK

On the religious side, the more definitive break with Hinduism came from Ambedkar in 1935. He then announced at a conference of Depressed Classes in Yeola, a town in Maharashtra, that although he was born a Hindu, he would not die a Hindu (Zelliot 1992: 170). The next year, he published *Annihilation of Caste*[30] in which he again condemned not only the caste system, but also Hinduism on the ground of its being the basis for the caste system. Originally, the publication was written as a speech which was to have been delivered as the presidential address at the annual conference of a Hindu caste-reform organization in 1936 in Lahore. But the speech was not delivered, the reason being that Ambedkar made it clear again in this speech that he was about to leave Hinduism: 'I am sorry, I will not be with you. I have decided to change' (1979 [1936]: 80). This was something that the organizers of the conference could not accept.

To understand the cold relationship between the Hindu caste reformers and those belonging within the autonomous anti-caste tradition, represented by Ambedkar, let me quote from the prologue in *Annihilation of Caste*:

The Jat-Pat-Todak Mandal, I was given to understand, to be an organization of Caste Hindu Social Reformers, with the one and only aim, namely to eradicate the Caste System from amongst the Hindus. As a rule, I do not like to take any part in a movement which is carried on by the Caste Hindus. Their attitude towards social reform is so different from mine that I have found it difficult to pull on with them (1979 [1936]: 27).

The prologue contains the exchange of letters between the organizers and Ambedkar. He explains why he was in the

---

[29] The text of the Poona Pact and Ambedkar's comments can be found in Ambedkar 1991a [1945]: 88ff.

[30] The same year he also founded the Independent Labour Party.

end not welcome to deliver the speech that he, in spite of his hesitation, had been persuaded to make. The prologue ends in the following way:

This is I believe the first time when the appointment of a President is cancelled by the Reception Committee because it does not approve of the views of the President. But whether that is so or not, this is certainly the first time in my life to have been invited to preside over a Conference of Caste Hindus. I am sorry that it has ended in tragedy. But what can any one expect from a relationship so tragic as the relationship between the reforming sect of Caste Hindus and the self-respecting sect of Untouchables where the former have no desire to alienate their orthodox fellows and the latter have no alternative but to insist upon reform being carried out? (Ambedkar 1979 [1936]: 35).

After the publication of *Annihilation of Caste*, Gandhi (1976a [1936]: 134ff and 1976b [1936]: 153f) wrote two reviews of it in his paper *Harijan* (11 and 18 July 1936) in which he expressed his difference of opinion regarding caste. There was one main difference between them. According to Ambedkar, the ideals of Hinduism were not in accordance with an equality of status between different categories of people, and accordingly the so-called untouchables would never get equality as long as they stayed within Hinduism. This was not the opinion of Gandhi. He found the ideals of Hinduism to be against the inequality in status between caste groups. Gandhi believed in the law of varna, which he found to have nothing to do with inequality between castes. In one of his review articles he makes his stand clear:

The law of varna teaches us that we have each one of us to earn our bread by following the ancestral calling. It defines not our rights but our duties. It necessarily has reference to callings that are conducive to the welfare of humanity and to no other. It also follows that there is no calling too low and none too high. All are good, lawful and absolutely equal in status. The callings of a Brahmin— spiritual teacher—and a scavenger are equal, and their due performance carries equal merit before God and at one time seems to have carried identical reward before man. Both were entitled to their livelihood and no more (*Harijan*, 18 July 1936, in Gandhi 1976b [1936]: 153f; also cited in Ambedkar 1979 [1936]: 83).

To Gandhi it was possible to keep Hinduism and the four varnas, incorporating the 'untouchables', on equal terms within the varna system. He requested a rethinking on the part of the caste categories higher in the hierarchy. Gandhi's view was that one should be loyal to one's varna regarding choice of occupation, but all occupations should be regarded as equal in status, none as more polluting than another.

Gandhi was, as already mentioned, born a Bania within the varna category of Vaishya. In 1927, he himself was accused of not himself keeping to the principle of 'following one's ancestral calling', which he held in high esteem. It was pointed out that he was involved in politics rather than, owning a grocery shop, which would have been more in accordance with his ancestral calling of the trading Vaishyas (Gandhi 1969b [1927]: 534f). He then specified his position; everybody was free to carry out any useful service, as long as he did not demand any compensation for it (*Young India*, 17 November 1927, in Gandhi 1969b [1927]: 260).

In *Harijan* (18 July 1936), Gandhi (1976b [1936]: 154) accuses Ambedkar of picking out doubtful Hindu texts and taking as examples those Hindus who are 'no fit specimens of the faith' when criticizing Hinduism. He comments that every known living faith will probably fail if the standards of Ambedkar are applied to them.[31] In reply Ambedkar points out that his criticism is first directed against the *ideals* of Hinduism:

...a religion has to be judged not by its worst specimens but by the best it might have produced. I agree with every word of this statement. [...] The question still remains—why the worst number so many and the best so few. To my mind there are two conceivable answers to this question: 1) That the worst by reason of some original perversity of theirs are morally uneducable and are therefore incapable of making the remotest approach to the religious ideals. Or 2) that the religious ideal is a wholly wrong ideal which has given a wrong moral twist to the lives of the many and that the best have become best in spite of the wrong ideal—in fact by giving to the wrong twist a turn in the right direction. Of these two explanations I am not prepared to accept the first and I am sure that even the Mahatma will not insist upon the contrary (Ambedkar 1979: 88).

---

[31] Also quoted in Ambedkar (1979: 83f).

The reply is written in a sarcastic tone and shows that Ambedkar first and foremost is critical of the ideals of Hinduism, and not of Hindus not living up to the standards of the Hindu ideals. This is confirmed a few pages later when he states:

I like to assure the Mahatma that it is not the mere failure of the Hindus and Hinduism which has produced in me the feelings of disgust and contempt with which I am charged. I realize that the world is a very imperfect world and any one who wants to live in it must bear with its imperfections. [...] If I am disgusted with Hindus and Hinduism it is because I am convinced that they cherish wrong ideals and live wrong social lives. My quarrel with Hindus and Hinduism is not over the imperfections of their social conduct. It is more fundamental. It is over their ideals (ibid.: 94).

This may be seen as the end of this controversy. They had come to a standstill. The differences in opinion over ideals were never solved between them. Ambedkar found the ideals of the varna system impossible to combine with equality. Gandhi, on the other hand, in accepting the Hindu ideals of the varna system, found this system able to bring in equality in status between the different varna categories.

INDEPENDENCE

THE CONTRADICTION BETWEEN INDIAN LAWS AND SOCIAL PRACTICES

In 1947 India gained its independence. Ambedkar was nominated as Law Minister, and before the Constitution was adopted in 1950 he expressed worries regarding the contradictions that would arise:

On January 26, 1950, we are going to enter into a life of contradictions. In politics we will have equality and in social and economic life we will have inequality...We must remove this contradiction at the earliest moment, or else those who suffer from inequality will blow up the structure of political democracy which this Assembly has so laboriously built up (Ambedkar 1994: 1216).

The drafting of the Indian Constitution, between 1947 and 1949, coincided with the UN Declaration on Human Rights in 1948, and one could see the similarities. I shall cite the section of the

Indian constitution on Fundamental Rights and the Directive Principles:

[It is solemnly resolved] to secure to all citizens: JUSTICE, social, economic and political; LIBERTY of thought, belief, faith and worship; EQUALITY of status and of opportunity; and to promote among them all FRATERNITY assuring the dignity of the individual and the unity of the Nation.[32]

According to the Indian constitution it now became illegal for the state to discriminate against anybody on the basis of his or her caste.[33] Article 17 deals especially with untouchability and declares its practice, in any form, to be forbidden. But the state should not only passively refrain from discriminating, it should also take action on behalf of the weaker sections.[34]

Five years later additions were made and according to the Untouchability (Offences) Act (UOA) of 1955, the enforcement of any disability arising out of 'untouchability' became an offence punishable by law. In 1976, two decades later, this Act was made even more effective in the Protection of Civil Rights Act (PCR Act).

Did the constitution and the new laws change the circumstances for the SCs in civil society? In 1989 the Scheduled Caste/ Tribes Prevention of Atrocities Act came into existence. The reason for this was that the PCR Act of 1976 had been shown to be inadequate because it did not take into account many of the crimes that were committed against SCs and Scheduled Tribes (STs). Looking more closely at this Act of 1989 we get, if not any statistics, at least some idea about what kind of atrocities the SCs and STs had to be protected against half a century after the Indian constitution came into existence.

[32] For an appendix with an extract from the constitution and a discussion see, for example, Galanter (1991 [1984]).

[33] In Article 15 (1) about Fundamental Rights it is stated that: 'The State shall not discriminate against any citizen on grounds only of religion, race, caste, sex, place or birth or any of them'. (Galanter 1991 [1984]: 569).

[34] In the Directive Principles of State Policy, Article 46 adds that: 'The state shall promote with special care the educational and economic interests of the weaker sections of the people, and, in particular, of the Scheduled Castes and the Scheduled Tribes, and shall protect them from social injustice and all forms of exploitation' (ibid.: 571).

The Act specifies 18 types of atrocities as illegal. To mention just a few, it became illegal to force SCs and STs to eat obnoxious substances, to dump waste matter on their land, to keep them as bonded labour, to destroy their buildings, to foul their water resources, and to denude them. The reason that the Act of 1989 came into existence was the large number of incidents directed against SCs and STs. They had been forced to eat human excrement, carcasses had been dumped in their premises, their drinking water had been polluted, women had been 'paraded naked'[35] in the villages, etc. (Gupta 1991: 3ff; Thorat and Hardtmann 2003). In the late 1990s, after yet another decade, the same kinds of atrocities were reported by Narula (1999) to be still prevalent against SCs across India.

DALIT SAHITYA AND DALIT PANTHERS: FROM SILENCE TO FURY

The Dalit movement with its claim for an identity separate from the Hindus could be said to begin with the Adi movements in the 1920s. It crystallized more clearly during the time of Ambedkar, mainly from the 1930s to the 1950s. In the 1960s and 1970s the movement took a new turn. The context was now different, in the sense that the SCs had obtained constitutional protection. Nevertheless, they continued to experience caste discrimination in civil society in much the same way as they did during colonial rule. On the whole, the revival of the movement may be seen as a reaction to the contradiction that had arisen. The Indian constitution and the additional laws were protecting the SCs against discrimination, but a government commission self-reflectively stated in 1980 that the police and

[35] To be 'paraded naked' is a well-known form of abuse against SCs. It means that you are forcibly taken through the village without clothes, to be exposed to everybody, with the sole aim of humiliation. In 1989, Scheduled Castes and Scheduled Tribes (Prevention of Atrocities) Act (Section 3[1][iii]) explicitly made this abuse illegal. 'Forcibly removing clothes from the person of a member of a Scheduled Caste or Scheduled Tribe, or parading him [sic] naked or with painted face or body, or committing any similar act which is derogatory to human dignity'. (Section 3[1] [iii]) (Referred in Narula 1999: 184).

the juridical agencies were incapable of ensuring that these laws were enforced.[36]

The dissatisfaction with this situation came to be expressed in the 1960s and 1970s by activists in Dalit Sahitya (Literature) and Dalit Panthers in Maharashtra. This was the first real revival after independence of the movement led by Ambedkar. With both Sahitya and the Panthers, the concept of dalit—'oppressed'—came to be used in a more deliberately and also in a different sense from before. The concept came gradually to be transformed into expressing self-respect and strength. This seems to be more than a matter of a change in language; it was closely connected with a process of self-understanding.

Dalit Sahitya and Dalit Panthers may be seen as two sides of the same coin. It was at end of the 1960s that Dalit Sahitya achieved the status of a school of literature (Zelliot 1992: 274), but already from the 1950s, Dalit authors and poets wrote Dalit literature prolifically.[37] The authors and poets in Dalit Sahitya were closely linked to the social and political activists in the Dalit Panthers, formally organized in 1972. Many authors and poets were simultaneously active in Dalit Sahitya and in Dalit Panthers. In other cases Dalit Panther members, not writers themselves, were strongly influenced by the literature and poetry; likewise, the poets and authors came to be influenced by the sociopolitical activities taking place and this was reflected in their writings. The fused networks of Dalit Sahitya/Dalit Panthers also involved social workers at the grassroots level, with their workplaces among the urban poor. Furthermore, the movement involved Dalit students and unemployed Dalit youths as well as urban workers and agricultural labourers in Maharashtra (Guru 1992).

[36] In 1979 the Government of India set up the National Police Commission. Its recommendations included a chapter in which SCs were dealt with. For more about the National Police Commission, see Government of India (1980: Ch. XIX), also quoted in Narula (1999: 33). For a related discussion, see also Thorat and Hardtmann (2003).

[37] The first English analysis of Dalit literature appeared in the *Times Weekly Supplement*, 25 November 1973. For references and a discussion about Dalit Sahitya, see Zelliot (1992: 267–333).

Dalit Sahitya/Dalit Panthers were Marxist and Buddhist in orientation, and the authors and activists were militant in their rhetoric.[38] Much of their inspiration came from the Black Panthers in the US, from whom they also took their name.[39] The activists, authors, and poets came to produce something new within the autonomous anti-caste tradition. The publicly expressed emotions were put into a socio-economic and political framework in which the past, present, and future were dealt with. They combined the poetically expressed with the politically framed. To some extent this had already been done by Ad Dharm and some of the Adi movements in the 1920s and 1930s. The difference with the Dalit Sahitya and Dalit Panthers was that they not only expressed the emotions of the Dalits, but they also wrote about these emotions in a self-reflexive way. And, not least, they consciously grabbed hold of the concept of 'Dalit', moulded it to their own design, and turned it into a central concept.

Ambedkar is often referred to as the one who introduced the concept of 'Dalit' into the movement, but he used the word 'dalit' in a similar way to his contemporaries and never made the concept itself a concern. It was with Dalit Sahitya/Dalit Panthers that the concept was first consciously put forward in a radical new sense. In the 1990s the concept reached further beyond the Dalit counterpublic than before. 'Dalit' became established among journalists as well as the public in a sense similar to that ascribed to it by Dalit Sahitya/Dalit Panthers two decades earlier. It came to public knowledge that 'Dalit' was a self-ascribed choice before any other address.

The Dalit Sahitya and Dalit Panthers took off from a platform that was formed historically, and they used the history of protest to further articulate arguments and to evolve a reflective stylist writing about emotions. Lutz and Abu-Lughod (1990), as noted

[38] The Marxist and Buddhist orientation is also to be seen in the publishing circumstances. The volumes of Dalit poetry in the 1970s were published by Maharashtra Buddhist Literature Committee, Asmitadarsh Press or the Marxist Magova Press, with a few exceptions (Zelliot 1992: 274).

[39] For more about the relations between Dalit Panthers and Black Panthers, see, for example, Murugkar (1991) and her Marathi as well as English bibliography (ibid.: 241–60). See also Zelliot (1992).

earlier, suggest that emotions can be studied in discourses. They follow Foucault, who finds discourse to be 'practices that systematically form the objects of which they speak' (Foucault 1972: 49, referred to in Lutz and Abu-Lughod 1990: 9). Their usage is reminiscent of the sociolinguistic usage of the concept. But they add: 'yet it goes further by looking at more than speech, by recognizing the local, contradictory, and fragmented character of discourses, and by insisting that discourses be understood in relation not just to social life but to power' (ibid.: 10).

Studying emotions in this way does not primarily tell us something about an individual's inner state, but it gives us the opportunity to understand how, in the case of the Dalit activists, discourses on emotions challenge power and status differences, and how these discourses may serve as loci of resistance (see the discussion in Lutz and Abu-Lughod 1990: 14ff). Emotion talk is seen, according to Wittgenstein, as 'in and about social life rather than as veridically referential to some internal state' (Wittgenstein 1966, also quoted in Lutz and Abu-Lughod 1990: 11). I am not going further into the question of discourses and emotions but will be content, for my own purposes, with seeing emotion talk as discursive practice and as a creative force in challenging hierarchical structures.

DALIT POETRY

Through the studies of discourse we may understand not only how emotions are socially construed, but also how emotions, when expressed, may play a part in a restructuring of power relations. Discourses (including expressed emotions and emotion talk) may be seen as constrained by habitus (Bourdieu 1977), but emotion talk and emotions that *are* expressed (breaking the constraints of habitus) may, on the other hand, be seen as contributing to a questioning of, or rather a self-reflexivity regarding, this same habitus. Let me cite the poem *Habit*:

Once you're used to it
you never afterwards
feel anything;
your blood nevermore
congeals
nor flows

for wet mud has been slapped
over all your bones.
Once you're used to it
even the sorrow
that visits you
sometimes, in dreams,
melts away, embarrassed,
Habit isn't used to breaking out
in feelings.

(A poem by F.M. Shinde, translated by Priya Adarkar, in Dangle (ed.), 1992: 69)

This poem is a reflection about the situation of Dalits, a situation that has become an embodied habit, and also a comment on the lack of emotions attached to the habit. The body used to habits does not feel anything: 'Your blood never more congeals nor flows' and further 'Habit isn't used to breaking out in feelings'. Sorrow, even in the dream 'melts away, embarrassed'. We find reflections about a silence, not only regarding expressed words and emotions, but an embodied inner silence where not even in dreams are emotions heard.

In Dalit poetry emotions and also the body are often expressed as absent or non-existent:

Don't look at me as if you were an orphan.
We are more than refugees
  without homes here
  a burden of centuries on our backs
  and even with that no footprints
  on this muddy piece of land
If the earth is not ours
How can we speak of the sky?

('Poem' by Mina Londe, translated by S.K. Thorat and Eleanor Zelliot, in Anand and Zelliot 1992: 109)

In this poem by Mina Londe we find another kind of silence. It is the silence or absence of the body, which is 'leaving no footprints'. This absence of the body is further related to an absence of visions.

In *Bosom Friend* by Hira Bansode, reproduced below, silence and self-accusation are tightly knit together, and although it does not go so far as to express any visions, we can follow a change in attitude:

Today you came over to dinner for the first time
You not only came, you forgot your caste and came
Usually women don't forget that tradition of inequality
But you came with a mind large as the sky to my pocket size house
I thought you had ripped out all those caste things
You came bridging that chasm that divides us
Truly, friend, I was really happy
With the naive devotion of Shabari I arranged the food
On your plate
But the moment you looked at the plate, your face
Changed
With a little smirk you said Oh My—Do you serve chutney—
      koshimbir this way?
You still don't know how to serve food
Truly, you folk will never improve

I was ashamed, really ashamed
My hand which had just touched the sky was knocked
Down
I was silent
Towards the end of the meal you asked
What's this? Don't you serve buttermilk or yoghurt with
The last course of rice?
Oh My Dear, we can't do without that . . .
The last bit of my courage fell away like a falling star
I was sad, then numb
But the next moment I came back to life
A stone dropped in the water stirs up things on the bottom
So my memories swan up in my mind
Dear Friend—You ask about buttermilk and yoghurt
What/How can I tell you?

You know, in my childhood we didn't even have milk for
tea much less yoghurt or buttermilk
My mother cooked on sawdust she brought from the
      lumberyard wiping away the smoke from her eyes
Every once in a while we might get garlic chutney on
Coarse bread
Otherwise we just ate bread crumbled in water
Dear Friend—Shrikand was not even a word in our Vocabulary

My nose had never smelled the fragrance of ghee
My tongue had never tasted halva, basundi
Dear Friend—You have not discarded your tradition
Its roots go deep in your mind
And that's true, true, true
Friend—There's yoghurt on the last course of rice
Today the arrangement of food on your plate was not
*   properly ordered*
Are you going to tell me what mistakes I made?
Are you going to tell me my mistakes?

('Bosom Friend' by Hira Bansode, translated by Jayant Karve and Eleanor Zelliot, in Anand and Zelliot 1992: 27–9)

Take a look at the last lines of this poem again: 'Are you going to tell me what mistakes I made? Are you going to tell me my mistakes?' This poem is chosen because it illustrates very well, in the second verse, how an explicit sadness and numbness is changed into how someone 'came back to life'. What happened in this poem? The woman in the poem is happy that a higher caste woman, forgetting about caste differences, is coming to her 'pocket-size house' as a friend. The guest soon makes some insulting comments about the food not being served in the 'proper' way. The happiness of the host changes into sadness and numbness. In this first instance she blames herself for not serving the food in the right way. But the comments of the guest dropped like a stone in water and stirred up things at the bottom, memories from her childhood. She 'came back to life'.

From sadness, numbness, and self-accusation, she starts to remember her childhood and also explains why she is serving food in the way she does. The poem could be seen, at the beginning of the third verse, to be directed as a remembrance to herself *and* to the guest: 'You know, in my childhood we didn't even have milk for tea much less yoghurt and buttermilk'. And as the poem goes on, remembering the sensations she has been denied, her 'nose had never smelled the fragrance of ghee' and her 'tongue had never tasted halva, basundi', we could foresee between the lines an awakening, a still unexpressed feeling of anger about the injustice. She then accuses the guest directly: 'Dear Friend', and 'friend' now has another feeling attached to it—'You have not discarded your tradition. Its roots go deep in your mind'. The poem has now taken another turn. She is not sad and numb any longer. She is not accusing herself and her own tradition for not serving food in the right way. The accusation is directed outwardly, against the guest and her insulting comments.

In the following poem we can see how Jyoti Lanjewar more explicitly expresses a change of attitude:

> Their inhuman atrocities have carved caves
>   in the rock of my heart
> I must tread this forest with wary steps
>   eyes fixed on the changing times
> The tables have turned now
> Protests spark
> now here
> now there.
> I have been silent all these days
> listening to the voice of right and wrong
> But now I will fan the flames
>   for human rights.
> How did we ever get to this place
>   this land which was never mother to us?
> Which never gave us even
>   the life of cats and dogs?
> I hold their unpardonable sins as witness
>   and turn, here and now,
>   a rebel.

('Caves' by Jyoti Lanjewar, translated by Shante Gokhale, in Dangle 1992: 22)

There is no self-accusation in this poem, unlike in the poem by Hira Bansode. The accusations are instead directed outwards. In one of the last lines we read: 'I hold their unpardonable sins as witness'. It is interesting to see how the poem is framed in this newly awakened and outwardly directed accusation. Beginning, middle, and end tell us about the past: 'Their inhuman atrocities have carved caves in the rock of my heart...I have been silent all these days...I hold their unpardonable sins as witness...'.

The moment or process of change is expressed as 'The tables have turned now'. The change that is taking place, which many Dalit poems express, is formulated in different ways by the individual poets, but what is described is strikingly similar. Through the poems we can follow the process in which self-denial is changed into a right to exist on equal terms, self-accusation is changed into accusations directed outwards against those who are found guilty of the atrocities in the past. A feeling of invisibility turns into a right to have a place on earth to call one's own, and silence turns into protest.

The poets deal with the past and the present, as we have seen, but also with the future in terms of visions, as in a poem by J.V. Pawar:

> These twisted fists won't loosen now
> The coming revolution won't wait for you.
> We've endured enough; no more endurance now.
> Won't do letting down your blood's call to arms
> It won't do:
>> the seeds of revolution have been sown since long
>> no use awaiting the explosion now;
>> the fire-pit is ablaze; it's for tomorrow
>> even if you take to your heels now
>> no use; life's certainty is no more.
> How will they snuff the fire within us?
> How will they stop minds gone ablaze?
> No more reasoning now;
>> unreason helps a lot
>> once the horizon is red
> What's wrong with keeping the door open?

('It's Reddening on the Horizon', by J.V. Pawar, translated by P.S. Nerurkar, in Anand and Zelliot 1992)

The poets and authors in Dalit Sahitya not only expressed emotions, but also reflected on emotions in the past, present, and future. We have seen how they were reflecting on: (a) the absence of emotions in the past, (b) the awakening of emotions in the present, and (c) the vision in which emotions are the sources behind a social revolution. The poets in Dalit Sahitya were, as already noted, closely intertwined with Dalit Panthers whose message was mainly about the socio-economic and political situation of the Dalits. When Dalit Panthers referred

to the past, it was in terms of the time before India's independence when Dalits were economically deprived and lacking
in political power. The present was described as the time
after independence, with the Congress now in power but
without any changes regarding the situation of the Dalits. The
future was, in their vision, the time after a socio-economic and
political revolution when the Dalits themselves had come to
power as the rulers.

DALIT PANTHER MANIFESTO 1973

The Dalit Panthers were formed in 1972 and in 1973 they published their Manifesto. The reason was that they wanted to
clear some misunderstanding about the 'Panthers' which had
developed: '... "Panthers" no longer represent an emotional
outburst of the dalits. Instead, its character has changed into
that of political organization' (Dalit Panthers Manifesto, Bombay
1973; Appendix in Murugkar 1991: 232).

Next, after an explanation of why the Manifesto has taken
shape, the Congress is dealt with: 'The present Congress rule is
essentially a continuation of the old Hindu feudalism which kept
the Dalits deprived of power, wealth and status for thousands of
years. Therefore, this Congress rule cannot bring about social
change' (ibid.). This 'Hindu feudal rule', of which the Congress
is seen to be a continuation, is explained as being even more
ruthless 'today' than it was in the Muslim or British period:

Because this Hindu feudal rule has in its hands all the arteries of
production, bureaucracy, judiciary, army and police forces, in the
shape of feudals, landlords, capitalists and religious leaders who
stand behind and enable these instruments to thrive. Hence the
problem of untouchability of the dalits is no more one of mere mental slavery (Dalit Panthers Manifesto, Bombay 1973; Appendix in
Murugkar 1991: 233).

Phule and Ambedkar are explained as being the two great leaders of the Dalit Panthers and 'Gandhism' is severely criticized:

The struggle for independence was a struggle under the leadership
of national capitalists, landlords, feudals, for their own benefit. It
was not under the leadership of the people, or of the Dalits....
Babasaheb [Ambedkar] used to say, Gandhism means preservation

of religious authority, Gandhism means traditionalism, Gandhism means casteism, Gandhism means preservation of traditional division of labour, Gandhism means incarnationism, Gandhism means the holy cow, Gandhism means worship of images, Gandhism means an unscientific outlook.

... Giving independence to Gandhi and Gandhians meant that the British wanted their own interests in the country to be looked after. This was the sort of borrowed independence we got (Dalit Panthers Manifesto, Bombay 1973; Appendix in Murugkar 1991: 235).

In the Manifesto the Left parties are criticized for their attempts to gain recognition from the Congress, and for not combining the class struggle with a struggle against untouchability. However, the problems of the Dalits could not be solved within the framework of religion and caste, it was said, but '[a] scientific outlook, class consciousness and a completely atheistic approach and fighting humanism alone could add an edge to the struggles of the dalits'. This, it is further explained was the purpose of Ambedkar when he founded the Scheduled Caste Federation and wanted to make it into a broad-based party. The Scheduled Caste Federation was turned into the Republican Party of India (RPI) after his death, however, and the RPI is criticized in the Manifesto for leaving the way of Ambedkar and destroying his revolutionary voice. The leadership of the party passed into the hands of the middle class, which took part in intrigues and made capital out of Ambedkar's name, at the same time as the atrocities against Dalits grew endemic: 'In a period of one to one and a half years, 1,117 dalits were murdered. The land grew barren, not a drop of water was available. Honor was violated, houses gutted, people killed. Along with the very question of living, physical indignities grew sharper' (Dalit Panthers Manifesto, Bombay 1973; Appendix in Murugkar 1991: 237).

Dalit Panthers proclaim that they belong within a broader struggle. They relate their own struggle to that of the Black Panthers and also comment on the Vietnam war: 'Due to the hideous plot of American imperialism, the Third Dalit World, that is, oppressed nations, and dalit people are suffering' (ibid.).

In the Manifesto, Dalit Panthers ask for a complete and total revolutionary change for Dalits, in social as well as economic, political, and cultural fields. In this context there are three

often-cited sentences from the Manifesto: 'We will not be satisfied easily now. We do not want a little place in the brahmin
alley. We want to rule the whole country.' In revolutionary and
visionary terms they explain how this rule will come about, and
their disappointment with the legal system is clearly visible:

When we gather a revolutionary mass, rouse the people, out of the
struggle of this giant mass will come the tidal wave of revolutions.
Legalistic appeals, requests, demands for concessions, elections,
satyagraha—out of these, society will never change. Our ideas of
social revolution and rebellion will be too strong for such paper-
made vehicles for protest. They will sprout in the soil, flower in the
mind and they will come forward with full force with the help
of steel-strong means (Dalit Panthers Manifesto, Bombay 1973;
Appendix in Murugkar 1991: 238).

In the last lines of the Manifesto they once again express their
disappointment with the legal system and criticize the state.
They foresee the final struggle:

The present legal system and state have turned all our dreams to
dust. To eradicate all the injustice against the dalits, they must
themselves become rulers. This is the people's democracy. Sympathizers and members of the Dalit Panthers, be ready for the final
struggle of dalits (ibid.: 239).

What could the discourses by Dalit Sahitya and Dalit Panthers
make us understand about social life (rather than about the
inner life of an individual) following Lutz and Abu-Lughod
(1990)? How could Dalit poetry and the Dalit Panther Manifesto, when published in books and pamphlets or read out at
conferences, challenge power and status differences? How do
these publications and conferences serve as loci of resistance?

The concept of 'Dalit' (oppressed) came to express self-respect
and strength and was related to external sociopolitical and
economic relations. Hence, the accusations changed from being
directed against the 'self', to being directed outwards, against
those who were seen as representatives of an oppressive system.
In the poetry the self-accusations were associated with a period
already past, in which silence dominated. This was seen in
contrast to the present time, which was a time of 'rebellion'.
The reason why the 'untouchables' were placed at the bottom of

the caste hierarchy was generally not explained in racial terms by Dalit Sahitya/Dalit Panthers, as was the case in the Adi movements, where the 'untouchables' were seen as defeated by Aryans. Instead, the present economic and political exploitative system was now explained as the source of the situation of the Dalits.

TWO CONFLICTING TRADITIONS OF CASTE PROTEST

Looking back into history, two lines of protest against the caste hierarchy could be discerned. On the one hand, we could find those groups or movements in which activists wanted to reform Hinduism and get rid of the practice of untouchability within the framework of this religion. Many of these groups, organizations, and movements during the twentieth century were inspired by the bhakti movement, the Hindu reform movement working for the abolition of caste, among other issues. Among the caste sabhas taking shape from the end of the nineteenth century onwards, many belonged within this Hindu caste-reform tradition. The phenomenon of 'sanskritization',[40] which is dealt with by Srinivas (1952), falls within this tradition as well, since it involves attempts by so-called untouchables to climb in status within the framework of the traditional caste hierarchy. Gandhi clearly belonged within this tradition, working against the hierarchical aspects of the caste system, but wanting to keep the Hindu varna system, for example, in terms of labour. This is a tradition of protest against caste hierarchy within the framework of Hinduism. It is furthermore a tradition that is closely related to the Congress Party, as I have shown in this chapter.

On the other hand, there were groups and movements in which activists were working against the caste system, but with the aim of annihilating Hinduism, which they found to be the ground from which the caste system emanated. They not only worked against the caste hierarchy, but against Hinduism as

[40] Using this concept of sanskritization, a Dalit activist and student of sociology in Bangalore told me: 'We are not trying to sanskritize ourselves'.

well. In this tradition we find many of those Adi movements which, from the 1920s onwards, argued that the 'untouchables' were the 'original inhabitants' of India, with a religion different from the Hindus. This tradition stood outside of and in conflict with the Indian National Congress. In the 1930s an autonomous anti-caste stand crystallized with B.R. Ambedkar as spokesman, in opposition to M.K. Gandhi. With Dalit Sahitya and Dalit Panthers in the 1960s and 1970s, there was a revival of this stance and they not only *expressed* emotions, but also wrote self-reflectively *about* the emotions of the so-called untouchables. Furthermore they weaved these emotions into a political framework.

Omvedt (1994a) has made a clear distinction between different forms of protest against the caste hierarchy, so let me take a closer look at her analytical framework. The Dalit movement she defines 'as part, in many ways the leading part, of a broader *anti-caste movement*' (ibid.: 10). A few pages later she puts it in this way: 'The anti-caste movement with its Dalit leading section...' (ibid.: 13).

According to Omvedt, the Dalit movement in particular and the anti-caste movements in general should be seen as 'anti-systemic' movements (Omvedt 1994a: 10ff). That is, these movements wanted to transform the basic structure of the Indian social system. She writes: '...these movements [the Dalit movement and the anti-caste movements in general] have been seen as basically reformist by the dominant left intellectual trends in India...' (ibid.: 13). Omvedt is criticizing Marxism from within. Her point is that the anti-caste movements in India have not been given due respect, neither historically among activists in the Marxist movement, nor among Marxist scholars. What she wants to emphasize is that the anti-caste movements, in the same way as the class movements, *could* be anti-systemic and should not only be seen as peripheral to a restructuring of Indian society. She wants to turn this Marxist assumption on its head, and points out that the Dalit movement in particular and the anti-caste movement in general are basically anti-systemic, but with reformist trends within them.

My concern is with her statements that imply that the 'reformers' and 'anti-caste radicals' belong to the same movement. She puts it like this: 'There were of course reformist trends

in the [Dalit and non-Brahmin anti-caste] movement as in other
social movements of Indian society'. Although Omvedt makes a
distinction between what she calls the anti-caste radicals and
the reformers, she does not find them so different that they are
not able to be put analytically within the same movement. The
reformist trends, she says, 'were represented *within* the Dalit
movement' by Congress Dalit leaders as well as Hindu
Mahasabha Dalit leaders (Omvedt 1994a: 10, italics mine).

I think Omvedt is right in questioning the Marxist assumption
that movements based on caste are peripheral to a restructuring
of Indian society, but that is not my main concern just now.
Rather, what I want to point out is that she underestimates the
differences between two conflicting traditions of protest against
the caste system, in her effort to show Marxists the anti-systemic
potential in movements also based on caste (and not only on
class). I find it misleading to speak of a Dalit movement and
include what Omvedt calls the 'reformist trends'.[41] In this regard
she is putting completely different complexes of ideas together.
The 'anti-caste movement (with its Dalit leading section)'
seems to be defined on the basis of two criteria; first, that of
encompassing specific categories of people (independently of
political and religious ideas),[42] and second, as having protests
against the caste system as the most important ingredient,
regardless of political and religious contexts. This seems to be
against her general approach of taking political as well as
religious ideas and contexts as points of departure when
analysing processes in colonial India.

To sum up, what Omvedt calls reformist trends within the
anti-caste movement I prefer to see as religious and political
complexes of ideas belonging to a very different tradition,

[41] I am not concerned here with the labelling of the movement as
'Dalit movement' or whatever, but with Omvedt not being clear enough
in differentiating between the 'anti-caste radicals' and the 'reformers'.

[42] Omvedt uses 'Dalits' synonymously with the so-called untouchables, 'Depressed Classes' or (SCs). In the 'general anti-caste movement'
she also includes 'Other Backward Castes [or Classes]' (OBCs) (Omvedt
1994a: 10). It should be noted though, that my objection is not in putting
the categories of SCs and OBCs together under the common label of
'general anti-caste movement', but against putting the 'reformists'
analytically within the same movement as the anti-caste radicals.

better understood if they are analytically dealt with in terms of
a Hindu caste-reform tradition. Activists in this tradition have
historically been in constant conflict with activists belonging
to another tradition, which I have labelled the autonomous
anti-caste tradition. My attempt in this background chapter has
been to show how activists protesting against the caste system
historically have belonged within two different traditions, and
have confronted each other, for religious and political reasons
that I have tried to clarify.

4

Movement Perspectives
Dalit Discourses across the Country

In the early 1990s Dalit activities across India intensified and
Dalit networks were activated. From then on the Dalit movement received more attention from the media and the public.
Small Dalit groups were formed and others revived in villages
as well as cities, uniting in the name of Ambedkar.[1] Activists
studied the writings of Ambedkar, took part in politics, and
worked to educate their relatives, friends, and others about
Ambedkar's ideas and writings. During the 1990s they spread
information about Ambedkar within India and even abroad, and
like the Dalit Sahitya/Dalit Panthers they emphasized their
Dalit identity and culture.

[1] There were two important circumstances that coincided at the
beginning of the 1990s, which caught the interest of the media across
the country and contributed to a revival of the movement. The first
was in August 1990 when V.P. Singh, then Prime Minister, announced
that he would implement the Mandal Commission Report, which
recommended extended reservations for 'Other Backward Classes'
(OBCs). Although these extended reservations did not directly concern the 'SCs', the Dalit activists argued in favour of them, and
this was a highly debated topic in the media for several years. Some
students from caste groups higher up the hierarchy, not included among
SCs or OBCs, even set fire to themselves on university premises to
oppose the extended reservations, which would diminish their own
possibilities in the labour market. The second occasion of importance
was the centenary celebration of Ambedkar's birth, in 1991, which was
celebrated on a large scale in India as well as, for example, by the
diaspora in Britain.

The contemporary Dalit activists declare themselves to belong within the tradition of Ambedkar and the Dalit Sahitya/ Dalit Panthers, but there are variations within the movement; this chapter will attempt to describe some of these. I begin by presenting three influential perspectives within the movement to show the heterogeneity and also the geographical spread of the movement. The three perspectives are: first, Dalit Buddhism which originated in Maharashtra in western India; second, Dalit (Christian) theology with its roots in the south of India; and finally the perspective of Dalit politics, as represented by the BSP, with a stronghold in north India, mainly in Uttar Pradesh. Among the Dalit activists, though, different perspectives may in practice be fused in different ways and I shall make the picture even more complicated by mingling some of the clearly separated perspectives at the end of this chapter.

To place the discussion in a theoretical framework it may be useful to think in terms of a 'subaltern counterpublic' (Fraser 1992).[2] I have chosen to talk about an 'alternative counterpublic' although my use of it is in consonance with Fraser's concept. Subalternity, in the Indian context, has by and large referred to a Marxian notion of a working class, by the influential School of Subaltern Studies (*Subaltern Studies* I–IX, 1982–96). It may then add confusion to use it in relation to the Dalit movement, a movement among the SCs. An 'alternative counterpublic' will in this context refer to the discursive arena where the Dalit activists, mainly from among the SCs, are bringing forward a counterdiscourse. Fraser writes: '[The] subaltern counterpublics... signal that they are parallel discursive arenas where members of subordinated social groups invent and circulate counterdiscourses to formulate oppositional interpretations of their identities, interests and needs' (1992: 123).

Alvarez, Dagnino and Escobar (1998b: 19), inspired by Fraser, talk about the same kind of public in terms of 'movement-based

---

[2] Habermas (1989[1981], 1992) has been criticised for the glorification of one overarching public sphere and he has been convincingly contested by Nancy Fraser with her introduction of the concept of 'subaltern counterpublics' (1992: 140, note 21). Fraser coined this expression by taking the term 'subaltern' from Spivak (1988) and 'counterpublic' from Felski (1989).

public' or 'movement-inspired public'. They also use 'alternative social movement public' or simply 'movement public' (ibid.: 20). These expressions could also have been a way of coming to grips with the counterpublic that concerns me.

The varied Dalit discourses of this chapter may be seen as different movement perspectives, all expressed and presented within the same alternative counterpublic. The focus on diversity is a way of emphasizing that people manage meaning from their positions in various social contexts (cf. Hannerz 1992a: 64f).[3] I would say that the movement perspectives, or the internal variation expressed within the counterpublic, are of greatest importance for the dynamic processes of confirming and recreating a Dalit identity, which has been taking shape since the 1920s. I shall return to this in the concluding chapter. The Dalit movement may thus be seen as a network of diverse movement perspectives, constantly in the process of being created and recreated by interacting activists, who socially organize and reorganize informal and formal networks of groups and individuals.

Again, three significant perspectives of the Dalit movement are the Dalit Buddhist perspective, the Dalit Christian perspective, and the Dalit party-political perspective. These movement perspectives or other movement perspectives, parts of perspectives, or fused aspects of some chosen perspectives are presented by activists in thousands of publications. Booklets and periodicals are published from small, often one-man, publishing houses across the country. People holding different perspectives interact regularly with each other. They read each other's publications and meet at conferences and seminars, to discuss questions related to the movement. Since the end of the 1990s, Dalit discussion groups on the Internet have become the forums that most clearly show that the three movement perspectives belong, among others, to one and the same counterpublic.

In what follows I have chosen to present some writings of importance that are constantly referred to by Dalit activists.

[3] See Hannerz' use of the concept 'perspectives' in *Cultural Complexity*, and his discussion in Chapter 3, called 'A Network of Perspectives' (1992a: 62–9).

The state of Maharashtra in western India has been the main area for Buddhist activities since the 1950s, although conversions to Buddhism have spread to other areas. I shall take the conversion of Ambedkar and his followers in 1956 and also *The Buddha and His Dhamma* written by Ambedkar (1991b [1957]) as a point of departure. Furthermore, I shall show how it was referred to in one of the larger Buddhist conversions during the 1990s that took place in Patna, in the State of Bihar. In this connection I shall further see how Ambedkar was similarly referred to during the WSF in Mumbai in 2004, a decade later. Next, I shall look at some pioneering works of Dalit Christian theology with its historical roots in south India.

Finally, I shall deal with a Dalit discourse within party politics, more specifically within the BSP, which has presented itself as a Dalit party since its foundation in 1984. The stronghold of the party has been Uttar Pradesh in northern India, where it came to power for a short time in 1995, 1997, and 2002 and then surprisingly regained the majority in the state election in 2007. *Chamcha Age* is a book often referred to by Dalit activists, written by the late party leader Kanshi Ram (1982), and one of the few writings in which the ideas of the party are presented. The following is not an exercise in literary analysis, but an attempt to present some of the content in the literature that is constantly commented on by Dalit activists, and to relate it to the discourses in the contemporary Dalit movement. This means that the writings are not presented in their totality, but the focus will be on the parts that are most often taken up by the Dalit activists.

DALIT BUDDHISM

Ambedkar led a famous mass conversion to Buddhism in Nagpur in Maharashtra in 1956, the same year he passed away. During the 1990s and 2000s, India has seen quite a few mass conversions to Buddhism, inspired by the one in Nagpur. I was present at one of the larger ones that took place in central Patna, in the state of Bihar, in 1993. Between 5,000 and 10,000 people had gathered, many of whom arrived a day in advance, by bus, train or on foot from all over the state and also further afield. They had spent the night in large open tents, put up for the purpose by the organizers. The main organizer of this conversion was Inspector-General of Police, Maiku Ram long active in the Dalit movement. Surrounded by Buddhist prayer flags on the stage, he made an introductory speech to the crowd: 'Today we free ourselves from Hindu religious slavery.' He turned to the 20 monks in ochre robes, seated behind him on the floor of the stage, and continued: 'Now the monks have to get out of the monasteries. We demand from them—bring Buddhism to our people in the villages!'

The conversion in 1956 spread rapidly, mainly to those areas where Ambedkar's political party, the Scheduled Caste Federation, had some influence—today's Maharashtra, Madhya Pradesh, Punjab, and Uttar Pradesh. The main conversions took place in Maharashtra, the home state of Ambedkar; while the census of 1951 showed 2,487 Buddhists, the number in the 1961 census was 2,789,501, which made the community almost as large as the Muslim community (Zelliot 1992: 126). Altogether in the country the number of Buddhists rose from 180,823 in the 1951 census to 3,250,227 in 1961 (ibid.). The conversion was a final attempt by Ambedkar, before his death two months later, to take the 'untouchables' out of Hinduism.[4]

In a speech in 1935 Ambedkar had already made his stand clear regarding his future conversion:

Because we have the misfortune of calling ourselves Hindus, we are treated thus. If we were members of another Faith, none would dare treat us so. Choose any religion which gives you equality of status and treatment. We shall repair our mistake now. I had the misfortune of being born with the stigma of an Untouchable. However, it is not my fault; but I will not die a Hindu, for this is in my power (Ambedkar 1979 [1936]).

During the years to come Ambedkar studied the religions of Islam, Sikhism, Christianity, and Buddhism. Representatives of different faiths negotiated with him, as a leader of the SCs, since they understood the numerical advantage if he led millions of SCs to convert to their religion. The final choice of Ambedkar came to be Buddhism.

[4] For more about contemporary Buddhism in India and the place of Ambedkar in Buddhist activities, see Zelliot (1992: 222–48).

Returning to the conversion ceremony in Patna in 1993, the main ceremony took about half an hour and was led by Bhante Gyaneshwar, a Burmese monk. Those who wanted to convert got up and closed their eyes, folded their hands, and read the ceremonial words together with the monk.[5] The oaths were the same as those taken in Nagpur in 1956, written by Ambedkar for that occasion. The crowd in Patna read these 22 oaths together with the monks on the stage:

(1) I will not regard Brahma, Vishnu, and Mahesh as Gods, nor will I worship them.
(2) I will not regard Rama and Krishna as Gods, nor will I worship them.
(3) I will not accept Hindu Deities like Gauri, Ganapati, etc., nor will I worship them.
(4) I do not believe that God had taken birth or incarnation in any form.
(5) I do not believe that Lord Buddha was the Incarnation of Vishnu. I believe this propaganda as mischievous and false....[6]

As seen above, the first oaths are about abandoning a belief in Hindu gods and a commitment not to worship them any longer. Hindu representatives often picture Buddha as an incarnation of Vishnu and Buddhism consequently as a part of Hinduism,[7] something which is dealt with and proclaimed to be false propaganda by the converts in oath number 5. The oaths of the conversion ceremony are to a large degree occupied with details about dissociation from Hinduism. Not until the 11th oath, 'I will follow the Eightfold Path of Lord Buddha', is Buddhism taken up more directly.

[5] For something on the psychological dimension of conversion to Buddhism, see Zelliot (1992: 218ff). For an account from a Dalit perspective, see, for example, Thorat (1979).
[6] For the complete oaths taken in Nagpur in 1956, see Zelliot (1992, Appendix: 215).
[7] Hellman (1993: 176ff) and Guru (1991) have shown how Hindu fundamentalists, like the Vishwa Hindu Parishad (VHP), incorporate Ambedkar and Buddhism in Hinduism and picture Ambedkar as a reformer of Hinduism.

During the ceremony in Patna the speakers made constant references to the conversion in Nagpur almost 40 years earlier, and Ambedkar was mentioned in almost all the speeches. *The Buddha and His Dhamma*, written by Ambedkar (1991b [1957]), was often cited and commented on. In bookstalls put up in the park, this script, as well as other literature about Buddhism and Ambedkar could also be bought.[8] Together with *What Congress and Gandhi Have Done to the Untouchables* (1991a[1945]), *Riddles in Hinduism* (1987b), and a few others, *Buddha and His Dhamma* is one of the most cited books by Ambedkar. It is often referred to among contemporary Dalit activists and for this reason I shall say something more about its contents.

BUDDHA AND HIS DHAMMA

Buddha and His Dhamma, was first published a year after Ambedkar's death. To Ambedkarite Buddhists it is often compared to the Bible or the Koran. Similar to these holy books, it is written in the form of chapters and verses. It is a reinterpretation of Buddhism and based on a selection of texts, mainly from Pali sources. It was logical that Ambedkar should prefer Pali and not the Sanskrit scriptures, according to Zelliot (1992: 250), as Sanskrit was the religious language of Brahminism. Ambedkar did not subscribe to any specific Buddhist school but gave his own interpretation of Buddhism, which has become known as Ambedkarite Buddhism.

Uke is a Dalit activist and a retired government employee, who lives in New Delhi and subscribes to Ambedkarite Buddhism. The way he expresses himself is characteristic of many Ambedkarite Buddhists. He explains that Buddhism according to Ambedkar differs from other branches:

There are so many factions of Buddhism, but Ambedkar has given us an easy way to find out if a statement is Buddhist or not. If you find something to be irrational Buddha never said it. In this way I am not just a Buddhist but also an Ambedkarite. Ambedkar has given a new direction to Buddhism (Personal interview with N.G. Uke, New Delhi, 13 April 1994).

[8] For more about Indian Buddhist literature, see, for example, Zelliot (1992: 249–63).

The opinion that Ambedkar gave a new direction to Buddhism is in line with the opinion among most Ambedkarite Buddhists, who do not have any specific interest in similarities and differences between Buddhist schools, such as Hinayana, Mahayana or Theravada. Furthermore, like many Ambedkarite Buddhists, Uke also emphasizes that *Buddha and His Dhamma* is written in understandable language. About the spread of the script among SCs he says, 'The book has spread because Ambedkar has given an interpretation for today's society, in a language that everybody understands. We rely on the words of Buddha as interpreted by Ambedkar.'

Ambedkar found Buddhism to be too unworldly, and his own interpretation of Buddhism was, according to Omvedt, 'meant for a community of super-exploited men and women seeking their place in a new millennium, a community with a fighting tradition' ('Ambedkar's new Buddhism' *The Hindu*, 25 February 1999). She compares Ambedkar's interpretation of Buddhism with liberation theology (ibid., 2001: 147f). The latter, with its origin in Latin America, was influenced by Marxism, which is also the case with Ambedkarite Buddhism. When Ambedkar converted in 1956, while still working on *Buddha and His Dhamma*, he gave a speech in Nepal to the World Fellowship of Buddhists titled 'Buddha or Karl Marx' (Rodrigues 1993: 308). Although the speech was given in a Buddhist context, it was directed to Marxists as well; it attempted to show the similarities between Marx and Buddha, and how Marxism and Buddhism could benefit from each other. This speech is closely related to *Buddha and His Dhamma* and still circulates in the form of cassettes and booklets among Dalit activists.[9] In Patna, on the occasion of the conversion in 1993, cassettes with the speech were put out for sale, side by side with *Buddha and His Dhamma*. The speech begins in the following way:

A comparison between Karl Marx and Buddha may be regarded as a joke. There need be no surprise in this. Marx and Buddha are divided by 2381 years. Buddha was born in 563 BC and Karl Marx in AD 1818.... Having read both and being interested in the ideology of both a comparison between them just forced itself on me. (Speech delivered at Kathmandu in World Fellowship of

[9] The speech is also included in Ambedkar (1987a: 439–62).

Buddhists on 20 November 1956. See also the printed speech in Ambedkar, [1987a: 441]).

In the speech Ambedkar points out that many premises within Marxism have proved to be wrong, but that there remains a surviving core of importance:

What remains of Karl Marx is a residue of fire, small but still very important. The residue in my view consists of four items:

(1) The function of philosophy is to reconstruct the world and not to waste its time in explaining the origin of the world.
(2) That there is a conflict of interest between class and class.
(3) That private ownership of property brings power to one class and sorrow to another through exploitation.
(4) That it is necessary for the good of society that the sorrow be removed by the abolition of private property (ibid.: 444).

He then goes on to compare these four points with Buddhism. 'On the first point there is complete agreement between the Buddha and Karl Marx', Ambedkar argues. He illustrates this by quoting a dialogue between Buddha and the Brahmin Potthapada. Potthapada asks some questions of Buddha, such as 'Is the world not eternal?', 'Is the world finite?', 'Is the soul one thing, and the body another?'. To each of them he gets the same answer from Buddha: 'That too, Potthapada, is a matter on which I have expressed no opinion.' The point made by Ambedkar is that Buddha, like Marx, did not find these questions to be of any relevance, because the answers could not contribute to the reconstruction of the world (Ambedkar 1987a: 444f).

The second point, regarding conflict of interest between classes, is also, according to Ambedkar, in agreement with Buddha, who 'recognises that class conflict exists and that it is the class conflict which is the cause of misery' (ibid.: 445). In comparing the third point of private ownership and property bringing power to one class and sorrow to another through exploitation, Ambedkar refers to the same dialogue as before between Buddha and Potthapada; when they are talking about sorrow and misery, Ambedkar concludes that 'If for misery one reads exploitation, Buddha is not away from Marx' (ibid.: 446). Regarding the fourth point that private property should be abolished so that sorrow should be removed for the good of society, Ambedkar finds the rules of the Bhikshu Sangh, the community of Buddhist monks, to be the best testimony. According to the rules, a bhikku (monk) can have as private property only eight articles for his most basic needs (Ambedkar 1987a). He concludes that 'These rules are far more rigorous than are to be found in communism in Russia' (ibid.: 447).

Communism is said to extend its hatred for Christianity to Buddhism without examining and understanding the differences between the two. Buddhism may be helpful to Communism according to Ambedkar. The Communist idea that 'religion is the opium of the people' is based on the Sermon on the Mount in which Christ sublimates poverty and weakness and promises heaven to the poor and the weak. This is not to be found in Buddhism, according to Ambedkar, but the aim of the Eight-Fold path in Buddhism is to 'establish on earth the kingdom of righteousness...'. The French Revolution was welcomed because it laid a new foundation summarized in three words 'fraternity, liberty, and equality', Ambedkar notes, but it failed to produce equality. Communism aims to produce equality, but manages it only through dictatorship. Only in following the way of Buddha can equality be attained without dictatorship (Ambedkar 1987a: 459–62).

Let me now turn to *Buddha and His Dhamma*, which has been controversial and is debated with regard to its free interpretation of the traditional sources. Queen (1994: 119), like Omvedt (1991; 2001), compares the message of *Buddha and His Dhamma* with liberation theology, and with works such as *A Black Theology of Liberation* by James H. Cone (1970) and *A Theology of Liberation* by Gustavo Gutierrez (1971). Queen quotes from a review of *Buddha and His Dhamma* in the Buddhist organ *Maha Bodhi* journal, in which it is stated that the book is '"enough to shock a real Buddhist", particularly in its denial of the Buddha's infallibility, its rejection of Karma and enlightenment, its omission of the Four Noble Truths, and its reduction of the dhamma to a "social system"' (*The Maha Bodhi* 1959: 352f; also cited in Queen 1994: 101).

It is obvious, when reading *Buddha and His Dhamma*, that Ambedkar finds Buddha to have a mainly social message. He writes as follows:

16. The question that arises is—'Did the Buddha have no Social Message?'
17. When pressed for an answer, students of Buddhism refer to the two points. They say—
18. 'The Buddha taught Ahimsa [non-violence].'
19. 'The Buddha taught peace!'
20. Asked—'Did the Buddha give any other Social Message?'
21. 'Did the Buddha teach justice?'
22. 'Did the Buddha teach love?'
23. 'Did the Buddha teach liberty?'
24. 'Did the Buddha teach equality?'
25. 'Did the Buddha teach fraternity?'
26. 'Could the Buddha answer Karl Marx?'
27. These questions are hardly ever raised in discussing the Buddha's Dhamma.
28. My answer is that the Buddha has a Social Message. He answers all these questions. But they have been buried by modern authors (1991b [1957]: 158f).

Religion and Dhamma are poles apart, according to Ambedkar. The purpose of Dhamma is to restructure the world, while the purpose of religion is to explain the world. Dhamma is equated with morality, and the part of the book that deals with Dhamma ends in the following way:

37. The group set-up leads to stratification of classes. Those who are masters remain masters and those who are born in slavery remain slaves. Owners remain owners and workers remain workers. The privileged remain privileged and the serfs remain serfs.
38. This means that there can be equality for a few but none for the majority.
39. What is the remedy? The only remedy lies in making fraternity universally effective.
40. What is fraternity? It is nothing but another name for brotherhood of men which is another name for morality.

41. This is why the Buddha preached that Dhamma is morality and as Dhamma is sacred so is morality (1991b [1957]: 233f).

According to Ambedkar, Gautama's (not yet the enlightened Buddha) conclusion, when he reflected on the root of sorrow, was that an end of war was not the end of his problem: 'The conflict between nations is occasional. But the conflict between classes is constant and perpetual. It is this which is the root of all sorrow and suffering in the world.... I have to find a solution for this problem of social conflict' (ibid.: 45).

Gautama's way to enlightenment is described in the following way:

On the night of the last day of the fourth week, light dawned upon him. He realised that there were two problems. The first problem was that there was suffering in the world and the second was how to remove this suffering and make mankind happy (Ambedkar 1991b [1957]: 55).

At the root of suffering Buddha finds greed and craving. 'The poor' are not meant to be content with their situation, Buddha says in *Buddha and His Dhamma*, and if greed and craving among the rich are not controlled, they will lead to class struggle:

5. The Buddha has not said, 'Blessed are they who are poor.'
6. The Buddha has not said that the sufferer should not try to change his condition.
7. On the other hand, he has said that riches are welcome and instead of listless suffering he taught Virya which is energetic action.

...

11. Avarice or possession due to uncontrolled acquisitive instinct calls for watch and ward.
12. 'Why is this craving or greed [by rich men] to be condemned? Because of this,' said the Buddha to Ananda, 'many a bad and wicked state of things arises—blows and wounds, strife, contradiction and retorts; quarrelling, slander and lies.'
13. That this is the correct analysis of the class struggle there can be no doubt.

14. That is why the Buddha insisted upon the control of greed and craving (1991b [1957]: 168f).

Queen states that Ambedkar in his interpretations of the traditional sources makes repeated use of 'omission, inter-polation, paraphrase, shift of emphasis, and rationalization' (1994: 102). He means that when Ambedkar has chosen what is to be included and how to interpret the Buddhist material, he has applied three criteria. These were the criteria that Ambedkar found to be recommended by Buddha himself to be applied to all statements: reasonableness, social benefit, and subjective certainty (Ambedkar 1991 [1957]: 254f). The point Queen is making is that *Buddha and His Dhamma* is written with the so-called untouchables of India in mind so that it is, intelligible and relevant to them. The traditional presentation of the Four Truths, where the individual causes himself suffering, is for that reason omitted. Karma and rebirth connected with the idea of misconduct in former lives has taken the form of suffering as a result of structural inequality. About the Eight-Fold Path, Queen writes that it is seen not as the means to Nirvana, but as the way 'to remove injustice and inhumanity that man does to man' (1994: 113).

Fuchs (2001: 258) has commented that dhamma is seen both as a moral code (for the individual's conduct of life and for social interaction) *and* as a constitutional necessity for society. He quotes: 'Morality in Dhamma arises from the direct *necessity* for man to love man' (Ambedkar 1991b[1957]: 231, quoted in Fuchs 2001: 258, Fuchs 2004: 297, emphasis added by Fuchs). *Buddha and His Dhamma* may be seen to serve as a 'third idiom' in the Dalit struggle for recognition, according to Fuchs. He adds to Queen that it is also written with others than the so-called untouchables in mind so as to bridge the distance between two conflicting positions, discourses or frames of references (Fuchs 2001: 266), that is, between a Hindu idiom and a Dalit counterdiscourse.

THE CONVERSION IN PATNA

Returning now to the Buddhist conversion in Patna, *Buddha and his Dhamma* and its message were constantly referred to V.T. Rajshekar from Bangalore, the editor of the *Dalit*

Voice,[10] had come to Patna on the occasion of the conversion, and his speech is illustrative of how socialism and Buddhism are combined: 'Today we convert to Buddhism. We are ready to meet the Brahmins, man against man, woman against woman'. And he went on to predict that 'The caste war has already begun, and that paves the way for socialism in this country'.[11] It was emphasized by most Dalit activists in Patna during the day of the conversion that Buddhism should be less unworldly, more engaged in the social sphere, and should aim to change the inequalities in Indian society.

Although Rajshekar converted to Buddhism in Patna, he is better known for his disposition in favour of Islam. He encourages Dalit-Muslim unity in his magazine. In this respect he resembles many Dalit activists who want to make clear to society that they readily cooperate with Muslims. Islam is seen as the most forceful threat to Hinduism among many groups in India. The message about cooperation between Dalits and Muslims comes across strongly to anyone familiar with the contemporary Indian situation; expressing willingness to cooperate with the Muslims tacitly implies dissociation from the Hindu community. And, further, in expressing themselves as allied with the Muslims they are also implying that they are not on the defensive, but are allied with forces regarded among many Hindus as threatening Hinduism. Islamic youth groups were consequently also present in Patna during the conversion and sold books, booklets, and cassettes from their stalls.

During the day in Patna many speakers referred to Gandhi as a contrast to Ambedkar and Rajshekar was no exception in this regard. In his magazine as well as in the booklet entitled *Mahatma Gandhi and Babasaheb Ambedkar—Clash of Two Values* (Rajshekar 1989) Gandhi is also questioned:

[10] For more about *Dalit Voice* and an interesting discussion on identity, see Charsley and Karanth (1998).

[11] It should be noted that the Dalit activist Balley from Punjab, whom I shall return to in Chapter 6, was also present in Patna on this occasion. He was the one who translated the speech by Rajshekar into Punjabi for the Punjabis present. This is one example of how activists from different networks across the country may meet and interact.

Many Mahatmas have come and many Mahatmas have gone. They raised a lot of dust but did not raise the level of the people. History does not take note of the dust-storms. It takes note of only earthquakes that up-root men and matters. It is concerned with social change. Did Gandhi cause any earthquake? No. He caused only dust-storms. Did he bring about any social change? No. He might have made the Birlas, his Bania jatwala richer. He might have brought 'independence' to the 'upper caste nation'. But to over 85% of India's persecuted nationalities devoid of human rights his contribution is nil (ibid.: 8).

In 60 pages Gandhi is criticized and Ambedkarism is put forward as India's most revolutionary philosophy.

Bhante Surai Sesai, a monk from Nagpur, pointed out in his speech at the conversion that Dalits are indigenous and pre-Aryan, in contrast to the Hindus or Aryans who invaded the country. He is known among Dalit activists for leading the Liberate Bodh Gaya Movement. The activists in the movement demand that the leadership of the temple in Bodh Gaya, where Buddha received enlightenment, should be transferred from Hindu priests to Dalit Buddhists and that all Hindu gods and rituals should be forbidden on the premises (Lynch 1998).[12]

The reactions were strong when the Buddhist conversion took place in Patna. The day before the conversion, an advertisement could be found in the Patna newspapers, under the heading 'Conversion: some questions'. Hindu representatives had bought advertising space on the front page in several local Hindi newspapers. The advertisement first warned against Buddhism. Next, it addressed the administration and asked

[12] The Buddhist conversion in Patna is an example of when elements from different research contexts popped up and converged (see discussion on 'serendipity' in Chapter 2). Dalit activists from different localities had for me unexpectedly arrived in Patna, like Balley from Jullundur, Rajshekar from Bangalore as well as a group of senior people belonging to Republican Party of India (RPI) from Maharashtra, who converted together with Ambedkar in 1956. Discourses on Buddhism, socialism as well as the discourse on Dalits as the original people of India converged during this day. A group of Muslims were selling their books and pamphlets side by side with books of Ambedkar. I was not left in any doubt, as far as fieldwork was concerned, that I was at the right place at the right moment.

how they could make the park, Gandhi Maidan, available for a conversion to Buddhism. Finally, followers were requested to meet at 5 pm the same day to discuss future programmes and the consequences of a conversion (see, for example, *Sandhyaprahri*, Patna, 5 December 1993).

Dalit activists have become more offensive towards Hinduism, which was obvious with the formation of the Dalit Sahitya/Dalit Panthers in the 1970s. The conversion to Buddhism in Patna was probably seen as a threat, and that may have been the reason why the reactions to it were so strong.

THE ASHES OF AMBEDKAR— WSF MUMBAI 2004

The World Social Forum (WSF) in Mumbai took place a decade after the conversion in Patna and I will give an idea about the role of Ambedkar in this context. On 6 December 2004, the death anniversary of Ambedkar, Dalit activists began a march, 'Swadhikar rally' from across India; Jammu and Delhi in the north, Kolkata in the east, and Kanyakumari in the south. Activists in four buses, 50 in each one, partly rode and partly marched through fourteen Indian states. They reached Mumbai about one month later on the inaugural day of the WSF. The main aim was, according to the organizers in NCDHR, to inform people in the villages about the negative impacts of globalization for the SCs in terms of economic liberalization.[13]

The Swadhikar rally entered Mumbai from four directions. Before going to where the WSF was being held, they met at the Chaityabhumi. This is the place where the body of Ambedkar was taken after his death. The symbolic significance of this meeting place should be understood. The Indian government has proclaimed the stupa, where parts of Ambedkar's ashes are kept, as a sacred Hindu place. This is something Dalit activists protest against with the explanation that Ambedkar condemned Hinduism, which he found to be intricately entangled with the caste system, as discussed earlier.

[13] For a related discussion on Dalit activists in the World Social Forum in Mumbai, see Jackie Smith *et al.* 2008: 42–4.

The buses with the rally activists arrived at Chaityabhumi. The Dalit activists walked the small distance to the stupa with their placards and took off their shoes before entering the area to pay homage to Ambedkar. The Indian media had been reporting about the rally from the different states. Now, the interest was not only from the Indian media, but also from foreigners—some photographers, journalists, some academics, including myself, and also the French organization No-Vox, representing the urban homeless in France among others. Two representatives of No-Vox had joined the rally during the last days before entering Mumbai.

During this occasion Danielle Mitterand, founder of the NGO France Liberté, and wife of former French President Francois Mitterand, was a guest of honour. She gave a speech and expressed her sympathies with the cause of the Dalits. One representative of No-Vox gave a speech in French, which his friend simultaneously translated into English and he compared the situation of Dalits to the condition of the homeless in France. The national convener of the rally reminded the participants of the oaths taken by Ambedkar in 1956 and led them in reading aloud some similar oaths written for this occasion:

Dalit Swadhikar Rally Pledge

We Dalit Activists, hereby affirm and agree to profess, practice and propagate the Right to Life, Liberty, Equality and Dignity of every human and other living beings.

We believe that all human beings are equal and there shall be no discrimination on the basis of race, caste, descent, gender and colour, religion, language, work, or any other grounds of discrimination.

We honor the Constitution of India and I will perform my duties to protect the human rights as enshrined in it.

We believe that 'Dalit Rights are Human Rights'.

We commit ourselves to opposing and challenging all dominant, exploitative and oppressive forces that thrive on casteism, racism, patriarchy, religious extremism, communalism, imperialism and neo-liberalism.

We dedicate ourselves to the Liberation, Empowerment and Assertion of Dalits, Women, Children and other disadvantaged communities in India and other parts of the world.

We vow to be part of all progressive movements, campaigns and initiatives that strive to eliminate all sorts of discrimination and promote equality, justice and peace.

We take a vow of our own will and accord to honor and abide by the morals, ethics and values set by this Dalit Swadhikar Rally and conform to them to make this rally a success. (Recorded during fieldwork, Chaityabhumi, Mumbai,16 January 2004).

The oaths outside Chaityabhumi in January 2004 were not taken by 300,000 people like in 1956, but by a relatively small crowd of a few hundred activists from different parts of India, many of them Dalit leaders in their own states. The oaths were written in the vein of Ambedkar, but were taken one step further in its nonreligious content compared to the ones in 1956. They further related to other discriminated people in the world and commented on imperialism and the neoliberal order. In this sense it was reminiscent of the Dalit Panther manifesto from 1973, which related to Black Panthers and condemned American imperialism and the Vietnam war.

DALIT CHRISTIAN THEOLOGY

I met the Protestant Bishop Azariah, a charismatic man with a huge silver cross on his chest, in Madras at the beginning of the 1990s. He explained to me that he found the Christian message of treating your fellows like yourself to be directed more to the high-caste Hindus than to the Dalits: 'Dalits have a wounded psyche. The message of Christianity is meant for those who find themselves to be superior, and not for the Dalits' (personal interview, Madras, 10 March 1992).

Bishop Azariah was of the opinion that the Christian faith should aim at a restructuring of society. In his book *Mission in Christ's Way in India Today* (1989), he explicitly subscribes to the ideas of liberation theology and like Queen he refers to some of its leading names, such as James Cone (1970) and Gustavo Gutierrez (1973). Discussing the question of peace, Azariah argues in his book that 'peace necessarily becomes a struggle with the forces of conflict and violations that dominate every place (space) and every period of history (time) on this earth' (Azariah 1989: 75). He concludes that 'peace is possible only through human struggle' (ibid.). In the chapter 'Doing Theology in India today', he refers to Kappen, a leading Roman Catholic theologian, and his book *Liberation Theology and Marxism* (1986). Azariah quotes: '...it is in the action and fashion of our people, in their condition of bondage to systems of exploitation and domination, in their struggles to fashion a more just and human society that we have to meet the living God' (ibid.: 21, also quoted in Azariah 1989: 91). He argues that Asian theologians have to dissociate themselves from a theology legitimating the status quo: 'For theology can become power only if it is appropriated by the oppressed masses in whose interest it is to change the world' (Kappen 1986: 29, also quoted in Azariah 1989: 91).

Gandhi is accused of not having identified the deeper cause of poverty in India, and Azariah quotes from the magazine *Harijan* to show Gandhi's preferences for a system where profession comes by inheritance:

I believe in Varna Ashrama-Dharma which is the law of life. ... The Law of Varna is nothing but the Law of Conservation of energy.... Why should my son not be a scavenger if I am one? (Gandhi, *Harijan*, 6 March 1937, p. 27 also cited in Azariah 1989: 41).

Azariah (1989) questions how Gandhi, who tried to banish untouchability from Hindu society, could justify the caste system, and in contrast he is in favour of a Dalit (Christian) theology.

'What is Dalit theology?' and 'Why Dalit theology?' are the two questions raised in the introduction to a compilation with the title *Towards a Dalit Theology* (Prabhakar 1988). This book is something of a pioneer in Dalit theology and the result of two seminars, in Madras and Guntur in 1986.[14] What is emphasized in the introduction, as well as in different articles in the volume, is that Dalit theology is a countertheology (Nirmal 1988) or counterculture (Ayrookuzhiel 1988: 5) in relation to the Brahminic system, which is seen as serving the privileged sections in society.[15]

[14] The seminars were arranged by the Christian Dalit Liberation Movement with assistance from the Christian Institute for the Study of Religion and Society. According to the organizers, the people present in these seminars came from different places in South India and from Uttar Pradesh. There were representatives of the Catholic Church, the Church of South India, the Lutheran Church, the Baptist Church, the Salvation Army and the Bible Mission (Prabhakar 1988: 157).

[15] For a broader historical context, where Dalit theology is analysed in relation to a more general history of Christians in India, see Webster (1994).

Throughout, the authors make references to Gandhi and Ambedkar. Buddhism and not Christianity was the choice of Ambedkar, but the emphasis here is not on the choice of religion, but on the fact that Ambedkar left Hinduism while Gandhi still believed in varna-dharma. Ambedkar's conversion to Buddhism is seen as an attempt to revive a countercultural stream (Ayrookhuziel 1988: 100), and whether it was Buddhism or Christianity is, in this context, of less importance. Prabhakar (1988: 43) takes the Poona Pact as an example of how Ambedkar also tried by political means to take the SCs out of Hinduism. Ambedkar as well as the Dalit Panthers are referred to, and there is a clear attempt to show that Dalit theology is part of the broader Dalit movement.

The caste system has its roots in the theology of Hindu culture, and the critique must be theological, according to Prabhakar:

The principles and practices of caste are rooted in the religious-philosophical-theological traditions of the dominant Hindu culture. The theory of varna (ritual ranking) provides the doctrinal basis for hierarchy and discrimination between jatis or castes (functional groups) and exclusion of certain 'impure' castes as untouchables and outcastes. The critique of this system of inequality has to be theological (ibid.: 2).

In the same volume Gandhi is cited by Chatterji (1988) to show how Hinduism is inevitably interlinked with the caste system and notes that although Gandhi proclaimed himself to be against untouchability, he believed in the system of varnas:

How can a Muslim remain one if he rejects the Quran, or a Christian remain Christian if he rejects the Bible? If *Caste* and *Varna* are convertible terms and if *Varna* is an integral part of the *Shastras* which define Hinduism, I do not know how a person who rejects caste i.e. *Varna* can call himself a Hindu (Gandhi, cited in Chatterji 1988: 17f).

According to Prabhakar, Dalits throughout history have struggled to escape 'the prison of the Hindu caste system', and he refers to Ambedkar who warned against the idea that the Hindus and Untouchables have a common religion (1988: 41ff).

Chatterji points out how Dalits have chosen what he finds to be varieties of egalitarianism:

Many untouchables became Muslims during the Moghul period, later on joined Sikhism, converted to Christianity during the colonial period, and adopted Neo-Buddhism along with Ambedkar in 1956 in Independent India. All these were egalitarian traditions (ibid.: 42).

Dalit theology is a reaction against the 'dominant Hindu culture', and it demands social justice in society at large. At the same time it aspires to social justice within the Christian church, and finds Indian Christian theology to be insensitive to Dalit issues. Dalit theology is two-edged. It is directed against the caste system and the Hindu culture and also criticizes the missionaries and the upper-caste Indian Christians for not having taken care to train a Dalit leadership in proportion to their numerical strength within the church (Gladstone 1988: 104ff). Zelliot (1992: 194) noted the same tendency among the new converts in the Nagpur Buddhist conversion in 1956. They rejected the leadership with a high-caste background in the Maha Bodhi Society, involved in the revival of Buddhism in India. In the same way Dalit theology rejects the leadership, influenced by Brahminic ideas, within the church.[16]

Although the caste system 'has crept into the Indian Church', much has also been done *on behalf of* the Christians of SC origin, according to Bishop Azariah (1988: 113ff). The difference with Dalit theology is that the latter is not *on behalf of*, but is *emanating from* the Dalits themselves, he argues (Azariah 1988: 120). The same thing is expressed by Prabhakar: 'It is a people's theology, and a particular people's theology, i.e., that of the Dalits, therefore, a theology *of* the Dalits, *by* the Dalits, *for* the Dalits' (Prabhakar 1988: 43). With reference to the concept of Dalit Power, introduced by the Dalit Panthers in the 1970s,

[16] It is not only the broader Indian society and the church that are criticized by Dalit theology, but also the leadership within the Dalit movement itself. Ruth Manorama, to whom I shall return when discussing Dalit feminism in Chapter 8, demands opportunities and platforms for Dalit women in the broader society and within the church. She also points out that the Christian Dalit Liberation Movement itself is imbued with a patriarchal structure (Manorama 1988: 146ff).

Prabhakar argues that Dalit consciousness is an integral part of Dalit Power. This consciousness means becoming aware 'that Dalit humanity is constituted by their dalitness'. He goes on: 'It means that the Dalit people are no more ashamed of being Dalit, and that they have a proud history and culture of their own, from ancient times, beginning earlier than and distinct from that of their caste-oppressors!' (ibid.: 45).

Nirmal takes the discussion further and states that Dalit theology necessarily has to be exclusive in character. The reason is that dominant traditions—cultural or theological—have a tendency to include and assimilate with the final aim of conquering others. Countertheologies have to be on their guard and shut off the influence of the dominant theological traditions (Nirmal 1988: 76). In this case it is the Brahminic tradition that has to be kept at a distance. Also Indian Christian theology took shape under the influence of caste converts to Christianity and has perpetuated within itself the Brahminic tradition, according to Nirmal. 'The protest note of the Dalit Christian theology will be so harsh', he writes, 'that the non-Dalit Indian Church will feel shaken and will fail to see it [Dalit theology] as a viable Christian option' (Nirmal 1988: 76). Nirmal foresees a critique from the non-Dalit Indian church regarding Dalit theology. This may be compared to the critique that is directed against *Buddha and His Dhamma* from among the wider community of Buddhists, as was seen in the review in *Maha Bodhi*.

Many Dalit activists argue that Dalit theology is also a political theology for social action to liberate Dalits from oppressive structures. At many points it seems, in the same way as with Dalit Buddhism, to come close to Latin American liberation theology (see also Webster 1994). According to Nirmal (1988), Dalit theology should be in dialogue with liberation theology in Latin America, but he proposes that Dalit theology should find its own solutions in India. The Marxist analysis of Latin American liberation theology did not need to take the caste factor into account, he says, which Dalit theology necessarily has to do (Nirmal 1988: 64ff).[17]

---

[17] For more about liberation theology, generally, see Christopher 2007.

DALITS IN THE PARTY-POLITICAL SPHERE

In the 1990s the SCs became more visible than ever in the political sphere. They became a category which politicians were forced to take into account in order not to lose votes. In the north of India the political situation changed radically when the BSP in coalition with the Samajwadi Party (SP), the regional Socialist Party, came to power in the 1993 Uttar Pradesh state elections. The coalition succeeded in what many had failed to do before, to get the votes of a broad category of Muslims and groups low in the caste hierarchy. While 'low caste' votes and Muslim votes went to the SP-BSP coalition, the Congress lost 'upper caste' votes to the Hindu nationalist Bharatiya Janata Party (BJP). This meant an increased caste polarization in politics in Uttar Pradesh.[18] The BSP has been successful not only in Uttar Pradesh but also in other north Indian states, such as Punjab and Madhya Pradesh.[19] The importance of the SC votes was manifested, and the SCs became a vote bank which the politicians were forced to acknowledge. Since then the BSP has been a strong political force in northern India.[20]

The BSP was at the time directed by one man, Kanshi Ram and, more explicitly, since the mid-1990s, also one woman, Mayawati. In 1995 the BSP made history by presenting Mayawati as the first ever Dalit woman Chief Minister of Uttar Pradesh. The BSP was known to have an anti-Hindu stance at the beginning of the 1990s, and Mayawati made it a habit to tell Brahmins and other 'upper caste' Hindus to leave the premises before she started her speeches. She became popular among the members for her relentless methods against the 'upper castes'. Mayawati was unknown to many people until she made a controversial statement about Gandhi at a press

[18] The SP-BSP coalition broke in 1995, but the BSP has continued to play an important role in Uttar Pradesh.

[19] For the percentage of votes polled by the BSP in five north Indian states during the 1989, 1991, and 1996 general elections with comments, see Jaffrelot (2003). For state-wise electoral performances of the BSP in these years and also in the 1999 general elections to the national parliament with comments, see Inkinen (2003).

[20] For more about the organizational aspects of the BSP and its enormous significance since the mid-1990s, see Chapter 5.

conference in March 1994. She criticized Gandhi for being patronizing when he coined the concept of 'Harijan', the children of God, for the SCs, and questioned why Gandhi never applied the label to himself. She is said to have asked rhetorically whether Gandhi is then the son of '*saitan*' (the devil) if the Dalits are the children of god. Whatever her precise utterances in the press conference, she apparently put Gandhi forward as an enemy of the Dalits.

Among Dalit activists the discussions had for a long time been focused on the status of Ambedkar versus Gandhi. The criticism of Gandhi and his concept of 'Harijan' came from within the movement, but it was with Mayawati that it was covered by the media and came to public knowledge. The reactions to her statement were strong. This was the beginning of a debate about Gandhi in the press. Some of India's leading intellectuals, as theoretically different as the post-modern Ashis Nandy and the Marxist historian Bipan Chandra expressed their opinions in *The Times of India* in defence of Gandhi (27 April and 13 April 1994). The well-known Indian journalist Arun Shourie (1997) also published a book a few years later to defend Gandhi. Although they differed in their criticism of Ambedkar, they were all of the opinion that his choice of Buddhism for the SCs was not a good alternative to Hinduism.

Chandra was critical of Ambedkar's propaganda in favour of conversion to Buddhism as this religion had in any case, in his view, been reduced to a sect within Hinduism. Nandy (1994) argued that Ambedkar was influenced by a westernized ideology. According to Nandy, anti-Gandhism is not restricted to the BSP, but spans the political spectrum, and includes Hindu fundamentalists as well as liberals and leftists. They are all 'wedded to modernism', he says, in favour of the modern nation state in human affairs, and positive towards western science and technology. Furthermore, they share an urban-industrial vision that dominates the globe. To these people, Nandy argued, Gandhi represents the 'ordinary, "superstitious", sceptical, tradition-bound, wily Indian' and in rejecting Gandhi, they reject 'everyday politics' and the 'ordinary Indian'. The disregard for the 'plural culture of Hinduism' is, according to Nandy, something inherited from an unofficial European parentage.

Arun Shourie's book *Worshipping False Gods* attracted much attention when it was published in 1997. In more than 600 pages Shourie sharpens the arguments in favour of Gandhi and portrays Ambedkar as an anti-nationalist and a collaborator with the British. In a review of the book, the Dalit intellectual Kancha Ilaiah (1997) argues that Shourie has failed to understand that the images of Ambedkar and Gandhi symbolize two diametrically opposite nationalist perspectives. According to Ilaiah, Ambedkar saw Gandhi and Nehru not just as nationalists but as Hindu nationalists and the Gandhian agenda as remaining within the varna-dharmic framework, in spite of Gandhi's criticism of untouchability. Ambedkar opposed Congress and did not see independence just as freedom from the colonial oppressors, but also as freedom from the upper-caste landlords and the bourgeoisie. Contrary to what Shourie (1997) maintains, Ambedkar wanted the untouchables to play a leading role in nation building, according to Ilaiah (1997: 7f).

An anti-Gandhism described as anti-nationalism could be called part of the 'dominant narrative of Indian nationalism', in the words of the historian Clarke (1998). In this dominant narrative nationalism is identified with the Indian National Congress and the Congress with Gandhi.[21] Ilaiah, belonging within a Dalit counterpublic, delivers an alternative to this dominant narrative when he argues that a nationalism that is not in favour of Gandhi, that is critical of Congress, and furthermore is opposed to Hinduism exists. It is actually possible to be an anti-Gandhian nationalist, according to Ilaiah. The anthropologist Owen Lynch (1998) also shows what an alternative nationalist discourse might look like when he describes the Dalit activists within the Liberate Bodh Gaya movement. In this movement a nationalist discourse takes place in terms of an indigenous, pre-Aryan Buddhist culture, which is an alternative to a national discourse in terms of a Hindu culture.[22] These Dalit activists do not equate Hinduism/Gandhi/

[21] For an interesting discussion of how Indian nationalism has historically been constructed around the idioms of the majority Hindu community, see Upadhyaya (1992).

[22] For more about Dalit activists regarding themselves as indigenous, pre-Aryan Buddhists see, for example, Zelliot (1992).

Congress with nationalism, but in contrast regard themselves as anti-Hindu, anti-Gandhian, and anti-Congress. Nevertheless, and this is the point, they still find themselves to be nationalist.[23]

The responses to Mayawati's statement were not just to be seen in the media, but were also expressed in other ways. Leading Congress members fasted in protest against Mayawati and in the Parliament, in both the Lok Sabha (Lower House) and the Rajya Sabha (Upper House), opponents demanded that Mayawati be punished. A petition was sent to Allahabad's High Court demanding that all printed material, as well as discussions and lectures, dealing with Mayawati's statement should be forbidden. There was a demand for a change of the law, so that Gandhi should be made equal to the national flag, and insults to the 'Father of the Nation' should be regarded as criminal (*The Times of India*, 24 March 1994).

A few weeks after Mayawati's controversial statement I participated in a seminar titled 'Gandhi, Ambedkar and now Mayawati' at Jawaharlal Nehru University in New Delhi. The seminar had attracted many Dalit students and the debate came to be dominated by criticisms of Gandhi. In the press Mayawati's language has often been commented on as 'bad language' and her tone has been described as aggressive. In the seminar a female Dalit student expressed her support for Mayawati. 'I don't say she did it in the right form', the student said, 'but it is her style'. 'She is expressing the feelings of the Dalits', the student added, 'then the language becomes necessarily bad and aggressive'.

During the seminar Gandhi was hotly debated and questioned. Another Dalit student questioned the status of Gandhi: 'Why can't we criticize Gandhi? He is like a god. Nobody is allowed to criticize him.'

When the seminar had come to an end the discussions continued outside the seminar room. A male Dalit student belonging

[23] It should be recognized that the argument takes place in a context where nationalism is seen as something positive, in contrast to 'anti-nationalism' which is a term of abuse. In a global context, on the other hand, Dalit history is most often expressed in terms of global solidarity with comparisons, for example, with African Americans in the United States or the Burakumin in Japan. I shall come back to this in Chapter 9.

to the Janata Dal[24] echoed the press: 'She [Mayawati] does use a bad language. She gives us a bad reputation.' In Chapter 8 I will discuss more specifically how Mayawati, who reached an economic and political position has, in different ways, been described in terms of lacking morality—accusing her of using 'bad language' is just one example of this rhetoric, which deprives her of a traditional 'femininity'.

THE CHAMCHA AGE

Through the media coverage of the BSP and not least the attention given to Mayawati and her statement about Gandhi, the name of Ambedkar and the antipathies against Gandhi were marketed in the mid-1990s on a large scale. Already in the early 1980s, however, Kanshi Ram had expressed his opinion on the Ambedkar-Gandhi question. When I asked him about his party programme, in an interview in 1994, he sent a young party member to fetch it who returned with a copy of Kanshi Ram's book *The Chamcha Age—An Era of the Stooges* (1982), which he put into my hand. This is one of the very few documents where the ideas of the BSP are presented. Although I never again heard it referred to as a party programme, it is often mentioned by BSP members in a more general sense when talking about the party, Kanshi Ram and his background.

The theme of the book is the conflict between Ambedkar and Gandhi in 1932 resulting in the Poona Pact. The latter is frequently cited by Dalit activists, not least among BSP members, to explain how Gandhi betrayed them. In the *Chamcha Age* Kanshi Ram made the content of the Poona Pact available with constant references to Ambedkar. At the same time he explained the meaning of the Poona Pact and placed it in relation to the contemporary Dalit movement. The book was released as a protest against Gandhi and the Poona Pact, on the 50th anniversary of the pact in 1982, to focus on what happened 50 years earlier.[25]

[24] The political party competing with the BSP for the votes of the SCs at this time.

[25] Kanshi Ram was clearly taking a stand in favour of Ambedkar and against Gandhi regarding reservations and the Poona Pact. When discussing Kanshi Ram and reservations, Pai (2001: 272) writes that he is 'against permanent job reservation', as the only comment on his

The Chamcha Age comprises four parts: 'Prelude to Poona Pact', 'Ambedkar on Poona Pact', 'The Chamcha Age', and 'The Way Out'. Speeches by Kanshi Ram are often expressed in the spirit of visions. In the same vein he contrasts in the book the 'Chamcha Age' with the 'Bright Age', which is to come in the future. According to Kanshi Ram, a chamcha is a tool, an agent or a stooge of the high-caste Hindus. The Chamcha Age started with the Poona Pact; but today the chamchas are not only to be found in the political field, but can easily be detected every-where in society, he writes. To get out of this dark Chamcha Age, a capable and educated leadership must be recruited. To this end the Backward and Minority Communities Employees Federation (BAMCEF) was developed. The disease of the Chamcha Age was the 'alienation of the elite' and the cure was BAMCEF (Ram: 122).

In the first chapter, Kanshi Ram delineates a prelude to the Poona Pact, with the exchange of letters between Gandhi, Samuel Hoare (the Secretary of State for India at the time), and Ramsay MacDonald (the British Prime Minister). Gandhi explains why he cannot accept separate electorates for the 'depressed classes'. This part of the book also contains Ambedkar's statement in response to the exchange of letters.

The second part deals more directly with the Poona Pact. The Communal Award gave the 'depressed classes' the benefit of separate electorates and a double vote in elections. Kanshi Ram presents the meaning of the Communal Award and the reactions of Ambedkar and Gandhi. He takes a clear stand in favour of Ambedkar and harshly criticizes Gandhi and his 'fast to death' against the proposal.

The third part has the same title as the book itself, 'The Chamcha Age'. It begins with a quotation from Ambedkar, who

---

stand on this question. Out of context it is misleading. Kanshi Ram wrote *Chamcha Age*, a book that he regards as a party programme, with the purpose of defending a specific form of reservation. He was critical of today's form that is the result of the Poona Pact, but defended the more radical form that was originally proposed in 1932, with separate electorates and double votes for the 'depressed classes'—during a time span of twenty years, until the 'depressed classes' had gained political power.

is commenting on the joint electorate: '[It is] a "rotten borough" in which the Hindus get the right to nominate an untouchable to sit nominally as a representative of the untouchables but really as a tool of the Hindus' (Ram 1982: 89).

No 'untouchable' who did not agree to be a nominee of the caste Hindus, 'a chamcha in their hands', could be elected in a joint electorate. The reason for this, Kanshi Ram explained, was that the 'untouchable' voters were in a minority and outnumbered one to five (ibid.: 1).

In part four, 'The Way Out', Kanshi Ram differentiates between a short-term solution (social action), a long-term solution (political action), and a durable solution (cultural change and control). After the arrangement for a leadership (namely the formation of BAMCEF), the problem of the Chamcha Age has to be solved. The first way to solve it should be with the help of social action. To this end 'awakening squads', like Dalit Shoshit Samaj Sangharsh Samiti (D-S4), were trained in almost all the major languages of India, according to Kanshi Ram.[26]

An example of what Kanshi Ram meant by 'social action' and 'awakening' was the occasion when the *Chamcha Age* was released. To give publicity and criticism to the Poona Pact, an 'awakening programme' was conducted for one month in 1982, fifty years after the pact was signed. The programme was started in Poona and ended in Jullundur in Punjab. In 1998 a one-month programme named 'Bahujan March from Slavery to Empowerment' was conducted in Karnataka. It was similarly a way of announcing their stand and giving publicity to the disapproval of the Poona Pact. This programme was followed up for one month at the beginning of 1999 by 'Pedaling to Power', a cycle march, intended to 'prepare the Bahujan Samaj to become rulers of this land' (*Pedaling to Power*, a small booklet printed by BSP, Bangalore, Karnataka unit, 1999).

Next, after social action comes political action, according to Kanshi Ram in *The Chamcha Age*. Political action is the same as building a political party not led by high-caste Hindus. To this end the BSP was formed in 1984.[27] Finally, a durable

[26] Most often referred to as DS-4 in writings, but as D-S4 in *The Chamcha Age*. The meaning is 'Dalit organization for agitation'.

[27] For more about the organizational aspects of the BSP, see Chapter 5.

solution for the Bahujan Samaj will be achieved through cultural change and control. This is something that will probably not be solved during this generation. Still, it is the final goal to 'change a culture of perfect inequality into one of absolute equality', and caste is the core of the problem. Kanshi Ram refers to Ambedkar: 'As per his thought, caste system is a social system which embodies the arrogance and selfishness of a perverse section of the Hindus who were superior enough in social status to set it in fashion and who had the authority to force it on their inferiors' (Ram 1982: 131).

Kanshi Ram highlights in his book the conflict between Ambedkar and Gandhi in relation to the Poona Pact. He illustrates this by repeatedly quoting from *What Congress and Gandhi Have Done to the Untouchables,* by Ambedkar (1991a [1945]). To be anti-Gandhian is synonymous with taking an autonomous political stand in relation to the Congress and also Hinduism.

THE ORGANIZATIONAL ASPECT

CHOOSING AND FUSING PERSPECTIVES

Although a Dalit Buddhist, a Dalit Christian, and a Dalit party-political perspective have been presented as three separate and coherent value systems for the sake of making sense of some influential perspectives among the Dalit activists, this is not what the scene looks like in practice. It can happen that a Dalit group is purely Buddhist or Christian, for example, without any interest in party-political questions. A group may also have a solely party-political perspective without any interest in religion whatsoever. But most often Dalit activists choose bits and pieces or aspects of perspectives and combine and recombine them. For some activists a Dalit Buddhist perspective is combined with a party-political perspective, not necessarily that of the BSP, presented here as an example. Others find the Dalit Christian perspective to be a better choice, maybe in combination with some other party-political perspective or some aspects of one. On the other hand, the perspectives are not always smoothly combined and there are often tensions between Dalit groups with different party-political perspectives, as will be seen in the Chapter 5. At common conferences where Dalit activists from across the country come together, disagreement may also arise about which figure to put on the scene: Buddha or/and Ambedkar or/and Jesus.

There are thousands and thousands of Dalit groups across India and also abroad that differ from each other in many respects. Nevertheless they consider themselves to be part of the Dalit movement. Gerlach and Hine (1970a) were pioneers in dealing with geographically dispersed movements in an anthropological way. Although their work was carried out almost four decades ago, I have found many similarities regarding the organizational aspects on their study of the Black Power movement and Pentecostalism in the United States and my own study of the Dalit movement. They characterized the organizational structure of the movements they studied as decentralized, segmentary, and reticulate (ibid.: 33).

The movements were decentralized in terms of being polycephalous (many-headed), that is, guided by many leaders. Some of these leaders were influential, but none could be called *the* leader of the movement in which they worked. The leaders often disagreed about short-range goals and methods, and the same could be said about the leaders in the Dalit movement. They have an influence over some group or network of groups, but none can speak for the Dalit movement as a whole. Similarly none of the multitude of Dalit leaders have power to activate the whole movement or call a halt to activities, such as demonstrations that are outside their domain. Neither do any of the leaders know about all the groups that consider themselves to be part of the vast movement (Gerlach and Hine 1970a: 36).[28]

The Dalit movement is also segmentary in a similar way to that described by Gerlach and Hine (ibid.: 42), and processes of fission and fusion are constantly taking place, depending on the context and situational demands. There are a great variety of independent localized groups with their own ideas about goals and methods, but they may combine, as they did, for example, in the National Campaign on Dalit Human Rights (see Chapter 7).

[28] For more about leadership and social movements, see, for example, Eyerman and Jamison (1991), and Barker, Johnson, and Lavalette (2001).

In other cases they may divide or split to form smaller units. New groups may be formed under a new leadership, or groups may combine or recombine in new constellations. In Britain the Ambedkarites may be seen as an example of what Gerlach and Hine have called 'geographical peel-off', that is, people with relations to a movement who move to another geographical area for extra-movement reasons, usually for employment or family reasons, and initiate new movement networks (1970a: 46) (see Chapter 6). Other reasons for fission or splits may be personal conflicts, competition between leaders or ideological differences, of which I shall also give some examples later. This may not always have the negative effect of weakening the movement, but may result in intensified recruitment of people not previously involved (ibid. 1970b: 393).

The Dalit movement is also reticulate. Groups, or nodes, are tied together not through any central hub, but through 'intersecting sets of personal relationships and other intergroup linkages' (ibid. 1970a: 55). Individuals and groups are often linked through kinship, friendship, and community belonging. Activists cross back and forth between groups; sometimes they take part in more than one group and they attend the meetings arranged by friends or relatives. The linkages that tie the whole into a network cannot be overemphasized, according to Gerlach and Hine (1970a: 63), and I agree. Through personal ties of kinship, friendship, and other associations a flexible unity may be maintained in the Dalit movement, where there is no central headquarter and no single leader.

Contrary to the general view among researchers that organizational fission and lack of cohesion in a movement are a sign of weakness, Gerlach and Hine found these characteristics indispensable for the continuity of movements. They write, 'When the success of movements is reported as having occurred "because of" rather than "in spite of" organizational fission and lack of cohesion, we will have come to understand the nature of movement dynamics much more clearly' (ibid.: 64). They found, for example, that the organizational structure of the movements they studied made them difficult to suppress. The structure was flexible, constantly changing, with thousands of small groups and a multitude of leaders. The same may be said about the contemporary Dalit movement. Although Ambedkar after his

death has become a uniting symbol, the Dalit movement
consists of a wide range of groups in constantly changing and
flexible constellations, with an innumerable number of leaders.
This kind of organizational structure may be frustrating to
opponents who may feel that they are facing 'on the one hand, a
spontaneous explosion at the grass-roots level; and on the
other, a many-headed hydra' (Gerlach and Hine 1970a: 65). The
organizational structure further allows for mobilization within
a broad spectrum of political and cultural groups. It should be
noted, however, that Dalit activists do not usually find splits or
tensions or even heterogeneity more generally to be a favourable
state of affairs; they deplore them and regard them as weakening the movement.

INTERNET

Following Dalit discourses in cyberspace, it is apparent that
various Dalit movement perspectives belong within one and the
same counterpublic. Dalit activists representing Buddhist,
Christian as well as party-political perspectives (other perspectives, combinations of perspectives or combinations of just some
aspects) take part in the same Dalit discussion groups on the
Internet. It is obviously easier to discern that geographically
dispersed groups with different movement perspectives are
in constant communication with each other, when one looks at
these discussions in cyberspace, rather than when travelling
physically among Dalit activists. In the discussion groups and
on different websites[29] they inform each other about activities,
festivities, conferences, books, articles or atrocities taking place
in different Indian states against SCs. They also debate and
argue about goals and methods for the movement. Religious
and party-political topics are most often on the agenda, as well
as reflexive debates about their own identity. Dalit networks
are activated daily in cyberspace and the Dalit counterpublic is
thus strengthened.

Graham and Khosravi (2002: 223) have argued, in the context of the Iranian discourse on the Internet, that cyberspace
offers 'a space where other ways of acting and ordering [social

---

[29] For an overview of some Dalit websites, see Zelliot (2002).

life] than those which are permitted in official places exist
and indeed proliferate'. This is also true for the activists in the
Dalit movement, who to a large degree have been excluded
from the Indian public sphere. Now they can communicate
in cyberspace to reorder relations, not only between Dalit
activists in India and those in the diaspora, but also to connect
the Dalit networks within the counterpublic to a broader
international public of sympathizers. This will be seen later in
the case of the NCDHR and the International Dalit Solidarity
Network (see Chapter 7).

The communication between Dalit groups and individuals
with different movement perspectives has been intensified
through discussion groups on the Internet. The daily communication between activists in diverse Dalit networks, in spite
of geographical distances and also disagreements on many
points, has been of the utmost importance in refining and
strengthening a Dalit identity. For the Dalit activists the Internet
has provided a tool in 'building bridges in cyberspace' (Graham
and Khosravi 2002: 229), primarily between networks of groups
with different movement perspectives *within* a diverse counterpublic, but also in relation to a broader international public.
According to Alvarez, following Fraser (1992), 'social movement
webs constitute alternative or subaltern publics in which new
cultural and political meanings are produced, dissent is made
possible, and direct action can be imagined' (1997: 108). Dalit
activists in India have created an alternative counterpublic,
which they kept alive for decades even without the Internet,
but in cyberspace the Dalit networks have certainly been
activated since the middle of the 1990s. Through cyberspace
existing movement networks and webs are activated on a daily
basis and the creation of new ones is facilitated.[30]

THE POSITIVE IMPORTANCE OF
A NEGATIVE SYMBOL

As we can see, the religious as well as the political controversies that emerged between Gandhi and Ambedkar engage across

[30] For an interesting edited volume on women's activities on the
Internet in a global context, see Harcourt (2000). For more about
Internet and social movements, see for example, Wim Van de Donk,
et al. (2004).

different Dalit networks. In religious and political networks, in their own media and literature, and more recently in cyberspace, Dalit activists have been engaged in these questions and have formulated their identity in a different way from the rest of society and also the state. The Dalit activists provide what could be called a parallel and alternative discursive arena, where they 'invent and circulate counterdiscourses to formulate oppositional interpretations of their identities, interests and needs' (Fraser 1992: 123). With the Dalit Sahitya/Dalit Panthers in the 1970s, their message was spread in a new and more reflexive way. During the 1990s their controversial stand regarding their own identity has to a larger extent than before reached outside their counterpublic and been debated: Dalits—*are* they not Hindus?

Dalit activists regard Ambedkar as the one who broke away from Hinduism to achieve emancipation from the caste system. Gandhi, on the other hand, is accused of attempts to include the SCs among the Hindus. The Buddhist conversion in Nagpur in 1956 is taken as an example, by Buddhist, Christian, and party-political[31] Dalit activists alike, to show Ambedkar's antagonism towards Hinduism and the caste system. In the same way, the political decision taken in the Poona Pact in 1932, to deprive the 'depressed classes' of separate electorates and double votes, and instead include them among the Hindus (with just one vote at their disposal) is turned against Gandhi. Gandhi is criticized for his inclusive stand in the Poona Pact, not only among the political activists, but among the Buddhist and Christian Dalits as well. The widely held opinion that the SCs belong to the Hindu fold is challenged, and many Dalit activists point out their close relationship to Muslims to underline their autonomy from Hindus.

The Dalit activists are generally critical of the Marxist parties, which they accuse of being led by a high-caste Hindu élite, and they prefer to speak in terms of caste oppression rather than class oppression. Still, there is a strong Marxist influence and constant references to Marxist and socialist ideas, which make

[31] For Dalit activists in the political sphere, who refer to the Buddhist conversion in Nagpur, see the revival of the Republican Party of India in Lucknow, in Chapter 5, as these kinds of references are not to be found in the *Chamcha Age*, dealt with in this chapter.

Dalit Buddhism as well as Dalit theology resemble liberation theology. Dalit activists within Buddhism, Christianity, and the party-political sphere all speak of the social, political as well as economic exploitation of the SCs and share a vision of a total restructuring of society in which they are given justice. Questions on which they share a common view with each other, as well as with liberation theology, are, for example, land redistribution and equal opportunities with regard to work.

Anti-Gandhism is one theme that permeates the Dalit discourses in the various contexts. Historically Ambedkar is closely associated with Buddhism and the RPI.[32] Gandhi, on the other hand, is associated with Hinduism and the Congress Party. A negative attitude towards Gandhi makes it possible for activists in different Dalit networks which are negative to Hinduism and the Congress—but do not necessarily belong to Buddhism or the Republican Party of India—to unite. A pro-Ambedkar stance, on the other hand, may have made activists with world-views other than Buddhism doubtful about joining the movement. In the same way the political Dalit activists outside the circles of the RPI, with its strong associations with Ambedkar as well as the Dalit Panthers, may previously have hesitated to join the movement. In the 1990s Dalit activists from all kinds of networks united on the common theme of anti-Gandhism and anti-Hinduism. Individuals may have different preferences and belong to different religious and political networks, but still regard themselves as part of the same movement.

It may seem like a question of nuance as to whether a pro-Ambedkar/Buddhist stance or an anti-Gandhian/Hinduism attitude plays the more important role for the Dalit activists. But it seems that anti-Gandhism and anti-Hinduism came to offer something to the movement, which Ambedkar and Buddhism could not. First of all it offered exclusiveness, in the sense of making the Dalit movement narrower, excluding all those who held Gandhi in high esteem. Ambedkar as a symbol lost some of its unifying qualities when knowledge about him spread and was used outside the circles of the Dalit activists at

---

[32] RPI, when it was founded in 1957, was a continuation of Ambedkar's party, the Scheduled Castes Federation.

the beginning of the 1990s.[33] The debates and antipathies against Gandhi have reinforced a sense of 'us' against 'them', which was in danger of becoming blurred when others outside their own circles or counterpublic took up Ambedkar as a symbol. One side of an anti-Gandhism is obviously to highlight the frontiers of the movement and the differences of the activists in relation to those 'others', who do not share their basic values.

Secondly, anti-Gandhism has also been of importance in making the movement more inclusive and broad internally. The activists have managed to find a common point of reference for discussion. The antipathies towards Gandhi and Hinduism can be seen as a bridge between different religious, social, and political networks. In another formulation, the anti-stances have been uniting discursive themes and bridging the differences between movement perspectives. The anti-stances seem to be contributing to a strengthened belonging and identity, both as an indicator of demarcation in relation to 'outsiders', and also as a bridging sign uniting loosely connected networks or perspectives within the movement.

[33] The 14th of April, the birthday of Ambedkar, was gradually understood in India to be of importance for a mass of people, and was observed also in government ceremonial broadcast on television. Even among Hindu fundamentalists he was taken up and celebrated. In London I attended, a meeting among The Friends of India, closely related to RSS, on 14 April 1995. Ambedkar's writings were displayed to the audience in a well considered but distorted way. He was mainly presented as a friend of the Hindus and an enemy of the Muslims. Buddhism was, for example, said to be Ambedkar's choice, because this was the religion most closely related to Hinduism and also a part of it. For more about how Hindu fundamentalists have taken up Ambedkar as a symbol, see, for example, Gopal Guru (1991).

5

Dalit Activities in Lucknow
Buddhism and Party Politics in Local Practice

In Chapter 4 I was mainly occupied with some influential discourses within the contemporary Dalit movement. In this chapter I shall look more closely at some of these discourses to see how they may be expressed and combined in local practices among activists. The location will be Lucknow, the capital of Uttar Pradesh—the state where the Dalit movement has been most visible in party-politics since the 1980s.

Escobar (1992: 414) has commented that social movements are often cultural struggles about meanings, especially in the 'Third World' where they have been seen primarily as struggles about economic means of survival, for understandable reasons. Since the 1980s, it has been pointed out that the 'new social movements' differed from the traditional class-based movements, and it was argued that they were more sociocultural than sociopolitical. In many respects the Dalit movement is similar to these so-called new social movements.[1] It is not based on class, but on the ascribed caste membership of so-called untouchables. It is sociocultural, with the activists involved in conflicts regarding social control of basic cultural patterns (Touraine 1985: 778). There is further a self-reflexivity in the movement (Touraine 1985) as well as a consciousness of a global dimension (Melucci 1989). The Dalit activists produce information and they also

[1] Melucci, one of the most influential theorists dealing with the so-called new social movements, was the one who coined the concept, something that he later regretted. I prefer the concept 'contemporary movements', as the concept of 'new social movements' has turned out to be problematic (see Melucci 1998: 424ff).

integrate the private and [counter] public sphere (ibid.), to mention a few features that have been highlighted as typical of the 'new social movements'. Many researchers, influenced by Melucci, have pointed out that the 'new social movements' were formed as alternatives to party politics. They were seen as working increasingly autonomously in relation to the political system.[2] The Dalit activists, however, both focus on cultural struggles about meanings, which was said to be a characteristic of the 'new social movements' and, especially recently, have become more involved in party politics, the state, and the parliamentary system.

In spite of differences within the Dalit movement, activists are, through their own counterpublic, jointly challenging the interpretation of their identity as Hindus, ascribed to them by others. Dalit activists are obviously involved in what may be called cultural struggles about meanings, or 'wars of interpretation', in the words of Slater (1998), not least about their own identity as seen in Chapter 3. Simply by being part of a Dalit network and talking about themselves as Dalits (oppressed) and not as 'untouchables', Harijans (the children of God) or even SCs, they make power relations visible. They announce to society that a fundamental problem exists (Melucci 1985: 797) and challenge dominant symbols and meaning systems in every-day life (ibid., 1988: 250). They give clear indications to society, and most of all to the Hindu community, that they no longer accept an ascribed status at the bottom of the caste hierarchy. They find themselves not to be part of the Hindu

[2] Melucci shares with Habermas the view that 'new social movements' are defensive reactions to colonialization of the life-world by the system (Habermas 1981). The rational and strategic ideas that guide the state and the market were, according to Habermas, forced upon the understanding of the individuals in the social life, the life-world. Melucci, however, modified this view to some extent, pointing out that the welfare society, with health institutes giving information about AIDS, for example, may manipulate and control people, but may still have a positive side providing new important information (Melucci 1989: 196). For a criticism of Melucci, see, for example, Bartholomew and Mayer (1992). For a criticism of Habermas' view on social movements, see, for example, Cohen (1985). For a related discussion about 'new social movements' in the Indian context, see Larsson (2006: 14ff).

community, but outside it and oppressed by it. In positioning themselves in a relation of conflict with the basic values of Hinduism, converting to other religions, or laying claim to a separate indigenous cultural tradition, they offer a new self-definition (see also Zelliot 1992; Fuchs 1999).[3]

Again, then, similarly to the activists in the movements studied by Melucci in the 1980s and 1990s, the Dalit activists are involved in a cultural struggle. The Italian activists tried to escape state interference and in this regard the Dalit activists differ from them. They often struggle to get closer to state power and *want* state protection against caste discrimination. Melucci found that the activists created a new space between the public political world and the private world in which to conduct politics and solve questions that they thought the political parties could not manage. In these kinds of spaces the Dalit activists, instead, find a possibility of activating networks to prepare themselves for engagements with the state.

In India, contemporary social movements are often to be found among those people who are not well integrated into the mainstream institutional political life. They do not try to *reclaim* politics, in the words of Melucci, through the creation of a politicized sphere of action between the public political world and the private world. What they try to do is to *enter* the world of formal politics. Leslie Calman (1992: 197) observed the same process with regard to the Indian women's movement, in which Indian women prepare themselves for engagement in more formal political activities. The movements discussed by Melucci and his associates operate at a distance from party politics and the state because the activists are dissatisfied with formal politics. In the Dalit movements the activists did the same until recently, not mainly out of dissatisfaction but because they did not have the means to enter this sphere, which is something completely different.

The Dalit movement and the contemporary ('new') social movements as described in classic studies by Melucci and others thus look alike, but there are different processes at work. Dalit activists are similarly creating spaces between the formal

[3] For a related discussion about social movements and identity-formation among the Rabha or Kocha people in sub-himalayan Bengal, see Karlsson (1997: 288–300).

public political world and the private world, as already stated. When more closely scrutinized, however, the Dalit activists will be found to be moving in the opposite direction. That is, they are not moving away from formal politics, creating new spaces for political activities to escape the state. Rather, they reach out from 'everyday life' and informal politicized spaces in the direction of party politics and the state, to be able to touch and be touched by it.[4]

When discussing movements in Latin America, Alvarez points out that 'multiple strands of the social movement webs increasingly stretch beyond the terrain of civil society and into that of political society and the state' (1997: 109).[5] In this vein, I shall demonstrate how the networks to which Dalit activists belong are often, in everyday life and civil society, intricately interwoven with party politics and the networks of the state. The activities being carried on in alternative Dalit spaces in Lucknow that will be presented in this chapter are examples of how party politics and cultural struggle about meaning may in practice be inseparably interwoven.[6]

An Indian policy of affirmative action for the SCs (among others) in universities and government service is one of the reasons for the positive approach to the state among Dalit activists.[7] Most of them, as we shall see in the life histories of

[4] In Chapter 7 we shall see how Dalit activists in the NCDHR approach the state and demand its protection against the discrimination directed against them in civil society.

[5] Alvarez prefers the term 'web' to the more common 'network' 'precisely to try to convey the intricacy and precariousness of the manifold imbrications of and ties established among movement organizations, individual participants and other actors in civil and political society and the state...' (1997: 90).

[6] Networks may be fused in practice in one locality but also conveyed between localities in a fused way. This will be seen in the transnational connections between Dalit activists in Punjab and Uttar Pradesh in north India and Ambedkarites in Birmingham and Wolverhampton in Britain. The Ambedkarites in Britain will be seen to belong to the same fused Buddhist and party-political networks as the Dalit activists in India, with whom they interact and communicate. See Chapter 6.

[7] This is not to deny that the activists in the Dalit movement to a great extent direct criticism against the state, mainly for being

Chindrapal Mitra, Ishwar Sevak, and Mirajkar in this chapter, grew up in poor economic circumstances. Many have, however, been able to get an education and find a job through the government policy of affirmative action. This has led to better economic conditions for many of those who would otherwise never have been able to get into the labour market. There is no system of quotas in the private sector and, according to the economist Thorat (1996), the SCs have experienced difficulties in getting into this sector because of caste-based discrimination. He has pointed out how the privatization and liberalization of the Indian economy, beginning with a new economic policy in 1991, have increased unemployment and the poverty ratio among the SCs: 'Thus, unless some steps are taken to protect Dalits from job discrimination in the private sector, the positive trends Dalits have experienced through the government's planned efforts since Independence may be reversed' (Thorat 1996: 4). The 'scheduled castes' never had easy access to the private sector, nor to private property such as land, and this may be one reason why there has been a strong socialist influence in the Dalit movement, with demands for nationalization of land and industry, for example.

BAHUJAN SAMAJ PARTY

The growth of the Dalit movement during the past few decades may be seen as part of a political transformation which has taken place in India. The Congress Party has lost its total dominance and new regional groups and parties have come to the fore. Two trends can be discerned in this transformation, according to Zoya Hasan (1998); first, a greater participation and empowerment of previously excluded groups, and second, an assertion of exclusivist and communal identities. Uttar Pradesh is the state where the Congress Party most obviously lost power, and where identities were formulated in caste terms. This is the state where the upper castes have been most strongly challenged from below (Hasan 1998: 6).

---

dominated and governed by 'high-caste Hindus'. For more about Dalits and the state, see Shah (2002).

The Bahujan Samaj Party was founded in 1984; between 1989 and 2002 the party grew steadily in Uttar Pradesh. It increased its assembly seats from 13 (out of 425) in 1989 to the incredible number of 98 (out of 403) in 2002, which is about one-fourth of the seats in the state assembly. During the same period the Congress Party's strength declined from 94 seats in 1989 to only 25 seats in 2002 (Inkinen 2003: 51). Since the general election in 1998 the BSP has tried to gain the reputation of a national party. In 2004 the BSP contested 435 Lok Sabha seats in 25 different states. This was the largest number of seats contested by any party. Although the BSP is not a national party it has become nationally feared by other parties because of its potential to take the valuable SC votes away. In 2007 Mayawati regained the majority in the Uttar Pradesh elections and the BSP surprisingly came to power winning 206 seats (out of 403) without the support of other parties.

Uttar Pradesh is the most populous state in India, with 176 million people. The symbolic significance of the BSP's feat in capturing political power in the middle of the 1990s and working its way to the majority in the Uttar Pradesh elections in 2007 has to be understood. The party has been led by Kanshi Ram, who passed away in 2006, and Mayawati, who is now the party leader, both born as SCs. Although there have been previous attempts by the SCs to get into a political position, the RPI being an example, none ever came close to the success of the BSP.

The political success of the BSP has certainly challenged cultural values that historically put the SCs in invisible positions in relation to others. The BSP has given a face to SCs or Dalits in the public sphere. During her periods in power Mayawati has worked tirelessly to capture public places symbolically. This should be contrasted with the invisibility of the SCs historically in the public sphere, when they were confined to their own counterpublic. The BSP, with Mayawati as Chief Minister in Uttar Pradesh, made the SCs and Ambedkar simultaneously visible to the public. Mayawati has put up thousands of Ambedkar statues in villages and cities all over the state, renamed universities and colleges after him, and built a huge Ambedkar park in Lucknow, to mention a few of her activities.

One of the most important changes that has followed from the BSP capturing political power in Uttar Pradesh during

several periods in the 1990s and 2000s and with single majority in 2007, has been that of changing the Indian 'culture of
politics' (Alvarez *et al.* 1998a), mainly in Uttar Pradesh. First,
the BSP introduced the SCs as political rulers. The Dalit
movement further presented, through the BSP, ingredients of
their counterpublic discourse (such as anti-Gandhism) and made
it known to the public, not least through the media. Making
the Dalit counterpublic discourse public seems to have been a
conscious effort, and probably the primary one, from the side of
the BSP leadership. Their foremost aim seems thus to have been
that of making the SCs visible in various ways. This has been
accomplished by holding political power, independent of how
that power was achieved or to what other use it was put.

Many were surprised by the sudden success of the BSP in
the 1990s, but former leader Kanshi Ram had been building up
his support for a long time. He began his career as a scientist,
but left his job in a laboratory in Pune in 1964 when he came
into contact with the ideas of Ambedkar and decided to devote
his life to the movement. For seven years he worked for the
Republican Party before becoming disillusioned with it and
deciding to start something new. In 1978 he founded the trade
union, the BAMCEF. Its sympathizers were mainly the SCs
among government employees. Kanshi Ram's strategy was that
the relative economic success of this middle class among
the SCs should be shared by those in the category who were
less fortunate. A guilty conscience among these employees in
relation to their less fortunate caste mates could make them
contribute economically to a party working in favour of this
category. His plan was successful, and a few years later
BAMCEF had become the economic backbone of the BSP.
Kanshi Ram worked on many fronts simultaneously and on
6 December 1981 he founded the propaganda section D-S4. In
cycle campaigns, for example, with slogans about equality and
respect, D-S4 worked for mass mobilization. Three years later
in 1984, the political party the BSP was formed.[8]

[8] For an overview and more about the background of Kanshi Ram,
the BSP, and political trends in Uttar Pradesh during the 1990s and
beginning of the 2000s, see, for example, Hasan (1998), Omvedt (1998
[1994]), Pai (1998, 2000, 2001, 2002), Wyatt (2000), Jaffrelot (2003),
Jeffery and Lerche (2003), and Inkinen (2003).

In the middle of the 1990s I discussed the politics of the Bahujan Samaj Party with Kanshi Ram, and found him strikingly consistent in his attitude.[9] His aim was to capture power at the centre and not just in one or two Indian states. His vision was of a total transformation of Indian society and this was only possible, he said, when he had achieved power at the centre. Some minor things could be done in the meantime, he thought, but his energy and focus were clearly devoted to the future. He imagined a transformed India ruled, not by the BSP, but by bahujan samaj, a society of the majority.

His argument went as follows. Today 15 per cent of uppercaste people (that is, Brahmins, Kshatriyas, and Vaishyas) govern the country. Now the time has come for the majority, bahujan samaj, comprising 85 per cent of the Indian people, to take over. The ultimate aim of the BSP was to capture power and to use that power for social transformation and economic emancipation. Kanshi Ram aimed at building a strong bahujan samaj. Bahujan consisted of 'Dalits—the better part of the bahujan', he told me half-jokingly, 'and Shudras, Muslims and other groups who are depressed by the minority, the high castes'.

During the 1990s there was a tendency among many Dalit groups across the state to occupy government land under the BSP slogan *jo zamin sarkari hai, vah zamin hamari hai* (government land is our land). Dalit activists put up Ambedkar statues on government land in the villages and claimed ownership of it. What did Kanshi Ram have to say about these activities?

Yes, I want to redistribute land. There should not be any big landowners and also no landless people. Everybody should have what he can cultivate, no more and no less. We have our own plan of how things should be done. When my ideas are carried out it should be done across the whole of India simultaneously, not just in one or a few states (Interview with Kanshi Ram, New Delhi, 9 April 1994).

Kanshi Ram was never very specific about his plans during interviews; he simply made it clear that he did not find it meaningful to work for minor changes in one or a few states. The vague way in which he spoke about ordinary local politics stands

[9] Interviews with Kanshi Ram, New Delhi, 9 April 1994 and Lucknow, 9 March 1996.

in sharp contrast to the detailed knowledge he seems to have had of the distribution of caste and religious groups in different districts and urban areas. People outside as well as within the party talked about this. It was claimed by Kanshi Ram, as well as by party workers, that close investigations were carried out at a grassroots level to find out which communities were living in the various areas. They prided themselves on being familiar with their potential voters, and asserted that this was one of the main strengths of the BSP. Party workers stated that because they knew exactly where to find the different communities at the grassroots level, they were able to approach them in the right way.

BREAKAWAY PARTIES FROM BSP IN LUCKNOW

The majority of Dalit activists see it as their main task to work against Hinduism and the caste system. Consequently there was widespread discontent when, in 1995, the BSP sought the support of the Hindu nationalist BJP, in order to claim the post of chief minister in Uttar Pradesh. For four months in 1995, Mayawati became the first Dalit woman ever to hold office as chief minister. Moreover, she was chief minister in the most populous and thus politically most important state in India.

She repeated this feat during a six-month period in 1997, and again in the elections in 2002, in more direct alliances with the BJP. Kanshi Ram, Mayawati, and many others in the BSP regarded it as legitimate to receive strategic support from a party whose ideology they opposed, in order to get into power. They thought they were encouraging the SCs and women to get into party politics by making a Dalit woman visible as power-holder in politics.

As already mentioned a vote bank of SCs had emerged in Uttar Pradesh, and the dissatisfaction with the BSP from 1995 onwards meant that there were 'scheduled caste' votes to be won for other parties. A number of breakaway factions—for small parties in Lucknow by the end of 1995—from the BSP were formed, but none of them attained anything near the importance of the BSP in the state.

During the autumn of 1995 the Kurmi caste group, within the BSP, was the first to become dissatisfied with the party.

They were of the opinion that Kanshi Ram and Mayawati, apart from making a mistake in allying with the BJP, were mainly loyal to their own caste group, the Chamars. The organization Kurmi Mahasabha was founded under the leadership of Ram Lakhan Verma and Jung Bahadur Patel. This organization was later transformed into the political party Apna Dal. The two small parties Bahujan Samaj Dal (BSD) and Bharatiya Loktantrik Dal (BLD) also hoped for a future in breaking away from the BSP, but they went all without success.

The most important of the breakaway fractions was the BSP(R), started by Raj Bahadur, for long a close associate of Kanshi Ram. When I met this thoughtful and articulate man, in his 60s at the time, the same age as Kanshi Ram, he expressed deep disappointment with the fact that Kanshi Ram had associated himself with a Hindu nationalist party. He had been loyal to Kanshi Ram since 1974, he told me; now he had no choice but to leave him, in spite of his wish to the contrary. Raj Bahadur found the collaboration with the BJP to be against the ideology of Ambedkar: 'I followed Kanshi Ram as long as he followed Ambedkar's principles, but when he left them and joined with BJP, I left him'.[10]

In this sense Raj Bahadur expressed an opinion that was heard among many former BSP members at this time. On the other hand, many were still loyal to Kanshi Ram, whom they saw as still ideologically opposed to the BJP and only strategically in alliance with the party. Many among the male BSP supporters were also of the opinion that Mayawati was the unreliable person, lacking in ideology and morality. Without her influence in the decision making of the BSP, everything had looked different. Kanshi Ram always remained one and the same, in their opinion, but he was strongly influenced by Mayawati. In 2003 Kanshi Ram suffered a stroke and Mayawati was accused of keeping him in captivity and against his will in their house.

It is interesting to note that the criticism of Mayawati has not only come from outside the party or from the fractions that broke away. Although she has been respected by a large section

[10] Raj Bahadur regards himself as a follower of Ambedkar's ideas, even though he belongs to Kurmi, a caste group classified as OBCs.

of the BSP voters, the criticism of her from the male activists within the party corresponded to a great extent with that directed against her from outside; Mayawati was mainly condemned on moral grounds. I shall return to these moral aspects concerning Mayawati in Chapter 8, when discussing the media coverage of the Dalit movement and more specifically of Dalit women.

THE REVIVAL OF THE RPI IN LUCKNOW

The effort to revive the RPI in Uttar Pradesh in 1996 must be seen in the light of the political situation in the state then. Its founders were well aware of the fact that the Congress had for some time lost its dominance and there were votes to be won among disappointed or former BSP supporters. At this time I already knew from different contexts the three initiators of the revival, who had long been active in the Dalit movement in different capacities. I shall give a brief account of the two initial meetings for the revival of the party, before presenting the life histories of the three initiators, Mirajkar, Ishwar Sevak, and Chindrapal Mitra.[11]

THE INITIAL MEETINGS

The sun was at its height, but on the third floor of the centrally located office building in Lucknow it was pleasantly cool. In a spartan room, rented for the purpose, about 50 people from different districts in Uttar Pradesh were gathered, seated on sheets spread on the floor. Seven large pillows marked a stage where 10 people had taken their places, among them Mirajkar, Ishwar Sevak, and Chindrapal Mitra, who were the main persons behind this meeting and had been among the last to arrive. This was the re-establishment of the RPI in Uttar Pradesh, which had seen its best days a little more than 30 years before.[12]

[11] These are pseudonyms.

[12] It is mainly in Maharashtra, where the party was founded in 1957, that it has had some impact and enjoyed support primarily among Buddhists. In Uttar Pradesh in the early 1960s when Muslims and Buddhists were temporarily united in an alliance, the party was of some importance (Zelliot 1992). In Maharashtra the party has been divided into several smaller factions with rivalry between the leaders.

A recurrent theme during the afternoon was the policies of the BSP, which were severely criticized. Many participants pointed out that the RPI was now revived as a reaction to the dictatorial BSP, ruled with an iron hand by the two people at the top, the President Kanshi Ram and the General Secretary Mayawati. Ishwar Sevak talked about the 'demands of the people': 'We shall be a party for minorities—SCs (scheduled castes), BCs (backward classes), minorities and women. It is a present demand from the people. There has been a vacuum since the BSP joined with the BJP.' The audience listened attentively and nodded in agreement. After the opening speech the people in the audience introduced themselves one by one, and gave their ideas about what the direction of the RPI should be. Many criticized the BSP and demanded that the revived RPI should be a more democratic party 'in the spirit of Ambedkar'. They also wanted the revived party to be anti-BJP and anti-Congress. Many spoke about Buddhism as the philosophy that should guide the party and quoted Ambedkar's (1991b) *Buddha and His Dhamma*.

Chindrapal Mitra had prepared a three-page draft of a programme, which he read out, for the others to discuss and comment on. It began by criticizing the BSP for damaging the Dalit movement through dictatorial leadership and a lack of clear direction. It was explained that the RPI should be decentralized and founded at all levels, from village to state level in Uttar Pradesh, and that a group leadership should be created in order not to centralize power and leave it in the hands of any one individual. Other goals were work for everyone, inexpensive and compulsory education, and the nationalization of all agricultural land, with the person cultivating it able to enjoy the proceeds of his own labour. Furthermore, according to the programme, the RPI should work for the acceptance of Buddhism. Those who stayed within Hinduism should be encouraged to marry across caste barriers in order to create a casteless and classless society.

At a second, smaller meeting a month later the debates were not about ideological issues, but mainly about organizational matters, like how the meetings in the districts should be arranged. Prakash Ambedkar (see also Chapter 6) was the main guest and shared the honour with Muzaffar Ali, a film director who has made a television film on Lucknow. Prakash Ambedkar was the president of one of the RPI fractions in Maharashtra, and had come to play a symbolic role in the party as the grandchild of B.R. Ambedkar. He could tie the Uttar Pradesh unit of the RPI into the broader networks of the party in the country, mainly to Maharashtra (but also to Tamil Nadu and Karnataka). The film director, Chindrapal Mitra hoped, would attract younger people to the party. The guests remained silent during the meeting and their role, in this context, was mainly to talk to the journalists at the press conference that followed.

THREE KEY FIGURES

I shall now look more closely at the three initiators of the RPI and use their narratives to illustrate how the change of identity during a lifetime is experienced and expressed. It will be seen how their activities in the private and public spheres are experienced as part of one and the same process.[13] For the three individuals in these examples, these strands are in some situations intertwined in such an intricate way as to make it difficult to distinguish between them. The networks of family and friends, of Buddhism, and of party politics are virtually inseparable from each other.[14]

The three activists have played a role in many locations and bodies, not only in several religious and social organizations but also in politics. In this respect they are typical of many activists in the movement. Like many others within the movement, they are also Buddhists. They are well-educated men raised in economically reduced circumstances, who are well represented among the activists. Women are in an obvious minority within the movement, but I shall come back to their role in the international arena in Chapter 7.[15]

[13] For a review of the literature which focuses on narratives of personal experience, see Ochs and Capps (1996). For a detailed account of the importance of narratives in social movements, see Davis (2002).

[14] Genberg (2002: 242ff) discusses in an interesting way the complications involved when defining spaces as 'private' or 'public'.

[15] As Fraser (1992: 15) has noted, 'even those subaltern counterpublics with democratic and egalitarian intentions are not always above practising their own modes of informal exclusion and marginalization'. In the Dalit movement there are women to be found, but they are clearly

What the three men also have in common is that their offices are crammed with books and papers, and that they spend a considerable amount of their income on new literature. On the shelves are to be found the volumes of B.R. Ambedkar and books about Buddhism, Marxism, sociology, and political science, among many others. In this they differ from most other Dalit activists in being better read with regard to politics, religion, and the philosophy of Ambedkar. These three persons all belong to an intellectual élite among the activists, interested in discussing various ideologies. Many Dalit activists have only read some of Ambedkar's minor publications or none at all, but still consider him as a role model.[16]

MIRAJKAR

Mirajkar was born in 1994, a Chamar, traditionally an 'untouchable' caste dealing with leather, and grew up in a small village in the north Indian state of Punjab. His parents as well as his grandparents worked as farm labourers. Together with his parents and six siblings he lived in a one-room kaccha (made of clay) house. All the Chamar houses in his village were situated together and segregated from the rest of the village, as is still the case in many Indian villages today.

Mirajkar tells the same story as that usually told by Dalit activists, about a childhood during which discrimination and a sense of non-belonging constantly made themselves felt. He was not allowed to touch the water in school, as he was considered 'unclean'. If he touched the water tap or the pitcher in school, the other children could not drink from it until it was purified. It was through this experience in school that he, like many others, for the first time became aware of his place in the caste hierarchy as 'untouchable'.

From these kinds of personal experiences many of the Dalit activists have come to be engaged on many fronts in the

---

the subaltern *within* a subaltern or alternative counterpublic, or 'the downtrodden among the downtrodden', as Ruth Manorama (1995), a women's activist, expresses it.

[16] It is important to remember that I am talking about *activists* in the Dalit movement. Among the SCs, generally speaking, the illiteracy rate is high.

movement. Mirajkar tells me about this kind of discrimination with a laugh, which underlines how unbelievable it all seems. He is now a respected person, with a high position, living in his own comfortable house. The laughter is perhaps also a way of talking in a more joking tone about memories which otherwise could give an impression of bitterness.

For a short period he did not attend school, but helped his parents in their work: cutting grass in the fields, rearing the cattle, doing household jobs. He was later sent to his *mama's* (maternal uncle's) place, where he continued his studies. Like the parents of many Dalit activists, his mother and father were poor, but he was the lucky one to be chosen for education in a family with many children. His parents were illiterate but became part of Ad Dharm, the movement which swept Punjab in the 1930s.

After his education Mirajkar moved to Delhi, where he had felt that the people were more aware and those who had migrated from Punjab were more in touch with the Dalit movement. For the first time he came into contact with people who had read the works of Ambedkar, and from a relative he borrowed *Who were the Shudras?* (Ambedkar 1990 [1947]), a book that made him more interested in the thoughts and philosophy of Ambedkar.

In Delhi he attended meetings every Sunday in Ambedkar Bhavan, where he met people interested in the philosophy of Ambedkar, Buddhism, and social questions. These included social workers and government employees, among others. At the Sunday meetings in Delhi, people got together and one of them would speak on a chosen topic. Sometimes they invited people from outside to deliver a lecture or give a course. According to Mirajkar, this was a good opportunity to get to know each other and discuss important issues. This was one of the arenas where he had an opportunity to meet people who were interested in the same kind of questions and this was the place where, in 1969, he first met Ishwar Sevak, one of the other initiators of the revived RPI in Lucknow. They are now also related, as Ishwar Sevak's daughter has recently become Mirajkar's daughter-in-law.

From his childhood Mirajkar had always been interested in religion and philosophy. He was interested in Hinduism, studied the Hindu bhakti movement, was influenced by Hindu religious texts such as the Bhagavadgita, and also read the philosophy of Mahatma Gandhi. Sikhism and Buddhism were also closely investigated. All along there was also an interest in politics. During the 1970s Mirajkar was employed in the Indian Police Service in Varanasi and as a policeman on the beat, he explains, he came into contact with a lot of people with different interests. Among them were some Marxist workers who had participated in the Naxalite movement.[17] Through discussions with Naxalites, many of them from SCs, he came to sympathize with their work and ideology. He continued to study the thoughts of Ambedkar and regards himself to have become a Buddhist at this time. The Naxalites have been known for using considerable violence but, in this respect, Mirajkar does not find any conflict between his Buddhist philosophy and his sympathies with them:

In self-defence you must resort to violence, but ideologically you should believe in non-violence. That is also what Buddhism preaches. The Naxalites are fighting for the cause of the poorest section of society, and making sacrifices for that. So I think they are the well-wishers of the poor, or their saviours in that sense. Of course, that is my personal conviction (Fieldnotes, 11 April 1996).

During our conversation Mirajkar stresses that his philosophy is a personal belief, and adds with a smile that it has nothing to do with his official duties. According to Indian law it is not permitted for government employees to take an active part in party politics.[18] Because of this he underlines his role as a

[17] Naxalism is a revolutionary Marxist-Leninist movement which began as an uprising among workers at a tea plantation in the village of Naxalbari in north West Bengal in 1967 and then spread, mainly to the states of Bihar and Andhra Pradesh. The members of the movement try by armed struggle to accomplish their goal of redistributing land ownership and in a revolutionary way changing society. The Communist Party of India (Marxist-Leninist) was formed in 1969, in support of the Naxalites, and the party is still influential in several regions. For the relation between the Naxalites and the Dalit movement in the 1970s and 1980s, see for example Omvedt (1994a: 336–8).

[18] It is worth noting that Mirajkar has a senior position in the police and also sympathizes with the Naxalites. When the Naxalites were most active at the end of the 1960s, they directed a lot of their aggression against policemen. Mirajkar's political philosophy seems to be highly unusual within the Indian police force.

sympathizer and a source of inspiration for the revived RPI, not as an initiator of the party. He is careful not to cross the borderline where he could be understood as a founder of the party. This means that he cannot have an official position in the organization. Instead, his son takes on this role in the newly founded party and engages with it in a more formal way. Similarly, his son is the editor of the Dalit magazine which is edited and published from his house and engages in the official contexts. Mirajkar was present when the RPI was revived, but as a spectator. He was also present during the press conference after the second meeting, but took a role similar to that of the journalists, putting questions to the founders. He maintains a strict line between his personal opinion, which he has the right to express, and more official engagement.

Although Mirajkar is not allowed to take an active part in party politics, he has been involved in various social activities since he arrived in Lucknow in 1984. For example, he became General Secretary of an organization known as the SC/ST Official Welfare Council in the same year. This comprises officials belonging to SCs and STs, and is a broad officers' organization, with the aim of fighting caste discrimination in the workplace.

Mirajkar was, as already noted, one of the initiators of the Ambedkar Mahasabha in Lucknow in 1991. Three years later, in 1994, he initiated a Buddhist mass conversion in the premises of the Ambedkar Mahasabha, together with some other people in the organization. Although Mirajkar began believing in Buddhism as far back as 1968, it was not until this occasion that he formally converted, together with his whole family. But he does not consider himself to be a traditional or orthodox Buddhist. He told me: 'We adopted Buddhism as a practical philosophy, as a progressive philosophy.' According to him the conversion to Buddhism aims at getting out of the caste system and giving Dalits a new identity.

ISHWAR SEVAK

Anyone taking an interest in the Dalit movement soon finds that certain names keep cropping up time and time again, in completely different contexts. Ishwar Sevak, a barrister living in New Delhi, is one of these, mainly because of the large number of books and articles he has written. He is one of those of whom a young Dalit activist said: 'There are three persons in India you can put on any stage to speak, and you will feel proud to be a Dalit.' As a 16-year-old, he joined the Scheduled Castes Federation (SCF), and was thus in contact with leaders of the SCs at an early age. He has been Chairman or General Secretary of a number of organizations associated with lawyers, Buddhists, and minorities. He is also one of the founders of the Dalit Solidarity Programme, an organization founded in 1992 and supported financially by the World Council of Churches among others. For this organization, he has organized conferences and 'educational camps' and also edited a book about the programme.

Ishwar Sevak was born in 1927 in Shimla into a community known as Chuhra (Valmiki), whose members traditionally worked as sweepers. Compared with Mirajkar, he comes from a family which was economically somewhat better off. His grand-father belonged to a family that worked as cooks for the British Army; his father worked as a watchman at electricity towers, and had his own house in Shimla. Ishwar Sevak started school at the age of five and, in addition, his father engaged a tutor for the children.

In a similar way to Mirajkar he speaks of the discrimination he experienced as a child, which later on made him join the Dalit movement. In school everybody was asked which jati they belonged to before they were allowed to drink water; in accor-dance with his 'untouchable' status he did not get any. In public places nobody could stop him from taking water, but after he had taken it the Hindus used to purify the well with cowdung. It is with pride that he recounts how his father refused to keep quiet in these situations: 'My father used to say: "You fools, you are so afraid of untouchables and untouchability, but you don't realize that the washer inside is made of leather."'[19]

When Ishwar Sevak was 15 years old he came in contact, through his father, with the man who was the acting president of the SCF in Shimla, and began to type documents for the party. At the age of 16 he met Ambedkar for the first time, and this was an encounter that inspired him to go on with political work.

[19] The washers were earlier made of leather, a material that was in itself considered to be unclean.

During the following years he worked in the Air Force, and when he was 26 years old, he came into contact with the Backward Classes Commission in Bombay. He wrote articles for various newspapers, studied different political philosophies, and had at that time, like Mirajkar, sympathetic learnings towards Marxists and Naxalites. He studied guerrilla warfare and became interested in international communism; Castro and 'Che' Guevara were among his heroes.

At the same time, he also had the idea of becoming a bhikku, an ordained monk. He wanted to set up a centre for Muslim and Buddhist studies, and even put down a deposit for a piece of land 50 kilometres outside Delhi. In the end he did not have enough money to realize his plans and was also discouraged by Ambedkar, who did not believe in the system of bhikkus.

Although Ishwar Sevak did not become a Buddhist monk, he converted when he was 30 years old, and after the conversion he became even more interested in Buddhism. Today he is critical of those Buddhists within the movement who identify themselves as Aboriginals:

Some people say we are the Aboriginal people, but I think they don't know very much about anthropology or history. This is history subjected to political thought. There has been so much mixture of blood in this country, that none can say that they are pure Aryans or pure Aboriginals. To say we belong to a race which is different from the Aryan group will not bring about unity. I believe unity can be achieved only on the basis of the majority, and common suffering. And then I go beyond it—unity can be brought about if we look at discrimination in the same way worldwide.

It is clear that Ishwar Sevak has always had the desire to draw the Dalit movement into broader transnational networks and relate it to discriminated people in other parts of the world; he was among the pioneers in the movement in this regard. He spoke in a committee for human rights at the UN on behalf of the SCs and tried to globalize the issue of the discrimination against them since 1983. Furthermore, he has invited representatives of minorities from different countries to discuss questions of discrimination.

On a personal level he is also in touch with Dalit activists in the diaspora. When the Ambedkar Centenary Celebration

Committee was founded in London in 1989, Ishwar Sevak was one of those appointed to serve on it. In other words, he has been working to internationalize the issue of discrimination against SCs and has also been part of the transnational Dalit networks. For a long time he has been one of the leading figures of the Dalit movement in northern India.

CHINDRAPAL MITRA

Chindrapal Mitra was born in 1921 in a small village in Bara Banki district in Uttar Pradesh. He belongs to Kewat, a Mallah community of boatmen, who ferried passengers between the shores and also fished. When he was born both his parents were agricultural labourers with a meagre income. They came to Lucknow in search of employment when he was three years old. His parents were employed as domestic servants and found a small one-room house where the family settled down.

Chindrapal Mitra's mother made an exchange arrangement with the people in the houses where she went to work. In return for herself and Chindrapal Mitra helping in the households with cleaning, shopping in the market, and other chores, her son was taught by the children in these houses. He had a great longing for learning, he explains, and he cannot emphasize strongly enough that it was his mother who gave him the opportunity to study.

His mother was active in the Congress Party and along with her, Chindrapal Mitra took part in various demonstrations and became part of the independence movement. His father was of the opinion that people belonging to the 'lower' castes should not take on the responsibilities of the 'higher' castes and be active in politics. But his father gave way to his mother and allowed Chindrapal Mitra to take part in the protests against the British.

Through his mother he got a clerical job in the office of the Congress Party and in this way became involved early on in party politics. He was arrested several times by the British, something he mentions with pride when talking about his life. Over the years Chindrapal Mitra has been involved and has held office in several different political parties. He met Ambedkar for the first time in the Buddha vihara in 1953. This is also the place where he converted to Buddhism as early as 1946, 10 years before the conversion of Ambedkar, something that he stresses to show that he understood early on how important it was for the Dalits to convert to Buddhism. The personal meeting with Ambedkar came to mean a lot to Chindrapal Mitra. He recounts how Ambedkar credited him with great capacity, and is immensely proud of the task Ambedkar entrusted to him: 'If you join me, as a soldier, you will be a commander of the party'. After this meeting Chindrapal Mitra became involved in Ambedkar's political party, the SCF. He came to be the first President of the RPI in Uttar Pradesh, when it was founded in 1957.

Over the years Chindrapal Mitra has been active in the Dalit movement in a number of ways. He had an indirect impact on the revival of the movement at the beginning of the 1990s because, in his capacity as a barrister, he was a member of the Mandal Commission, which was the Commission to recommend increased reservations for OBCs.

An activity that takes a lot of his time is his own small publishing company. Chindrapal Mitra publishes literature written by himself and by others, and over the years he has published a number of booklets and also a book in Hindi dealing with the 'untouchables' and the Dalit movement in Uttar Pradesh.

There are many similarities between the three individuals in this example, and they also have much in common with other Dalit activists. In their childhood, Chindrapal Mitra, Ishwar Sevak, and Mirajkar experienced caste-based discrimination, as a result of being born into the category of 'untouchables'. Mirajkar and Ishwar Sevak both refer to the occasion in school when they were not allowed to touch the water, as the first time they experienced exclusion. They were all born into economically poor families; the parents of Mirajkar and Chindrapal Mitra worked as farm labourers, while Ishwar Sevak's father worked as a watchman and was a little better off. Although their parents had very low incomes all three were given an education.

When they grew up they came into contact, through their parents and different networks of friends, with people working against caste discrimination and became active themselves. At a young age they were all interested in politics, and Mirajkar as well as Ishwar Sevak sympathized with Marxists and Naxalites, while Chindrapal Mitra through his mother came to work for the Congress Party and later on the SCF, and the

RPI. Chindrapal Mitra converted to Buddhism at the age of 25 and Ishwar Sevak at the age of 30. Mirajkar was a convinced Buddhist at the age of 30, but did not convert formally until recently.

A BUDDHA VIHARA IN LUCKNOW
ENTERING THE VIHARA

I now turn my attention to a Buddha vihara in Lucknow that has for a long time been connected with Dalit activities, both religiously and politically. In this small vihara, located in the old part of Lucknow, Ambedkar and his writings have a central role to play. Travelling by *tempo*[20] on the busy main road, you get off and walk just one block. Passing a cloth shop on the right, you will come to a small, calm green square surrounded by red brick buildings. Arriving at the square at 9 AM on a Sunday means that people are still busy with their morning tasks. A woman is washing some *saris* outside her house, a man is loading his donkey with colourful plastic buckets, and at the other side of the park some children are playing cricket. They are probably inspired by the cricket World Cup, which makes people all over the city crowd in front of available television sets—it may be in the *chai*-shop (tea-shop) or in front of the window of the radio and television shop. A win for India is celebrated with firecrackers during the night, frightening the dogs which run around barking endlessly on the streets.

Entering the vihara, embedded between the dwelling houses, you arrive first at the office room. This morning a monk is sleeping at the desk with his head on his arms, which are resting on the table. It turns out later that he belongs to a visiting group from Sri Lanka, which has just arrived. Two other monks are reading the newspaper and nobody takes any notice of me. This room is surrounded by about 15 glass-fronted cupboards, filled with books, mainly in Hindi but also some in English. Each cupboard has its own red, blue or metallic lock, and the keys are kept by the monks living in the vihara, who come when

[20] Tempos are common vehicles in Lucknow, running on specific routes. They take about six passengers and are slightly larger but similar to the auto-rickshaws.

someone wants to read or maybe buy a book published by the vihara's own publishing house. On the wall, behind the desk, two historical figures are displayed—a large framed picture of Ambedkar, and down to the left a small picture of Karl Marx. On another wall there is also a picture of the present head monk, Venerable[21] Prajnananda, and another one of the founder Venerable Bodhanand Mahastavir, who established the vihara in 1925. In a calendar with Ambedkar's picture, Buddhist feast days are marked.

Walking through the combined office and library, you enter the small courtyard. It is surrounded by luxuriant greens in pots and the temperature is pleasant in the morning hours. This morning I find another of the newly arrived monks from Sri Lanka, dressed in his yellow robe, sleeping on one of two *charpois*[22] in the courtyard. To the left is a sacred room divided into two parts and separated from the yard by a black lattice gate with a strong padlock, which today is opened and pushed aside, in the same way as the lattice gate that divides the inner room. In the outer part of the room 10 women from the visiting group from Sri Lanka are resting, sitting with their heads leaning against the wall. A Buddhist layman among the guests is being attended to by another woman who is wrapping his leg with a gauze bandage. When the bandaging is finished, he puts on his cap and disappears with his tourist bag on his shoulder to see the city. The woman, who has finished her task, leaves to wash her feet, returns to fetch her bag, and persuades the other women to go sight-seeing Lucknow with her.

The Vihara's Engagements

The history of the vihara is one in which religious, social, and political engagements have for long been closely intertwined. Venerable Prajnananda, the head monk, was chosen at the age of 13 from among five boys, to be the successor of Venerable Bodhanand Mahasthavir.[23] He has been responsible for the

[21] 'Venerable' is often added in front of the monk's name, to show respect.

[22] Wooden string-beds.

[23] Ambedkar in a conference in Mahova (close to Kanpur, in Hamipur district) in 1928 took *Venerable Bodhanand Mahasthavir* (1874–1952)

vihara since 1952. About his teacher and the ideas which still characterize the vihara he says: 'The main work for my teacher was the uplifting of the backward classes. Humanitarian work came first and Buddhism second.'

Prajnananda met Ambedkar on three occasions, of which he is of course proud. The first time was when Ambedkar visited the vihara in connection with a Scheduled Caste Conference in 1948: 'I had the chance to serve him water, and Bhante[24] introduced me as his successor.' The second time was at a Buddhist conference in Burma, and the third time was at the famous Buddhist conversion in Nagpur in 1956. Prajnananda was the youngest of the 10 monks on stage when the conversion took place, and says that he is the only one who is still alive today. During the two days of the conversion all the monks, and also Ambedkar, stayed at the same hotel/vihara. Prajnananda describes Ambedkar as follows: 'My impression of Ambedkar was that among children he was a child—and I was a child at that time', he added with a smile. Commenting on Ambedkar's religious and political activities Prajnananda says:

He was revolutionary in social, political, and also Buddhist lines. He did not want Buddha in lying or sitting figures, but in standing figures. He wanted a moving Buddha. That type of Buddha statues could also be found in Mathura Museum.[25]

Prajnananda is favourably disposed to Ambedkar's *Buddha and His Dhamma*.[26] In 1970, a Hindi edition of the book was published from this vihara by the Buddhist Education Society. For Prajnananda religiosity again is combined with a social and

---

as one of his own Buddhist teachers. At this conference Achchutananda and Ambedkar represented the SCs and Venerable Bodhanand Mahasthavir represented the Buddhists (interview with Prajnananda, Lucknow, 3 April 1996).

[24] Literally monk. It refers here to Venerable Bodhanand Mahasthavir.

[25] Interview with Venerable Prajnananda, Lucknow, 3 April 1996.

[26] Prajnananda is from Sri Lanka and does not belong to the 'SCs'. His positive attitude regarding Ambedkar could be compared with that of the monks in the viharas in Britain, who at times are quite critical of Ambedkarite Buddhism (see Chapter 6).

political interest, and he expresses a somewhat ambiguous trust in Mayawati:

When this woman came to power we had high hopes, but even after three months she did not do very much for Buddhists. She visited Buddhist countries like Korea, Japan and Taiwan. But fifteen days after her return she had to resign. We should hope as well-wishers that she comes back [laughter].

His political interest, though, was not restricted to one specific political party. Those parties in favour of depressed groups he found worth helping. He told me that he had hosted the BSP as well as the RPI in the vihara:

After Ambedkar's death, nine MPs from the Republican Party of India visited Lucknow and there was an Uttar Pradesh reception. The meeting was held in this vihara and in this room. I had to do the same thing to help BSP. Their first activity centre was here in the Buddha vihara. They used to come and hold their meetings here. Although I am not in the political line, I supported and gave them hospitality here. It all depends on the presiding monk.

In this same Buddha vihara the social organization Ambedkar Mahasabha was formed as a result of the Ambedkar centenary celebrations in 1991. The first three years Prajnananda was president and then he was patron for one year, together with another monk. The Ambedkar Mahasabha was an SC organization aimed at fighting caste discrimination. According to its programme, it was to 'educate the masses, put forward their problems and advise the government regarding policies and programmes'. The Ambedkar Mahasabha was a social and non-political organization, which made it possible for people in government service to take an active part in it. Many of the members, however, belonged to the Indian Administrative Service (IAS), and in their professional capacities had an influence on the political policies taking shape in the Uttar Pradesh government.

Initially the Ambedkar Mahasabha had no office of its own and members met in the vihara. Later on a small office was rented in central Lucknow, where two people were employed to take care of the administration. Chindrapal Mitra was chairman of the organization and every morning between 9 AM and 12 noon he or some other senior activist could be found behind a desk, with people queuing up waiting to present their problems. SCs came from different districts in Uttar Pradesh to get help with legal matters, mostly connected with land rights, or to ask how to handle different questions in the local branches of the Ambedkar Mahasabha, in the villages or small towns in the state. The organization also had a youth wing with its own premises, a tiny room in the backyard of the head office, without electricity or other amenities. The plan was to create a library with the books of Ambedkar. This project was started on a small scale with a few books on a shelf. Ambedkar Mahasabha split due to personal and economic issues and the office rooms, including those of the youth wing, were closed, and the organization was later run temporarily from other places in the city.

SUNDAY MEETINGS

During my fieldwork, a small group of Dalit activists used to gather in this vihara every Sunday between 9 AM and 11 AM The gathering followed the same pattern every Sunday. Shortly after 9 AM people started to arrive. Having taken off their shoes outside the shrine-room, they entered to put a candle and a stick of incense in front of the Buddha statue in the inner part of the room.

Two smaller Buddha statues flanked the main statue and behind the altar, in three niches, additional small Buddha statues were placed. On the altar the candles were burning, and the sticks of incense put in a bowl of sand filled the room with their characteristic smell. Fresh flowers were put side by side with plastic ones. The ceremonial bowls of water on the altar were surrounded by many small items that looked like souvenirs. It seemed as if many new things had been added gradually over a long period without the older ones being removed. On the wall to the left was a modern tourist tapestry from Singapore showing three Buddha viharas; the text above read 'Singapore' and the text below 'Instant Asia'. It may have been a gift from a guest.

After paying homage to Buddha, people sat down on plastic mats on the floor and engaged in small talk about family and work until everybody had arrived. At 9.30 AM Mr Nand Kishore, a middle-aged tranquil man who conducted the meetings, used to turn up. He had converted in 1956 in Lucknow on the occasion of Ambedkar's conversion in Nagpur. 'We first get to know Babasaheb Ambedkar and then we become Buddhists', he explained to me during a conversation about the relationship between Buddhism and Ambedkar.

One of the monks, either Bhanteji, the head monk, or *chota bhante*,[27] a 15-year-old monk, arrived in the shrine-room and under the guidance of a monk the chanting took place. Next there would be a reading from *Buddha and His Dhamma*. Two chapters or rather verses were read aloud each Sunday, and the reading rotated so that somebody else would take it up from where it had left off the week before. The reading of *Buddha and His Dhamma* was carried out at the suggestion of Prajnananda, who told me:

I have suggested that after the Pali puja and other things, half an hour should be spent reading his [Ambedkar's] book. After finishing *Buddha and His Dhamma* we should read Buddha *charitra*, the life histories of Buddha, by Bhadant Anand Kausalyayan.[28] After that we should read *Buddha and His Dhamma* again. It should be rotated like this, instead of one week this, another week that...*one* idea should continue.

After the reading of *Buddha and His Dhamma*, there was finally a quiz competition. Two different questionnaires were distributed, one for adults and another with more basic questions for the children. Both consisted of two types of questions, six of them dealing with Buddha, his life and teaching, and six others related to Ambedkar and his life. Three different answers to each question were given, one of which was to be chosen. The parents discussed with their children which answer they wanted to give, and younger children were given more help than the older ones. Finally the forms were collected and the correct answers counted. A small prize was given to the winning child or children. These prizes were often small booklets from the vihara's publishing house.

[27] Literally the 'small monk', which he was occasionally called.

[28] Venerable Anand Kausalyayan, originally from Punjab, became a bhikku in Ceylon in 1930. In 1970 he moved to Nagpur in Maharashtra, where he built a Buddhist training centre on the spot where the Ambedkar-led mass conversion to Buddhism took place in 1956 (Zelliot 1992: 229).

This specific Sunday the prize consisted of three booklets: *Hundred Truths*, a Buddhist script by R.D. Nar and *Civil Rights Defence Law, Separate Act about SC, 1955*, that is, a law regarding SCs formulated by Ambedkar. The third one was *State Socialism*, a booklet by Ambedkar published in 1990 from Jullundur in Punjab and sold in the vihara for Rs 5.[29] The 10-year-old girl who was the winner of the booklet was enormously proud of her prize; from the editor's introductory 'Note' she could learn that:

Socially oppressed and economically exploited poor Indians cannot expect justice, social, economic and political as enshrined in the Constitution at the hands of the powers that be. They must now rise so that the present structure, social as well as economic could be basically changed. They must now tell the rulers in the words of Thucydides, 'It may be your interest to be our masters but how can it be ours to be your slaves'. The only course of action left to the toiling exploited classes is the use of force, no doubt in a constructive manner. Will they rise to the occasion? Will they shoulder the responsibility in their own interest, to usher in a new era? (Balley 1990: 9).

Taking part in the Buddhist ceremonies in the vihara seemed to be a way for the Dalit Buddhists to learn more about Buddhist rituals and about Ambedkar. It was also a way to introduce Ambedkar and Buddhism to their children. At the same time, it was a forum for the adults to discuss political and philosophical questions critically outside a more formalized party-political setting and without necessarily taking a stand in favour of one specific political party.

This Sunday, after the common rituals had come to an end, one of the men took out a small red box with a cord around it. He had passed the sweet shop on the way to the vihara and now wanted us to share his joy as his son had obtained his PCS, that

[29] In Chapter 6 I shall return to the publisher of the booklet, who is living in Jullundur in Punjab, when I discuss some transnational connections between India and Britain. The publisher was also present at the Buddhist conversion in Patna, Bihar. With this note I just want to draw attention again to the fact that networks are linked together over large geographical distances, and the Lucknow vihara belongs within wider Dalit networks.

is Permit for the Civil Service. The box of *burfi*s was passed around and we were all urged to take two of them. Everybody congratulated him and asked about his son, who had now finally been guaranteed a good income.

DALIT ACTIVITIES IN THE PUBLIC SPHERE: CELEBRATING AMBEDKAR

I have dwelt on some regular activities within the Dalit movement taking place in an alternative Dalit space, the Buddha vihara, and will now take a closer look at some activities directed outwards to a broader public. Ambedkar was born on 14 April (in 1891), and this is of course a date for celebration among Dalit activists. During the 1990s the celebrations of his birthday also spread rapidly outside the circles of Dalit activists. One reason seems to be that politicians and journalists, for example, recognized the rising interest in Ambedkar among the SCs. He is nowadays officially celebrated on this day by all kinds of politicians in India, and there is certainly an element of populism in this focus on Ambedkar once in a year. In New Delhi a ceremony is held which is broadcast on national television to be followed by people from their homes.

Dalit activists also have their larger, more formal celebrations on this day, with politicians and other people of importance invited. I spent the morning of 14 April 1996 in a large hall just across the road from the state assembly in Lucknow. Ambedkar Mahasabha had arranged the celebrations. The hall was packed with about 300 people, many standing along the walls, and some 20 persons on the stage. The most prominent among the speakers was Moti Lal Vora, the Governor of Uttar Pradesh. Mirajkar, Chindrapal Mitra, and many others also gave speeches in honour of Ambedkar. The celebration followed the general pattern of an official function with speeches succeeding each other, but also had something of a family occasion to it, with many women and children present.

THE VILLAGE

Chindrapal Mitra and Mirajkar had also decided to hold a meeting in a village, 25 kilometres north of the city in the afternoon on this date, about two months after their revival of the RPI in Lucknow. In the village a Buddhist conversion had taken place a year earlier and there was also an active Dalit organization. I arrived at the house of Mirajkar in Lucknow, situated in an area 20 minutes by tempo from the city centre, at the appointed time for the departure to the village. He lives with his wife and three children in a two-storey house in a middle class area. I am shown into the living room to sit in one of the red arm-chairs, waiting for him to get ready. His college-going daughter is busy, sitting on the floor with papers and books all round her, about to complete her zoology essay of about 50 pages. Drawings of fish, copied from different books, are now cut into shapes and pasted into empty spaces left for the purpose. The living-room is furnished with small Buddha statues and there are some pictures on the wall. In the middle of the room is a small wooden table looking like a Buddhist wheel surrounded by four armchairs, and from over the door a reproduction of Mona Lisa smiles at us from her frame.

A beige puppy is following the activities on the floor, from under the 'Buddhist wheel', and takes the chance to snap up the glue for his entertainment. In a corner of the room the television shows a romantic Indian film. Mirajkar's two sons enter the room, dressed similarly in blue jeans and black t-shirts with a red border at the neck, and after some instructions they begin to help their younger sister. It certainly looks idyllic with the three teenagers, in this harmoniously furnished home, helping each other with their homework; the father also expresses his pride in his children when he enters the room and takes a glance at the daughter's almost completed essay.

Chindrapal Mitra and another friend from Bihar who has recently settled in Lucknow also arrive. The friend has been an active Naxalite in Bihar for 20 years and he is to join us on the trip to the village.[30] The friendship that ties these three persons

---

[30] In 1967, after the Naxalbari uprising, there was a huge Marxist meeting in Arrah (a village close to Patna in Bihar) where the friend of Mirajkar was born and brought up. When the Marxist leaders failed to make any mention of the Naxalbari revolt, the people present at the meeting, who sympathized with the revolt, became furious, and this was the day when he decided to become an active Naxalite, he had told me earlier. He left a well-paying job and together with 20 activists

to each other in the private sphere are essential for their decision to come together to hold the political meeting. We leave in Mirajkar's car, and on the way the three of them discuss everything from family matters to more political and philosophical questions. The daughter of Ishwar Sevak (the third initiator of the RPI who is absent today) has recently finalized her Ph.D thesis on Buddhism and Mirajkar is now considering publishing it. They begin talking about Buddhism. Mirajkar turns to Chindrapal Mitra and says in a half-joking tone: 'A monk is allowed to have only eight belongings. Everything should belong to Sangam. That is real socialism.' Chindrapal Mitra nods in agreement and Mirajkar goes on: 'Once Lord Buddha was offered a woollen shawl, but he didn't take it. You give it to Sangam, he said. That is true communism.' Their small talk glides easily back and forth combining different religious and political topics.

When we are about to reach our destination, one of the village organizers of the meeting is waiting some 100 metres away from the village, so as to arrive and be received together with the guests by the small 'reception committee'. A tent roof is placed over a small dusty square, situated in the middle of the village, surrounded by a few shops. Three charpois, covered with carpets, serve as a stage from which the three guests are to make their speeches. The central charpoi is higher than the other two, which are propped on bricks to come level with the middle one. In front of the stage is a microphone. Some carpets

---

moved out into the villages. It was decided that each of the activists should be responsible for the recruitment of people in one district and should concentrate on one village. He started at random and travelled between the villages to find a place where he could settle at the same time as he preached his message about revolutionary change. He came to settle down in a village in Bhojpur district in Bihar. The idea was 'to choose one trustworthy person in the village, who eliminated the worst enemy', who was often the landowner in the area. When the policemen arrived, they were killed or mugged and in this way the group laid their hands on weapons. People in the villages were not difficult to persuade because 'they were really oppressed in this area', but they were scared and it took about two years of persuasion, he explained to me. Discussing this period of his life, he talked about himself and his friends as 'extremists, who also made many mistakes', but also added that he did not regret his activities.

are laid in the gravel and about 10 men have taken their seats on the ground to wait for the meeting to begin. The organizers wait for more people to arrive, but the flow is not forthcoming. The square gives an impression of being even more desolate when the organizers finally declare the meeting open, with a volume that makes the loudspeakers vibrate.

To the left of the stage is a framed photograph of Ambedkar. A candle is lit in front of it and the guests are each given a garland to put over the frame. The speeches that follow are given in a familiar tone, with the guests seated on the charpois and facing the small gathering of men. They talk about Ambedkar's conversion to Buddhism and point out that the RPI is the political party that Ambedkar founded. Two other interwoven topics are how 'common people' need money to buy their rice, and how the greed for money and power among politicians combined with corruption makes the money absent when it should really be present. Some younger boys try to make themselves invisible while taking seats at the end of the 'stage'. They know that they will be turned away, and that is what immediately happens. Some of the elders from the village tell them harshly to sit down on the ground. Gradually some more men and boys have arrived and there is now a small crowd under the tent roof. But there are still no women to be seen.

The meeting continues for about an hour and then we move into the office of the Dalit organization in the village. It is a very small room, situated in the square with a map of India and two pictures on the wall; one of Ambedkar and the other one of Periyar. Next to the map '*Jai Bhim*', 'Long live Bhimrao Ambedkar', is painted in large black letters. There is a heated debate between the guests who are in favour of the RPI and the villagers who are loyal to the BSP. The villagers and their sympathies for the BSP are questioned by the guests: 'What did the BSP do? Did they build any roads? Did they give you electricity? Where are your leaders today? Do they come here?' The villagers are crowded outside the open door to take part in the debate with the guests who are seated together with the organizers in a circle on the floor. It is now twilight and an oil-lamp has been lit in the middle of the room. The men from the village are not easily persuaded: 'BSP made us feel like one big family in Uttar Pradesh, Madhya Pradesh, Maharashtra...'.

An hour later Mirajkar wants to return to Lucknow and we get ready to leave. The villagers accompanying us to the car are still arguing with the guests. In the small pharmacy, next to the Dalit office, a big poster with a picture of Mayawati is plastered on the wall. At times the debate has been harsh, but in spite of the disparate political opinions everybody seems to agree on one point: Ambedkar is their prominent role model and he should be honoured today, 14 April. Consequently they part on good terms, a smile on their lips, and 'Jai Bhim'.[31] It is now completely dark in the village and we get into the car for the trip back to Lucknow. Mirajkar is satisfied with the afternoon and comments: 'Just use logic and they will finally agree with you. I asked what the Mayawati government had achieved and in the end they were convinced. You just have to go to the villages and talk to people.' He suggests that we go via the celebrations in Hazratganj, just for the fun of seeing what is going on.

LUCKNOW CENTRE

Returning to Lucknow, the scene is a sharp contrast to the small gathering in the village. We park the car some blocks away from Hazratganj, the central shopping area, and walk back to the main crossing where the statues of Ambedkar[32] as well as Gandhi are to be found, each installed at one end of the crossing. Today, on 14 April, the Ambedkar statue is lit up by red and yellow light bulbs strung all around the construction that constitutes something like an open roof over the statue. The city centre is overwhelmingly crowded and we have some problems moving around in the throng. It's like a gigantic feast. Many people, not belonging to the SCs, have also come to take part in the festivities.

The centre becomes even more crowded as it is filled by a parade entering the crossing. People had come together in a park (Begum Hazrat Mahal Park) from different parts of Lucknow as well as from villages and towns nearby, earlier during the day. From here the procession had taken off and it has now

[31] 'Jai Bhim' is a form of address used among Dalit activists instead of traditional greetings such as namaste.

[32] For more about this specific statue of Ambedkar at Hazratganj crossing, in the context of Ambedkarites in Britain, see Chapter 6.

reached Hazratganj. From wagons pulled by bicycles small boys dressed like Ambedkar as he is usually shown on posters, in a blue suit, a tie, black spectacles and a book under his arm, watch out over the crowd. Bands are competing for attention. The music is loud and there is a swarm of people selling and buying balloons and toys fastened onto long wooden poles, exhibited for spectators to have a chance to choose between them.

For the hungry there is a multitude of choices. Small dishes can be bought from the many mobile wagons or the more stationary ones. The smell of spices fills the air. From everywhere, it seems, the vendors shout out their specialty, so that people know in which direction to head, according to their taste. Ice-cream vendors are clearly the most popular among the children. The employees' organizations from Bank of Baroda and the Allahabad Bank are distributing food and water for free. You have to tread carefully not to destroy the gypsum statues of Ambedkar displayed for sale on cloths on the ground. There are posters of all kinds to buy, with pictures of Ambedkar, Indian movie stars, grey kittens, cute crying children, and views of the Swiss mountains.

Mothers and fathers hustle with their kids to get in front of the large Ambedkar statue to garland it. The children are lifted to put their own garlands round the neck of the statue. Now and then the flowers are removed by organizers, so that the statue is not totally drowned in the homage. No doubt this is the most important day during the year for those paying their respect to Ambedkar.

COMMENT

The Dalit movement 'provide[s] the socially and politically excluded with critical, alternative public spaces in which they can re/construct culturally stigmatised, or even vilified, identities and claim a "right to have rights" not just to social services but to human dignity, cultural difference, and/or social equality', to cite Alvarez (1997: 109), speaking about the movements in Latin America. The Buddha vihara, the rented hall where the RPI was revived, as well as the private homes of the activists provided some of the counterpublic and private spaces, where activists had the opportunity to come together. In these sites they combined debates and activities related to Buddhism, social questions, family life and other personal matters with those about party politics.

We have seen how, in local practice, Buddhist and political movement perspectives may be combined in different ways. In the narratives of the three individuals it could be seen how they in their personal lives have experienced party politics and the Buddhist world-view of Ambedkar as intertwined since long before. In the revival meeting of the RPI that took place in Lucknow, it was stated in the party programme as well as emphasized by those present, that the party should work in favour of Buddhism. Finally, in the Buddha vihara the responsible monk hosted during the years the RPI as well as the BSP, both of which he found to be in favour of depressed groups. Political issues, not least related to Mayawati, were also a natural part of the relaxed small talk going on during the Sunday meetings in the vihara.

I have shown how networks at a local level may run from private to the counterpublic space, to also fuse with party politics. One example of this was how the networks of friendship and family relations among the Dalit activists, who spent time together in each other's homes, were closely related to the networks in a counterpublic space—in the Buddha vihara as well as in Ambedkar Mahasabha. These networks were further seen to be fused with party-political networks when the revival meeting of the RPI was held. The Dalit activists in this chapter were moving freely between different sites (private as well as counterpublic) with claims for human dignity and cultural difference.[33] These cultural demands were closely combined with claims for economic equality and political power.

---

[33] The claim for cultural difference in this context involves being respected and recognized as Buddhists who are culturally different from the Hindus. Cf. Fuchs (2000b: 80), who has commented (also in the context of the Dalit movement) that: 'To ask for recognition by some other implies the acknowledgement of difference.'

6

A Transnational Dalit Counterpublic
The Example of Ambedkarites in Britain

All over the world we find Indians who have emigrated to settle in new surroundings. Among the SCs who managed to find their way out of India, many settled in Britain and were employed by heavy industry, filling a gap when the country was short of labour in the 1950s and 1960s. This chapter talks about the Ambedkarites[1] among the immigrant SCs in Britain. They are spread across the country, but to a great extent keep in touch with each other. In Europe, in the same way as in India, many of them have converted to Buddhism and built their own Ambedkarite Buddha viharas where they celebrate specific feasts, such as the birthday of Ambedkar. Apart from Britain, Ambedkarites are also to be found in the United States and Canada, in smaller numbers in other European countries than Britain as well as in Australia, Africa, in Southeast Asia, and in South America. Thus, the Ambedkarites in Britain are part of a worldwide Dalit diaspora. During the 1990s networks between groups and individuals became more elaborate among the Ambedkarite diaspora, as well as between them and the Dalit movement in India, not least due to their communication via the Internet. They arrange Dalit conferences and seminars regularly in which Ambedkarites come together, often with invited non-Ambedkarite scholars, experts, and laymen from across the world, to discuss subjects related to the situation of the SCs in India.

[1] Ambedkarite is the concept preferred in Britain as a form of identity, instead of the more usual concept of Dalit in India. The reason given by the immigrants is that the concept of Dalit is unknown among the British.

This chapter aims to show how Ambedkarites in Britain belong within the framework of a transnational Dalit movement that transgresses state borders. It will describe how transnational Dalit networks between India and Britain have been created and how they are constantly in the process of being recreated. This will be closely related to the earlier chapters in the following way. Dealing with the transnational aspect of the movement, I shall argue that the Ambedkarite Buddhists in Britain take part in the same anti-Hinduism/Gandhi/Congress discourse that is found in India. The Dalit activists in India and the Ambedkarite Buddhists in Britain are thus interrelated transnationally within the same counterpublic. Consequently the Ambedkarite Buddhists in Britain also belong within the same autonomous anti-caste tradition as the Dalit activists in India.

To begin with, I shall trace the background of the Ambedkarites in Britain. Next, I shall demonstrate in more detail how the Ambedkarites dissociate themselves religiously from Hinduism. I will discuss the close relationship between the Ravidasis and Ambedkar in the 1930s, and the reasons for the ambivalence between the Ambekdarites and Ravidasis today.

In the final part, it will become clear how the Ambedkarites in Britain affiliate transnationally with Indian political parties, such as the RPI, the BSP, and the Janata Dal, that arose as alternatives to the Congress Party (and in opposition to Hindu nationalism). I shall touch on the relation between the Ambedkarites and the non-Indian Buddhist monks in their viharas.

SCs EMIGRATION FROM INDIA TO BRITAIN IN THE 1950s AND 1960s

Although Maharashtra was the state where the Dalit movement originally took shape, the influence of Ambedkar and his movement could also be seen in Punjab, which Ambedkar visited several times. Juergensmeyer (1982: 165) writes:

In 1956, shortly before his death, when Ambedkar created the Republican Party of India and his new Buddhist movement—political and cultural articulations, respectively, of his approach to social change—the Punjab branches of these movements became among the most active outside of Ambedkar's home state itself, Maharashtra.

The history of the Dalit movement in Britain takes its origins from the end of the 1950s when the first Punjabi immigrants arrived in search of a better life. This was a time when SCs in India had visions for a better life for themselves and their families. Thousands of villagers from among the SCs moved to the Punjabi cities with the dream of a better life after independence, or simply to escape the continuing poverty in the villages (Juergensmeyer 1982: 234). The reserved quotas in educational institutions and governmental jobs gave opportunities to the SCs, and by the mid-1970s over 12 per cent of Punjab government employees (almost 20,000 persons) were drawn from this category (ibid: 236).[2]

When independent India became a member of the Commonwealth in 1950 a liberal immigration policy was introduced, and Indians emigrated. Approximately 300,000 Indian immigrants came to Britain upto 1968, when the laws became stricter again. A large percentage of these people were Punjabis and remarkably, as Juergensmeyer comments, there was a large proportion, 10 per cent, from the SCs, especially from the Chamar community. Most of the immigrants originated from Jullundur doab (the area between two rivers) and settled in the industrial centres, such as London and Birmingham (ibid.: 245ff).[3] From the early 1950s until the end of the 1970s the British economy was acutely short of labour and the South Asians filled the gap (Ballard 1994: 6).

Discussing the Jat Sikhs in Britain, peasant farmers originating from Jullundur doab in Punjab, Ballard comments that something that could be called 'migration fever' swept rural Jullundur in the early 1960s. Almost all the young men dreamt of emigration (ibid.: 95). The SCs in rural Jullundur also seem to have been hit by this 'migration fever' and many managed to fulfil their dream. It was mainly the work of a few people that raised the proportion of SC emigrants from 1952 onwards. Before that year, this category had difficulties in obtaining the necessary emigration documents:

[2] In higher positions, however, they occupied only 2 per cent of the posts (Juergensmeyer 1982: 236).

[3] For a more detailed description of the geographical origin of South Asian immigrants in Britain, see Ballard (1994: 1–34).

One would not ordinarily expect Chamars to have access to international travel in such large numbers, and indeed in this case it was only that a fortunate selection of officials worked in their favour. Until 1952 it had been difficult for Chamars to thread the maze of upper caste bureaucracy and obtain the necessary emigration papers. In that year, however, the first Scheduled Caste gazetted officer in the Punjab, Ishwar Das Pawar, became the undersecretary for passports in the Punjab government and began handing out passports to Scheduled Caste applicants with an unaccustomed generosity. Pawar estimated that he helped five hundred Scheduled Caste applicants to emigrate each year (Juergensmeyer 1982: 246).

A common route among the SCs seems to have been from the villages in Punjab to New Delhi for a few years, and from there onwards to Britain. In New Delhi some of the young Punjabi men with 'migration fever' came in contact with people already involved in the Dalit movement. But for many, knowledge about Ambedkar and his movement came only after they had arrived in Britain.

Juergensmeyer writes that although life as a whole has become better for the SCs in Britain, 'in some ways it is disturbingly the same'. There is an obvious segregation, with immigrants living in their own areas separated from the others. Furthermore, the caste relationships between the caste groups seem to be upheld to a great extent (ibid.). Although many features of the traditional caste system have broken down, the rules of endogamy (that is, marrying within the caste group or caste category) are still strictly followed in the diaspora as well as in the subcontinent (Ballard 1994: 26). Rather than the status between caste categories becoming less important in the diaspora, the opposite can be observed. There has been an intensification of intercaste competition for status, and 'many settlers are still almost obsessively concerned with issues of rank' (Ballard 1994: 27).

THE COMMON HISTORY OF RAVIDASIS
AND AMBEDKARITES

Among the Chamars who arrived in Britain from Punjab, many had been touched by the Ad Dharm movement in India and belonged to the Ravidasi community. To recapitulate, the

organization Ad Dharm in Punjab and its members who were
called Ravidasis referring to the bhakti poet Ravidas, were part
of the broader Adi movement that swept India in the 1920s. This
movement, as I pointed out in Chapter 3, pioneered attempts to
form an identity among the 'untouchables' separate from
Hinduism. Let me quote a few lines from the first Ad Dharm
conference in 1927: 'We are not Hindus. We strongly request
the government not to list us as such in the census. Our faith is
not Hindu, but Ad Dharm. We are not part of Hinduism, and
Hindus are not a part of us' (cited in Juergensmeyer 1982: 74).
Ad Dharm was inspired from within Hinduism, that is, from the
reformist bhakti movement, but in their rhetoric, the original
Ad Dharm dissociated itself from the Hindu religion and the
Hindu community. They also supported Ambedkar in his political
demand for a separate electorate for the 'depressed classes'
in 1932. The connection between Ambedkar's stand in the
controversy and Mangoo Ram, the leader of Ad Dharm, is clearly
to be seen in the 1930s. On a local level in Punjab, Ad Dharm
was competing with the movement of Ambedkar, but on a
national level Mangoo Ram supported Ambedkar against
Gandhi. In a telegram sent in connection with the second Round
Table Conference in 1932, he wrote in part: 'Dr Ambedkar is
sole representative of all India's depressed classes. We demand
separate electorate. Joint electorate is detrimental to our
interests' (Juergensmeyer 1982: 127, note 9).[4]

As noted earlier, Gandhi started a fast against separate
electorates. But the leaders of Ad Dharm saw the 'epic fast'
as 'an underhanded trick, something he [Gandhi] resorted to
in time of extremity, the cynical ploy of a master politician'

---

[4] Compare the discussion by Lynch (1969) regarding the support
from the Jatavs in Agra who, like Mangoo Ram, sent a telegram in
favour of Ambedkar during the conference in 1932: 'They along with
Untouchable groups, wired London to insist that Ambedkar, not Gandhi,
was their leader. The political importance of this telegram was tremendous. It signalled that Jatavs had become aware of the national
implications of their problems and activities through a process of ana-
logical identification. That is, their problems, insofar as they were
matters peculiar to Agra, were local and unique; but insofar as they
were a matter of Untouchability, the problems were national and general' (ibid.: 81).

(Juergensmeyer 1982: 128). Mangoo Ram, in his turn, began a counterfast in favour of the Communal Award and separate electorates and in protest against Gandhi (ibid.: 163).[5] In this context Mangoo Ram also expressed his scepticism about Hinduism in the following way: 'Gandhi, if you are prepared to die for your Hindus, then I am prepared to die for these Untouchables' (ibid.: 129). He shared Ambedkar's opinion that Gandhi's movement and the Congress Party, in the same way as the Arya Samaj, mainly spoke for the Hindus and from the Hindu point of view (ibid.: 124ff).

THE GROWTH OF THE AMBEDKAR MOVEMENT IN BRITAIN (THE 1960s AND 1970s)

The Black Eagle, a pub in Handsworth (Birmingham) was the place where the first Ambedkarites among the Ravidasis used to meet. This was at the beginning of the 1960s before they had a place of their own. A small group of young men in their 20s and 30s, newly arrived in Britain, had begun to meet to discuss Ambedkar. In 1964 there was a handful of them, I have been told, who came together regularly for these meetings, separate from the ordinary Ravidasi meetings. It seems that the Ambedkarite networks in Britain grew out of informal contacts. Some of them who had arrived earlier helped and supported those who came later, who still did not know the English language, for example. There was a social network in which those people in need of help with regard to social services, problems at their workplaces, housing, etc., could phone the Ambedkarites at their homes. The help was given for free and in this way the informal networks grew and developed. In these contacts the knowledge about Ambedkar was transmitted, it was explained to me by an Ambedkarite Buddhist, formerly belonging within the Ravidasi community: 'We made a lot of friends, and got the possibility to explain what our aim was.'

In the mid-1960s a Dalit activist brought *Ambedkar: Life and Mission*, by Dhananjay Keer (1990 [1954]) with him from India

[5] In the Punjab census reports of 1931 the Addharmi was registered as a religion separate from Hinduism. Three decades later, however, in 1961, they were regarded as a caste within the Hindu religion (Nesbitt 1991: 9).

to Britain. Today this is a well known Ambedkar biography among Ambedkarites in Britain as well as in India. One of the Ambedkarite Buddhists in Britain told me about his first emotional meeting with Ambedkar that came via this book.[6] One evening he began to read the biography:

I kept reading, and I could not sleep that night. The discrimination and hatred that he [Ambedkar] went through, I have also gone through. I did not think of studying Ambedkar. I was just discovering myself. [Long silence. He wipes some tears away with a handkerchief]. It was very emotional, I tell you.

This man was moved to tears in remembering and telling me about this specific moment in his life. He knew about Ambedkar from the time he was living in New Delhi. At that time, in the late 1950s, he had met Ambedkarites from Punjab in the Dr Ambedkar Association, run from a building called Ambedkar Bhavan in central New Delhi. These people told stories about Ambedkar whom they had met. The turning point for his commitment, though, came through this emotional meeting, founded in a sense of recognizing himself in the lifestory of Ambedkar as told by Keer. He identified himself with Ambedkar.

It is not uncommon for Dalit activists to regard a specific occasion like this as the turning point when, for the very first time, they suddenly and revolutionarily recognize that they and their families, have been unjustly treated. Ambedkar's biography by Keer is today a classic among Dalit activists; it is referred to as having changed the life of many. It is an emotional identification with someone who has gone through the same kind of discrimination, combined with the feeling of recognizing themselves, for the first time, as unfairly treated, which gives them a sense of 'waking up' from a lifetime's 'indoctrination'. Prior to this emotional situation Dalit activists had not given the reason for their social status much thought, or if they had, their social situation had been seen as self-evident and caused by themselves.

For many this turning point in their lives is like an enlightened moment to which they can refer years later with all the

[6] This man was active in the Indian Republican Group in Britain when it was first formed, and was also one of the organizers of a Buddhist conversion in Britain in 1973.

details. They can remember the place where it happened, the time of day, what kind of emotions it aroused, and finally how this specific moment changed their lives completely from then onwards. For many, this was the first book they had ever read about Ambedkar and its impression on them was tremendous. They contributed 5 pounds each, which was a lot of money in the 1960s, it has been explained to me, to begin some kind of publication of Ambedkar's books.

There were, however, other Ambedkarite groups formed parallel to the groups from within the Ravidasi community. Already in 1956, the same year as Ambedkar passed away, the Scheduled Caste Welfare Association was formed in Britain, in 1962, the Indian Buddhist Society was founded, followed by the Indian Republican Group of Great Britain in 1965. It seems that the Ambedkarite networks that had developed within the Ravidasi community came to blend with some that were already in existence and in themselves fused Ambedkarite Buddhist and political networks. The networks grew and over just a few years, in the mid-1960s, the number of active Ambedkarites in Britain grew from a handful to a few hundred, with many more supporters.

These networks also extended to Punjab (from where the majority originated), and the idea with the foundation of the Indian Republican Group of Great Britain in 1965 was to support the RPI in Punjab and its candidate Balley in the election.[7] Balley is well known among Dalit activists, in India as well as in Britain, as the editor of the weekly *Bheem Patrika*.[8] During my fieldwork in Birmingham and Wolverhampton in the autumn of 1997 one of the early members told me:

In 1965 the Republican Group was founded, and we started to collect money, that is 50 pence or one pound from different people who sympathized. The money that was collected grew to an amount of about 300 pounds, which was a large amount at that time, for people with small salaries. We used to earn about 10 pounds a

[7] A growing hostility had erupted between Ravidasis and Ambedkarites in 1965 in Britain, and Ravidasis that year formed a registered association, 'specifically excluding Ambedkarites' (Juergensmeyer 1982: 250).

[8] It is worth noting that Ishwar Sevak, one of the initiators of the revived RPI, has been a frequent writer in *Bheem Patrika* over the years.

week at that time. The amount of 300 pounds was sent on different occasions, during a ten-year period, to Punjab.

In the beginning of the 1970s, Juergensmeyer (1982) visited Balley's office in Jullundur in Punjab, and described the personality, the office and the different roles of this Dalit activist in the following words:

L.R. Balley, who operates out of a tiny one-room office in the industrial area of Jullundur, exemplifies the dedication of that leadership. Although he is nominally only the editor of the *Bheem Patrika* and a member of the board of the Republican Party of India (Khobragade faction), his role in the lower caste community is much more multifaceted than that: he is a counselor, ombudsman, political organizer, spiritual leader, historian and educator. The tiny office is always crowded with visitors. But his ambitions are tempered by financial restrictions. He and other Ambedkarites have purchased a plot of land near Boota Mandi, where they eventually hope to build some sort of memorial to Dr Ambedkar; to date, however, there is only a cement wall around the property and a gate with the words Ambedkar Bhawan (Ambedkar Building) (Juergensmeyer 1982: 166).[9]

Due to different circumstances Balley, on whom the Ambedkarites in Britain had set their hopes, later on withdrew from active engagement in the RPI in Punjab. The money sent from Britain was partly invested in a piece of land, where Ambedkar Bhavan in Jullundur is built today.[10]

[9] When I visited the place 30 years later, Ambedkar Bhavan had materialized. Balley, still active, took his bike every day to the office in Ambedkar Bhavan to work on the paper: 'To run a paper is not a children's game', he told me, 'it takes a lot of energy and time'. Entering the gate that Juergensmeyer described, a proper two-storey building was now to be found behind the wall, with a few rooms to be used for meetings and other activities. There was also another smaller house close by, where Balley was to be found each day, reading the newspaper, writing, editing, and waiting for people asking for help in different matters. But the vision had now taken on larger proportions, and a huge new building was under way. The foundation was laid and the rest he said would hopefully be completed in about a year's time.

[10] The Indian Republican Group of Great Britain even ran candidates in British elections. Two Republican candidates contested from the Southall, Ealing Borough constituency in the 9 May 1971 election

Balley also cooperated in areas other than the party-political with the Ambedkarites in Britain. In 1969 the Dr Ambedkar Memorial Committee was founded with the purpose of publishing the writings of Ambedkar, available neither in Britain nor in India. This committee, which today runs the Wolverhampton Buddha vihara, came to cooperate with Balley also on this issue. The president of the Wolverhampton Buddha vihara told me about the Ambedkar Memorial Committee:

The purpose was to print literature by Dr Ambedkar in different languages and distribute it in India to the people free of charge. We are still doing that. We are spending thousands and thousands of pounds on that. We also had *Ambedkar: Life and Mission* reprinted in Punjabi. In two months they sold 3,000 copies, so it is ready for a second reprint. Balley translated it into Punjabi and reprinted it. More than half of the money was sent from here. Also *Buddha and His Dhamma* was translated into Punjabi and financed by us. Mahaboudh Society translated it. We had it printed and sent it on a non-profit basis (Interview 15 November 1997).

RAVIDASIS: A CATEGORY OF THEIR OWN

It is a complicated question to categorize the Ravidasis as Hindus, Sikhs or something in-between. Regarding Indian Punjabis generally, it is first of all notoriously controversial to draw a boundary between Sikh and Hindu, Nesbitt (1991) writes. Discussing the Ravidasis further complicates the picture when trying to describe the individual as either Sikh or Hindu (ibid.: 9). My aim in this chapter is fortunately not to categorize the Ravidasis as belonging to one or the other of the religious categories. Rather, I shall show how converted Ambedkarite Buddhists in Britain are ambivalent about the Ravidasis, depending contextually on which stand the Ravidasis take in relation to Hindu ideals and rituals. Although Mangoo Ram and the original Ad Dharm took a clear stand against Hinduism, Congress and Gandhi, Ravidasis are said to be ambivalent about these points.

In any case let me summarize some interesting observations by Nesbitt, who carried out her research among the Ravidasis

---

and received 265 votes out of a total of 42,000 (Juergensmeyer 1982: 249, note 12).

in Coventry, regarding caste hierarchy. Contrary to what is often supposed, it seems that caste affiliation still plays an important role in deciding social status among Punjabis and Sikhs in Britain (Nesbitt 1997: 213ff). One reason for this is that the Sikh emigration has been from villages within a small area in Punjab, Jullundur district. This makes it possible for the Punjabi immigrants to Britain to keep track of and know each other's family and caste background. Compared with the emigrants from Gujarat, there is a 'compact geographical/cultural base, coupled with the relative fewness of sizeable Punjabi castes in Britain...' (Nesbitt 1997: 214). The Valmikis and the Ravidasis are the most stigmatized among the caste groups. Thus, in practice, caste remains an observable dynamic, not only in the Hindu society, but also in the Sikh society in Britain. This is a fact, according to Nesbitt, despite bhakti sants like Ravidas preaching against the caste hierarchy (ibid.: 203f).

Among the Sikhs in Britain references are made to 'proper', 'pure', 'real' and 'true' Sikhs (ibid.: 210), and there is a caste-related ranking of 'Sikhs' and 'proper Sikhs'. Nesbitt quotes a Ravidasi boy whom she interviewed, who echoed the same ideas about caste ranking as the high-caste Sikhs:

There's three castes. The first one is—I've forgotten. The second is Jat and the third is Chamar. And the first one are true Sikhs, like they carry the Ks [the sacred attributes] at all times... They say their prayers. I'm not one of those: I'm not high caste (ibid.: 211).

This Ravidasi boy was aware of the difference in status between the different Sikhs. 'I'm not high caste', he said, and consequently he did not identify as a 'true Sikh'. In the same way, a Ravidasi girl who identified herself as Hindu distinguished between her own Ravidasi community and 'true Hindus', according to Nesbitt (1997: 212).

There seems to be some degree of consensus regarding the status of Ravidasis among the Sikhs, Hindus, and Ravidasis themselves. Among the Sikhs the Ravidasis are not seen as 'proper' ('pure', 'true' or 'real') Sikhs. In the same way the Hindus do not regard the Ravidasis as 'true' Hindus. Ravidasis echoed the same ideas about their own status in relation to Sikhs and Hindus in the interviews by Nesbitt. In Britain as well as in India, however, Ravidasis have built their own temples or *gurdwaras*, separate from both Hindus and Sikhs (ibid. 1991: 13ff).

THE AMBEDKARITE–RAVIDASI RELATION

Juergensmeyer (1982) has dwelt on the ambiguous relationship between the Ravidasis and the Ambedkarites mainly from a Ravidasi point of view.[11] I shall point out some aspects that I think Juergensmeyer has bypassed and in some instances I shall also give a different emphasis from his. One reason for these differences is probably that the Ambedkarite movement has undergone changes over the years. The Dalit activists have become much more visible during the 1990s and 2000s compared with the 1970s and 1980s, and their arguments are much more straightforward.

Juergensmeyer argues that those accusing lower-caste movements of separatism are only partially correct. In, for example, the famous case of separate electorates (the Poona Pact in 1932) the movement activists among the untouchables throughout India were of the opinion that the risk of being set apart from Hindu society was not a danger, as they *were* already isolated. The aim of separate electorates was to become integrated on equal terms (Juergensmeyer 1982: 271).

Juergensmeyer emphasizes the similar integral aspects of the Ravidasi and Ambedkarite movements for understandable reasons; these movements are ultimately not separatist but on

[11] I have been fortunate in having Juergensmeyer's book (1982) as a study to set my own data against. Juergensmeyer dwells on different stands among the activists among so-called untouchables and compares Ravidasis and Ambedkarites, among others. He has included a section on Ambedkarites in Punjab as well as one on Ravidasis in Wolverhampton. It may be seen as a strength of the argument that my ethnography as a whole is in accordance with Juergensmeyer's observations among the Ravidasis regarding the relationship between the two communities, although details may differ and changes of course have taken place since the 1970s. Juergensmeyer's book was also one of the first studies that made me interested in the Dalit movement. Balley, the Dalit activist in Jullundur whom Juergensmeyer visited in the early 1970s, also placed it in my hand. He took it off his bookshelf to show me, when I arrived in the city in 2001, 30 years after Juergensmeyer's fieldwork. Not much has been written about Dalit activists transnationally and Juergensmeyer may be seen as a pioneer in this sense.

the contrary are working for the integration of the SCs, as he has convincingly shown. Ambedkarites, thus, find SCs to be already separated from Hinduism on the basis of caste. I would like to emphasize that Ambedkarites find a break with Hindusim and the Hindu community to be the only way for SCs to be integrated on equal terms in the broader Indian society. To be clear, the Ambedkarites are separatists in relation to Hinduism and the Hindu community exactly for the reason that they want to be integrated in the Indian society on equal terms. They do not want to belong to the Hindu community—this is not equivalent to being separatists in relation to the wider Indian society, which encompasses many different communities and religions.

The ambivalence among the Ambedkarites in their attitude to the Ravidasis seems to be related to the double stance to be found within Ad Dharm. To the extent that the Ravidasis distance themselves from Hinduism, they are accepted among Ambedkarites. Juergensmeyer writes that the concept of Sanskritization, as coined by M.N. Srinivas, could well be applied to the Ravidasis but would then be called 'Sikhization'. For the Ambedkarites, however, Sanskritization or Sikhization will make all the difference. Sanskritization is a process of trying to achieve a higher status within Hinduism, while the concept of Sikhization signals a break with the Hindu system. The criticism in this regard from the Ambedkarites is that the acceptance of Sikh values is not complete among the Ravidasis. They are said to still preserve Hindu ideals.

Juergensmeyer argues that it might appear, superficially, that Ravidasis as well as Ambedkarite Buddhists adopt legendary heroes, namely Sant Ravi Das and the Buddha, to symbolize a separate cultural identity. However, he says that 'in fact such figures also face in the direction of the high tradition, so they provide linkages to the social and religious whole as well'. He points out that Ravi Das belongs to the Sant tradition within Hindu culture, and the Sant tradition has come to be understood 'as the heritage of all, suggesting a harmonious model of religious society to which all have access'. He compares this with Ambedkar's choice of Buddha, as Buddhism also involves the element of universal access: 'In this respect the Buddha and Ravi Das are parallel figures' (ibid.: 271ff). In the light of the 1990s Ambedkarite movement, I would say that this comment leads in the wrong direction. This is a focal point in understanding the ambivalence between the two communities.

Ravi Das and Buddha are not parallel figures, at least not for the Ambedkarites. Quite the opposite; they stand for conflicting ideals. Ravi Das is seen, just as Juergensmeyer describes him, 'fastened onto Hindu culture' (ibid.). It may be to Hindu culture in general or to the reformist Sant tradition of Hindu culture, but this does not make much of a difference to the Ambedkarites. Buddha is not first and foremost acclaimed within the Dalit movement for his 'harmonious model' giving access to all. Rather, he has become an icon because of his break and revolt against Hinduism.

Juergensmeyer emphasizes the similarities between the two communities, but let me continue to focus on the differences, for the sake of better understanding what is going on in the relationship. There was never an acceptance among Ravidasis of *normative* Hinduism, which Juergensmeyer has shown. They did not accept a *dharmik* model in which society was stratified into different castes with different status. Rather, they subscribed to a *qaumik* model, each group being equal in status relative to others. But, and this is important to note, the qaumik model was not the only alternative for the Ravidasis. Juergensmeyer writes that '[a]nother model of society found its way into the ideology and imagery of the Ad Dharm: the *panthik* model, an ideal society based on Hindu culture but thoroughly cleansed of caste' (1982: 273f).

From these models among the Ravidasis, which Juergensmeyer has described, it becomes easier to understand the ambivalence among the Ambedkarites. They do not accept Hindu culture, cleansed of caste or not. They do not believe, following Ambedkar, that Hinduism could ever be cleansed of caste, but think that caste and Hinduism are inevitably linked together. To the extent that the panthik model, an ideal society based on Hindu culture has found its way into the community of the Ravidasis, the Ambedkarites will oppose them. But in so far as the Ravidasis are qaumik—seeing the Ad Dharm as a qaum, separate from Hinduism, in line with Mangoo Ram and the mission of the original Ad Dharm—Ambedkarites will accept them.

Juergensmeyer finds the main disparity between the two communities to be with regard to social vision. He finds

Ambedkarites to be working in the direction of assimilation into a wider egalitarian culture and becoming more secular. The Ravidasis he perceives as more loyal to a religious heritage, and working more in the direction of a religious version of an ideal social order (Juergensmeyer 1982: 260).

In contrast, I want to set the difference between the communities in the broader context of what I have discussed earlier concerning the autonomous anti-caste tradition, and also contemporary Dalit discourse. The Ambedkarite Buddhists in Britain must be seen as part of the anti-Hinduism/Gandhi/Congress discourse among the Dalit activists in India. The ambivalence to Ravidasis may have come about for many reasons. However, the main reason given by the Ambedkarite Buddhists as to why they have a complicated relationship with the Ravidasis is that the latter are today not clear regarding their relation to Hinduism, Gandhi, and the Congress Party. On an analytical level, it seems, to repeat, that the Ambedkarites are close to the original Ad Dharm, the original ideas of the founder Mangoo Ram, and also to the qaumik model which he advocated. But their discourse stands in sharp contrast to the panthik model among the Ravidasis, built on an ideal Hindu society.

The activities among the Ambedkarites transnationally may be interpreted as an attempt to assimilate into a wider egalitarian culture Juergensmeyer (ibid.) suggests,[12] but even more important to note in this context is that to achieve this 'assimilation' they primarily strive to break away from a religious and political hegemony in which the caste hierarchy is found to be fundamental. This is a hegemony in which the India-born Ambedkarites in Britain have also been brought up, and although they have emigrated, they regularly relate to and discuss politics and religion in India with family and friends back home.

ENTERING THE BUDDHA VIHARAS

Although part of a British context, the discourse and practices among Ambedkarites in Britain are strongly reminiscent of what

[12] When the break has become a fact and their autonomous status has been widely accepted, their ultimate aim is, I agree with Juergensmeyer, to be assimilated into a wider, egalitarian culture.

goes on among Dalit activists in India. The break with Hinduism is combined with a political break with the Congress. In the following pages it will be seen that political parties that appeared in India as alternatives to the Congress, like the BSP, the RPI, and even the Janata Dal, also figure in the Ambedkarite Buddha viharas in Britain. Some of the transnational connections will be pointed out. The networks of Buddhism and politics among Ambedkarites in Britain also appear to be fused in a similar way to those among Dalit activists in India.

FROM CARNABY STREET TO THE
WOLVERHAMPTON BUDDHA VIHARA

At one end of the well known Carnaby Street in London there is a small fancy boutique, selling leather clothes as well as skirts made out of strings of pearls. The owner is a Chamar. I had met him earlier at a Dalit conference in New Delhi, where he noted me as the sole non-Dalit visitor. Before he disappeared in a black limousine together with Paswan and some other Dalit Sena[13] members, he invited me to celebrate Ambedkar's birthday, 14th April, in Britain. One year later when I entered the boutique in London, he was busy helping a young woman choose between skirts and asked me to take a seat while I waited. Some 20 minutes later when pearl skirts in different colours could be found in a bunch on the desk, the young woman left with her mother. 'These people, they just come to try everything on, but never buy anything', he said, nodding towards the door which had just closed behind the assumed customers.

This year the shop-owner, Vijay,[14] was the main financier behind the 14th April celebrations in the Buddha vihara in

---

[13] Dalit Sena is a conglomerate of different organizations from different states across India. The chairman of this organization was one of the most important Dalit politicians in north India during the 1990s. Dalit Sena was officially a non-political organization, but none could fail to notice that Ram Vilas Paswan, the President of Dalit Sena, was a Janata Dal politician. As an important Indian politician, Paswan had many friends and a wide circle of acquaintances, and one of these was the shop-owner in London.

[14] Pseudonym.

Wolverhampton.[15] It was decided that I should come with him and his family to Wolverhampton a few days later. On the day of the celebration I arrive at their house in London well on time. It is a luxurious house in an expensive area, and the first thing to catch my attention when entering was a gilt plate in the hall which said: 'This house was inaugurated by V.P. Singh in 1992'. The Janata Dal politician V.P. Singh is well known among Dalit activists in India and highly respected because he implemented extended reservations for OBCs during his time as prime minister. It was through his contact with Paswan in Dalit Sena that Vijay had been able to invite V.P. Singh to celebrate Ambedkar's birthday in London and at the same time seize the opportunity to have him inaugurate his house. Pointing at some pictures in the hall he comments: 'In this house there are just three persons—Ambedkar, Buddha, and my father.' I am shown into the spacious living room with thick, soft oriental carpets on the floor and modern pictures on the walls. Seated on a huge white leather sofa, I nonetheless find at least two more persons of importance in this home: from within framed photographs on the wall V.P. Singh and Paswan are looking at me. The son-in-law serves me some snacks and juice while waiting for the rest of the family to get dressed. He is working in the leather boutique together with Vijay's son. Joining us a little later, Vijay tells me that it took him twenty five years to settle in this posh area. When everybody is ready we pack ourselves into two cars—Vijay, his wife, daughters, sons-in-law, and grandchildren for the trip from London to Wolverhampton.

A few hours later we reach our destination. In the parking place, a large Ambedkar statue keeps an eye on the building. In an article about the history of religious sites in Wolverhampton, Frank Sharman writes about this statue that it must be the most unveiled one in Wolverhampton. The first time it was unveiled was in 1981, by the Buddhist monk B.A. Kausalyayan. Next time was in 1992, by V.P. Singh, during his visit to Britain. When a new community centre was opened, annexed to the vihara in 2000, the statue was unveiled a third time, by

[15] This was despite the fact that he was associated with the Janata Dal and the sympathies in the vihara were mainly with the BSP, something I shall return to later on.

the Mayor of Wolverhampton, Tarseim Singh.[16] The statues and pictures of Ambedkar have a strong significance for the Ambedkarites, mainly as a unifying symbol (or at least they used to have, as discussed in Chapter 4). This is also the case in Wolverhampton, as could be understood by the many unveilings.

For the 14th of April, an open tent is erected outside the vihara, where the food is served—chapatti, dal, and a variety of Punjabi dishes. Two men approach us when we get out of the car, with the intention of touching Vijay's feet in honour; Vijay is paying for the food for the ceremony this year, that is, for hundreds of people. The shop-owner makes a gesture, well in time, to show that it is not necessary to bow down.

The temple has associations with Japanese architecture. It has round, hand-painted windows with Buddhist motifs. Just to the right, as you enter from outside, is the kitchen. Today the women and children are crowded into the kitchen to prepare Punjabi dishes for the guests. The smell of Indian spices and also the voices and laughter of the women and children fill the vihara, and give the impression of a friendly and homelike atmosphere to an outsider. Punjabi is the language which is spoken since almost all people visiting the vihara are, as already mentioned, people from Punjab belonging mainly to the Chamar community.

Outside the kitchen on the notice board, two well known persons, one of them from Punjab, are depicted in a cutting from a newspaper: the BSP President Kanshi Ram, accompanied by Mayawati. This piece dealt with Mayawati's utterance about Gandhi as an enemy (see Chapter 4). Later on when I return to the vihara it is replaced with another article under the heading 'Statue Symbols', dealing with Mayawati's 'Ambedkarisation'[17] (*India Today* International, 28 July 1997).

[16] See Frank Sharman, 'Heritage and Cultural Roots', http://www.localhistory.scit.wlv.ac.uk/articles/electronic/roots/roots.htm.

[17] During her first two shorter periods as chief minister in Uttar Pradesh, in 1995 and in 1997, Mayawati began (and even completed) a large number of Ambedkar projects—ranging from naming or renaming institutes, colleges, universities, hospitals, guest houses, roads, and districts after Ambedkar, to implementing Ambedkar villages. She replaced the old statue of Ambedkar in Hazratganj, the central crossing in Lucknow, with a new one. The statue of Ambedkar

Further inside to the left is the meditation room. In contrast to the kitchen it is completely silent. The older of the two men, Dinesh Chandra,[18] a pleasant, unobtrusive gentleman who welcomed us, shows me around and we take our shoes off before entering. The room is bright, and the coloured windows lend a special atmosphere to it when the light from outside falls through. On the floor white pillows are arranged. Before taking a seat on a pillow, people go to the front and bow their heads for a few minutes, to pay reverence to the large gilded statue of Buddha, and also to put some coins in the donation box. Flowers, lighted candles, and the smell of incense surround the statue. In this room the classes for the smallest children are held once a week, I later realize. This is the place where the children of Ambedkarites listen to children's stories about Buddha and Ambedkar to learn about them. When story telling is over, they sit in small groups to paint scenes from Buddha's and Ambedkar's lives.

To the left of the Buddha statue is a picture of Ambedkar. It is placed slightly higher up than the Buddha statue. This may seem like a small detail but it is filled with meaning. The fact that a human being is placed higher than Buddha in the shrine room is often criticized by the non-Indian Buddhist monks working among the Ambedkarite Buddhists in Britain. Their interpretation is that the Ambedkarite Buddhists have too strong an influence in the Wolverhampton vihara and the non-Indian Buddhist head monk is accused of being too weak. The head monk, however, has no problems with the accusations of putting Ambedkar in higher esteem even in relation to the Buddha, I learn when I meet him later on.

Just outside the meditation room there is a room, or rather a hall, furnished like a small library with glass-fronted cupboards, filled with books about and by Ambedkar. There is Buddhist

---

has strong symbolism, not least in relation to a Gandhi statue nearby. Let me quote from the article on the notice board in Wolverhampton: 'An old statue of Ambedkar in Hazratganj, the heart of Lucknow, is being replaced by a mammoth bronze one. The Gandhi statue across the road was taller than that of Ambedkar. Boasts a civil engineer at the site: "With the new statue, we will dwarf Gandhi".'

[18] Pseudonym.

literature in Punjabi as well as in English and a table where one can sit and read. Dinesh Chandra takes me to the second floor. Upstairs is a room each for the two monks. My guide exchanges a few words with one of them in the hall before showing me their work room, with a writing table covered with piles of papers and some open books. An adjoining room is used for storage. This room is filled with cassettes of speeches by Ambedkar, piles of books, and booklets—Buddhist literature and literature about Ambedkar. Among the books in store many are produced in cooperation with Balley in Punjab, the editor of the magazine *Bhim Patrika* and also closely attached to the RPI. In the Buddha vihara in Wolverhampton the main political sympathies in the 1960s and 1970s were with this party, hence the connection with Balley. The activists in Wolverhampton and elsewhere in Britain even supported Balley financially because of his political engagement as said. They wanted him to build up the party in Punjab.

What happened, however, was that the RPI, which from the 1950s had already begun to split due to leadership tensions, was also fractured in 1969 when the leader Khobragade founded his own RPI. This RPI group opposed an alliance with the Congress, while the other RPI group led by Gaikwad was in favour of it. Balley took the same line as the majority within the Punjab Republican Party, in favour of the Khobragade group. The Gaikwad group came to cooperate with the Congress Party, while the Khobragade group never had any success in electoral contests. Balley consequently failed in the elections and became disillusioned with politics.[19] Instead, he began to direct his energy to working for social change.[20] The Wolverhampton Buddha vihara came to withdraw some of its support for Balley, and their political sympathies changed gradually in favour of Kanshi Ram.

---

[19] The picture Balley gave me in 2001 of his political engagement in the 1960s, is in accordance with the one he presented to Juergensmeyer in the 1970s.

[20] However, he still belongs to the RPI (Khobragade branch) and to some extent also sympathizes with the Marxists, although he never voted for them.

THE CELEBRATIONS

When I return outside, Vijay's family is still by the tent, about to finish their meal with some Indian sweets. Soon, however, we get into the two cars for the short trip to the rented hall where the main festivities are to take place. We reach our destination and are among the last to enter the hall to find our seats.

The ceremony begins with the president welcoming everybody. One of the Buddhist monks lights the candles in front of the Ambedkar picture and adorns it with garlands. The women move forward to leave their bouquets in honour of Ambedkar. A band on the stage is playing an accordion, *tablas*, and a windorgan. They play a few songs and are accompanied by a choir of five women in the background. The children come to the front, one by one, to recite some verses in English about Ambedkar which they have learnt by heart. The first small boy to enter the stage is five years old and has memorized a long piece, a feat that impresses all of us. Afterwards the children will come to the front again to receive diplomas from the president. A picture is taken of each child with his or her diploma and the president. The youngsters in the community who have cleared some examination also go onto the stage to receive a diploma for their achievements.

The speeches succeed one another. Some of the senior men are talking about the importance of Ambedkar. One of the young men, the general secretary in the newly started BSP-Overseas in Birmingham, gives a fiery speech about the importance of the BSP, Kanshi Ram, and Mayawati, its leaders at the time, and the shortcomings of the other political parties.[21] In between the speeches there is music and poetry. People show their appreciation by spontaneously going to the front to put some notes or coins on the podium. One small boy helps the men line up in a long queue. He is reciting a poem about Ambedkar in Punjabi, written by his father. 'The words are very moving', says Gita next to me.

At about 6.30 PM when the ceremony has still not come to an end, most children are tired of it and are in the corridor

---

[21] When I met this young man again a few weeks later he was just thinking about setting up a website for the BSP-Overseas.

outside the hall, running around, playing, and shouting. The women are unsuccessfully trying to keep them quiet.

This occasion was not the only time during my stay that support for Kanshi Ram and the BSP was expressed among the Ambedkarites in the Wolverhampton Buddha vihara. One of the Ambedkarites expressed his admiration for Kanshi Ram in the following way:

Everybody here, 99.5 per cent of the members support Kanshi Ram. We think it was due to Kanshi Ram and his movement, his social awareness programme, how he got the message to the people... It is because of him that now almost everybody in India knows about Dr Ambedkar.

Most people in the Wolverhampton Buddha vihara seemed to support Kanshi Ram (the BSP and also BAMCEF),[22] although they were disappointed that he took the support of the BJP. Nevertheless he was defended. The Ambedkarites in Wolverhampton, like many Dalit activists in India, defended Kanshi Ram with the argument that he was only taking support from the BJP for tactical reasons. Ideologically he was said to be against the party. Although the main political sympathies in the Buddha vihara in Wolverhampton, over the years, had shifted from the RPI to the BSP and Kanshi Ram, the Ambedkarites still wanted to maintain good relations with Balley (RPI).[23] They emphasized that the vihara was politically independent, although people had their personal preferences.

THE BUDDHIST MONKS IN BIRMINGHAM
GIVE THEIR VIEW

Talking to the Buddhist monks was for me one way to get an 'outside' perspective on the Ambedkarites from inside the Buddha

[22] One of the main leaders of BAMCEF, living in Punjab, was related to some Ambedkarites in the Wolverhampton Buddha vihara. He had visited Wolverhampton just prior to my stay.

[23] After my field studies in Britain, for the celebrations on the 14 of April 2000, both Balley, with sympathies for the RPI as well as Mayawati, the then general secretary of the BSP were, in spite of their enmity, invited to give speeches. Mayawati accepted the invitation. Balley, on the other hand, declined the offer because he did not want 'a clash on the stage', he told me when I met him in Jullundur in 2001.

viharas. The Buddhist monks were at times slightly critical of the strong position of Ambedkar in relation to Buddha within the Ambedkarite community and I shall now look at the community from the monks' point of view. I shall do this by presenting ethnography from one specific occasion, when I went with three monks related to two different Buddha viharas in Birmingham to a Monday meeting in the Wolverhampton Buddha vihara.

In Birmingham, as well as in other places in Britain, Ambedkarites have bought ordinary dwelling houses for the purpose of using them as viharas. The symbolic change from a dwelling house to a vihara could be said to take place when you find a Buddhist monk who is willing to live in the vihara and be responsible for its activities. In other words, when you have your own monk. Nagitha Thero[24] was a Buddhist monk from Sri Lanka who was responsible for one of the viharas in Birmingham. I used to accompany him in his car to the Wolverhampton Buddha vihara every Monday evening for the women's classes. He had lived in India for a long time and spoke Hindi that could be understood by the women whose mother tongue was Punjabi. The monks in the Wolverhampton vihara (from Thailand and Burma) used English, of which most of the Punjabi women had very limited knowledge.

On a cold, misty November Monday during my stay, I am standing outside Nagitha's Buddha vihara. Nobody opened the door when I rang the bell this evening, but 20 freezing minutes after our scheduled appointment, a small car appears round the corner. I am not forgotten. This Monday is a very special day, as two other Buddhist monks are to accompany us. Nagitha has just picked them up. One of them is the monk responsible for the other Ambedkarite Buddha vihara in Birmingham; with him is a guest, a visiting monk, originally from Kashmir and now living in Thailand. What is special, however, about this day is that the guest had been working and living in Punjab. Hence he knows Punjabi, the mother tongue of the people in the Wolverhampton vihara. I am let into the car and introduced to the visiting monk in the front seat.

Half an hour later we arrive in Wolverhampton some 10 minutes before the time announced for the procedure to begin.

[24] Pseudonym.

Everybody approaches the monks, their hands folded in respect. The Monday meeting takes a different form than usual, with many women, but also men and children, present. The monks from the Wolverhampton vihara as well as the visiting monks are seated on a podium, next to the Buddha statue and are greeted by the president of the organization. The monks all sing and offer brief speeches, but the main part is reserved for the visiting monk, who talks about Buddhism and the role of Ambedkar in Punjabi. Everybody is lyrical about it afterwards. The president explains to me: 'This was a very emotional moment for us, because this was the first time ever that a monk has spoken in Punjabi in our vihara.' The women present are keen to have the monk permanently in the vihara, and the president is of the opinion that he could double the membership in a few weeks time: 'He is the ideal monk for us. This uncle [pointing to another senior Ambedkarite present] is retired and spends his days here, although he does not understand English. Also for him this monk would be good.'

When the Monday meeting has come to an end the monks go upstairs to eat some food together. They are all tired and we soon leave for Birmingham. Back in the car the three monks relax. All of them are satisfied with the evening, and after some time the guest turns to me joking about the strong position of Ambedkar in the Wolverhampton Buddha vihara. He is happy about the appreciation among the Ambedkarites for his speech. It is not just the fact that he spoke in Punjabi, he says, that made them understand. He comments jokingly on Ambedkar's strong position in the vihara: 'You see if you speak of Buddhism, even if they like it they will not understand anything. But if you speak of *Ambedkarite* Buddhism, whether they like it or not they will understand'.

COMMENT

In this chapter I have shown how the networks of the Dalit movement have been conveyed transnationally from north India to Britain since the 1950s and 1960s.[25] Buddhism and politics

[25] Looking at the discourses among Dalit activists on the Internet, it may be assumed that similar processes have been at work among

were similarly fused in the Buddha viharas in Britain as in northern India. There were further transnational Dalit networks to be found, related to the RPI, the BSP, and even the Janata Dal in the Buddha viharas in Britain. The Ambedkarites in Britain, similarly to the Indian Dalit activists, expressed sympathies in relation to Buddhism and Ambedkar and antipathies in relation to Hinduism and Gandhi. This was seen not least in the ambivalent stance among the Ambedkarites in Britain in relation to the contemporary Ravidasis, who were said to not distance themselves from Hinduism as clearly as Mangoo Ram and the original Ad Dharm.

Many non-Indian Buddhist monks who worked among the Ambedkarites were more or less critical to the strong position of Ambedkar in relation to Buddha. In the Wolverhampton Buddha vihara, on the other hand, the responsible Buddhist monk defended the strong position of Ambedkar in the Ambedkarite community.

Regarding the Buddhist networks it should be noted that the Buddha vihara in Lucknow (Chapter 5) is related to the Buddha viharas in Britain as well as to Dalit activists in Jullundur in Punjab. Venerable Prajnananda, the head monk in the Lucknow vihara, visited Jullundur among other places in the 1950s and 1960s, and many among those who converted to Buddhism under his guidance in that time, have been living for a long time in Britain.[26] The fused political and religious Dalit networks are thus in a constant process of being recreated and not least activated transnationally.

Dalit activists among the diaspora in other countries, with networks stretched transnationally to India.

[26] During my fieldwork in Lucknow Prajnananda went as a chief guest to the Ambedkar celebrations in Birmingham.

7

Translating 'Caste Discrimination' into an International Discourse

THE NATIONAL CAMPAIGN ON DALIT HUMAN RIGHTS

In 1998 the NCDHR was formed; from the very beginning, the campaign reached a larger international audience than had previously been the case with national efforts within the Dalit movement. There are many reasons for this. Internet was in greater use worldwide, including in India. Dalit discussion groups were not in existence on the Internet in 1995, but were more visible in 1998. The home page of the campaign easily reached NGOs, human rights activists, Dalit activists in the diaspora, and interested others across the world. Many of the initiators were affiliated before the campaign started with Christian transnational networks such as the World Council of Churches and the Lutheran World Federation, which facilitated the internationalization of the issue. Furthermore, the NCDHR had professionals to design its folders, posters, and also the website. Internet presence made the message easily accessible to people not familiar with the issue. The campaign was also carried out in a consistent manner with, for example, a following-up of a first folder with a second similar one consisting of fact sheets and posters. Easily recognized symbols were repeatedly used as logos.

What picture did these activists want to project of themselves? By looking at the campaign schedule and the days chosen for the beginning and end of this campaign, we can find out something about the activists. The campaign was launched on 10 December 1998 on World Human Rights Day and closed (at the state and national level) on 14 April 1999, on the birthday of Ambedkar. They wanted to be seen as belonging to a global context, speaking the international language of human rights, combined with a belonging within the Ambedkar movement connected to the local/regional discourse about him.

The same could be said about the website (www.dalits.org, later changed to www.ncdhr.org) of the NCDHR. The image they put forward in 2001 was of a global human rights movement *and* a movement in the tradition of Ambedkar. At the top you found the letters 'NCDHR' with links to information about the campaign, and at the bottom the letters WCAR (World Conference Against Racism), with links to information about the World Conference in Durban. At the top was a picture of Ambedkar and the following quotation from him: 'You must have firm belief in the sacredness of your mission. Blessed are those who are awakened to their duty to those among whom they are born.'

The NCDHR has also since its foundation in 1998 systematically built up an international network. The International Dalit Solidarity Network (IDSN), with its office in Copenhagen, was formally inaugurated in March 2000 and consists of groups and networks in Europe and the United States in support of the campaign. Solidarity networks are to be found in Belgium, Denmark, France, Germany, the Netherlands, Sweden, the United Kingdom, and the United States. Let me now take a closer look at the material published and spread by the campaign, both within India but also internationally, for example in Durban.

THE MATERIAL: FIRST FOLDER

LET US CAST OUT CASTE. These are the words written in black block letters, top down on the left-hand side, on the first folder published by the NCDHR. The folder contains a campaign perspective, a charter of Dalit human rights, appeal sheets, a memorandum, and a poster.

Let me begin with the poster. By looking at the illustrations, associations turn easily to indigenous people. At the top are two black faces familiarly associated with aboriginal art. Under the faces, the folder's frontpage text is repeated: DALITS. A PEOPLE. A CULTURE. A HISTORY, but now all in block letters with some more information included. 'Dalit Rights are

Human Rights' is one of these additions, written in large white
letters. Another addition is: WE DEMAND FREEDOM FROM
CASTE BONDAGE FOR 260 MILLION DALITS OF ASIA,
written in black on a white background. This text is in the form
of a half circle building a frame for the two black faces. These
faces are repeated in the other materials in a manner that makes
them memorable and associated with the campaign, and they
seem to work as a logo. The background colour shades from
white at the top into violet as it reaches downwards. In the
left-hand corner is a small picture of Ambedkar.

The poster is a good example of how the NCDHR wants to
put Dalits into the global discourse on human rights. Furthermore they want to expose the problem not specifically as Indian,
but as an Asian problem, talking about '260 million Dalits of
Asia'. The tone is not defensive, but demanding in character:
'We demand freedom from caste bondage...' and 'Let us cast
out caste'. Finally, the picture of Ambedkar in the left-hand
bottom corner is also an addition in relation to the front picture
of the folder, now also placing the campaign in the tradition of
Ambedkar. Below is a Naivistic painting of human beings, men
and women, carrying pots or fishing, a child is seen reaching
after a bird, and the sun is shining. It may be interpreted as
a happy past, a happy future, and harmony between men
and nature. But first and foremost, Dalits are projected to an
international audience with associations with Aboriginals or
indigenous people in other parts of the world.

Already, even without opening the folder, we could see the
attempts to make the Dalit question an international issue in
terms of human rights, and in terms of having caste discrimination and untouchability included in the International Convention on the Elimination of All Forms of Racial Discrimination
(ICERD). On the back cover of this first folder are excerpts from
the 'Charter of Dalit Human Rights', one of the enclosed papers.[1]

---

[1] The first three demands are directed to an international audience:
(1) We assert that Dalit Rights are Human Rights. (2) We affirm
that the denial of basic needs of the Dalits is a gross violation of
Dalit human rights. (3) We seek the inclusion of caste discrimination
and untouchability in the International Convention on Racial Discrimination (Folder of National Campaign on Dalit Human Rights. 1998.
India: Secunderabad).

In the memorandum inside the folder, it is made clear that Dalit women and men together have launched and are leading the campaign.

SECOND FOLDER

The first impression of the second folder is that it is more demanding in character than the first, which is softer, not only in design but also in colours and language. On the upper right-hand corner of the second folder is a small illustration of the face of Ambedkar and in large white letters on a cracked black background is written: BLACK PAPER—Broken Promises & Dalits Betrayed.

While the first folder enumerates the demands of Dalits, the second one does the same but now explicitly directed to certain recipients; first, to the Government of India, second to the International Human Rights community, and third to the United Nations. On the folder it is made clear that the concept Dalit is used synonymously with SCs. It is also explained that to the official figure of 170 million SCs in India, the campaign adds some more categories of Dalits, namely, '20 million Dalit Christians, 50 million Dalit Muslims who have their roots in the Dalit community and 20 million Dalits residing abroad', which adds up, according to the campaign, to 260 million Dalits in the world.

In this second campaign folder the following interpretation of the symbols on the inside cover is written, which also gives an idea of what the campaign aims to express in the material it is distributing:

The twin figures [the same faces as were found on the first folder] lined up along the margins symbolise the community of Dalits gathered around the twin drums (shaded background at centre), the age old musical instruments of the Dalits. The beating of the drum symbolises for us here all that is expressed above—anguish, anger, protest, assertion, appeal, demand and proclamation.

On the inside of the cover in the first folder were given the facts about Ambedkar in one page. Here we can find one of the few mentions of Gandhi in the campaign material: 'For Gandhi, Dr Ambedkar was a *fierce and fearless man who has carved out for himself a unique position in society*, and a man who would not *allow himself to be forgotten.*' We could note an ambiguity in this sentence. The sentence quoted above has more than one message in it. It is directed to different audiences. Directed to an international audience, it wants to catch the interest of the reader. It appeals to the already well known, that is, to Mahatma Gandhi as a well known figure, talking in positive terms about the less well known Ambedkar. For those within the Dalit movement acquainted with the relationship and conflicts between Gandhi and Ambedkar, the above quotation from Gandhi is associated with the religious conflict between Ambedkar and Gandhi. In connection with Ambedkar's script *Annihilation of Caste* (Ambedkar 1979) in which Ambedkar denounces Hinduism, Gandhi was commenting on the script in his paper *Harijan*. In this context he was sarcastically and in critical terms commenting on Ambedkar, as 'a man, who has carved out for himself a unique position in society', further adding that 'Dr Ambedkar is not the man to allow himself to be forgotten' (*Harijan*, 11 July 1936 in Gandhi 1976a [1936]: 135). The meaning is that Ambedkar is taking too much space and seeking publicity. Ambedkar replied that it was not with the motive of gaining publicity that he printed the undelivered speech, but 'suppose it was my motive', he says, 'who could cast a stone on me? Surely not those, who like the Mahatma live in a glass house' (Ambedkar 1979: 86).

THE MANIFESTO

On the front page of the National Campaign Manifesto a red fist is shown breaking chains of steel accompanied by the text 'Dalit Human Rights'. The manifesto is a small-sized pamphlet of 40 pages.[2] The manifesto of the NCDHR could be compared with the Dalit Panther manifesto. There are similarities but also differences. In the manifesto the NCDHR clearly puts itself in the tradition of Ambedkar and Phule, as the Dalit Panthers did. It adds Periyar, the social reformer from south India, most probably because the main core of activists in the NCDHR is drawn from the south where Periyar has great influence. Phule, on the

[2] The pamphlet was drafted by M.C. Raj, author of *Dalitology: The Book of the Dalit People (2001)*, a book of 800 pages.

other hand, was born in Maharashtra, where he has inspired the Dalit Panthers among others. The NCDHR manifesto begins with two quotations taken from Ambedkar and ends with two others also by him. Also in the memorandum (in the first folder) they explicitly claim to belong in the tradition of 'our great leader Dr B.R. Ambedkar' and leaders like Jotiba Phule and E.V.R. Periyar: 'We are only attempting to carry on the great march that they have led decades ago.'

Early on in the manifesto (NCDHR 1998: 6) the NCDHR cites a poem by Namdeo Dhasal, one of the founders of the Dalit Panthers. He was, in the words of Zelliot, 'a forceful poet and the major figure in the Communist faction of the Dalit Panthers' (1992: 219). The poem by Dhasal in the NCDHR manifesto signals that it wants the campaign to be associated with the Dalit Panthers, at least in relation to the initiated. It is also clear that it wants the campaign to be recognized as continuing the tradition of turning against Hinduism, whose proponents include Periyar, Phule, and Ambedkar, and in the 1970s was revived again by the Dalit Panthers. The NCDHR places itself within the tradition, which I have called the autonomous anti-caste tradition. But in its discourse in relation to the government and to international forums, like the UN, some parts are played down and others are highlighted. A slight change of language is found when we compare the NCDHR manifesto with the Dalit Panthers Manifesto.

The Dalit Panthers clearly and explicitly express their criticism of Gandhi and the Congress Party in their manifesto of 1973. This is not the case with the NCDHR, which never criticizes Gandhi directly or mentions him by name, in its manifesto. On the other hand, he is indirectly criticized, in terms of 'our so-called nationalists'. In the last quotation on the inside of the backcover, he is also indirectly referred to in a quotation from Ambedkar: 'There have been many Mahatmas [sic] in India whose sole object was to remove Untouchability and to elevate and absorb the Depressed Classes: but every one of them has failed in his mission. Mahatmas have come, Mahatmas have gone. But the Untouchables have remained as Untouchables.' The manifesto also takes a stand in favour of separate electorates, which we have seen to be one of the main questions of conflict in the 1930s between Gandhi and Ambedkar. Two of the four quotations by Ambedkar on the inside cover are further strongly critical of 'the Hindu faith' and 'the Hindus'.

The NCDHR manifesto is directed more to an international audience than was the Dalit Panther manifesto, which was more of a statement internal to the movement. What is explicit in the Dalit Panther manifesto, the criticism of Gandhi, for example, is only to be read between the lines by the initiated in the NCDHR manifesto. The simple reason is probably that Gandhi is highly respected outside India, and the manifesto and campaign folders do not allow for elaborations to give the full context and make the conflicts between Ambedkar and Gandhi understandable to an international audience. The most obvious similarity between the two manifestos seems to be the explicit attempts to relate to discriminated people worldwide.

NEGOTIATIONS IN AN INTERNATIONAL CONTEXT, 2000–1

Even since the Dalit activists got to know about the United Nations World Conference against Racism, Racial Discrimination, Xenophobia and Related Intolerance in Durban they began to make preparations to attend (see also Chapter 1, pp. 5–11). They came from different local/regional contexts to a common state-related context and now wanted to enter into an international context, with many new actors and interrelations. Going all the way to the Durban conference in South Africa, taking the issue of 'caste discrimination against Dalits' to an international arena, was the outcome of a process of negotiations in many preparatory meetings. It is this process of negotiation that I want to highlight from the point of view of the Dalit activists.[3]

The following pages will attempt to give a picture of how the negotiations were handled by the activists representing the NCDHR in the meetings. They were reporting to the Dalit network they represented in India, as well as to the IDSN, which received reports of the meetings by email. I shall

---

[3] For related discussions see Berg 2007, Bob 2007 and Lerche 2008. In another context Madsen (1996: 265–97) discusses in an interesting way negotiations between Indian NGOs and the Indian government.

quote from their reports to show how the language of these activists had to be negotiated and how the discourse changed, as different meetings took place and the Durban conference was approaching.

The Dalit activists, the core of the NCDHR, taking part in the meetings preceding the Durban conference were in a situation in which they had to negotiate their language in relation mainly to four interests. These were (a) the Dalit networks in India which they represented; (b) the existing UN framework; (c) the representatives of the Indian government; and (d) human rights activists in other countries. This had to be done so as to: (a) retain the original ideas of the NCDHR and be able to discuss caste discrimination against Dalits; (b) fit caste discrimination against Dalits into the existing framework (organizational structure, themes for discussion, forms of presentations in terms of limited time schedules for oral presentation, and limited space in written documents) of the United Nations; (c) be accepted by the representatives of the Indian government (and its allies), at least to the extent of not being opposed and excluded before reaching Durban; and (d) build alliances with discriminated groups from other countries also planning to go to Durban.

Many of the Dalit activists, women and men, move easily across the landscape of discursive space within the movement and are familiar also with movement perspectives other than their own. They may as well communicate with others outside of their counterpublic. Many of them travel frequently to conferences abroad and are familiar with the UN language. They join at a local or regional meeting, come together later in a national Dalit campaign and travel abroad to unite in international conferences. The time-aspect of meeting each other repeatedly over a longer period of time, locally or in an international context will bring about a feeling of commonality, important to an identity-forming process.

'CASTE DISCRIMINATION'—THE FIRST HALF OF 2000
(FIRST PREPARATORY COMMITTEE)

The first meeting in which the NCDHR took part was the Bellagio Consultations to WCAR in Italy in January 2000, organized by the International Human Rights Law Group. This was a meeting in which representatives from different discriminated communities in various countries, human rights organizations, and UN human rights bodies came together. Among them were the Indian Dalit representatives, but also representatives of the Burakumin minority in Japan, for example. The resolution prepared by the participants recommended that caste discrimination against Dalits should be taken up at the WCAR and at the Preparatory Committee meetings, among other issues.

Four months later, in Geneva from 1–5 May, the UN First Prep (Preparatory) Com (Committee) for WCAR was held. The NCDHR sent a team of five to this meeting to lobby and make sure that caste discrimination would be taken up at the Conference. Human rights organizations such as Human Rights Watch were also making oral and written submissions to the Preparatory Committee that the issue of Dalits and caste discrimination should be part of the agenda at the Conference.[4] The Government of India was reported to be opposed to it, on the ground that caste is not race. Another delegation, including Dalits, was reported by the NCDHR to have been sent by the government to oppose the issue of caste discrimination being taken up in Durban. This delegation argued that caste discrimination no longer existed in India. An activist, just back from this meeting commented on it in a Dalit discussion group on the web. He quoted one of the individuals to have said during her intervention that '...there is no real problem in India on Caste System since the laws are in place and there are strong constitutional provisions. The problem (of untouchability and caste system) is a creation of the west.

Further he reports that he insisted at this meeting, supported by the Dalit Solidarity Forum, that the 'Caste System and Practice of Untouchability' should be a major theme and have a workshop. 'Anything less will not be acceptable'.

My point is that during the first five months of 2000 up to (and also during) the First Preparatory Committee meeting in Geneva, of the total 20 months of negotiations before Durban, the concept of caste was strongly in the picture, in spite of the

---

[4] Dalit Media Network from Tamil Nadu was another Dalit organization present at this meeting. Smita Narula spoke on behalf of Human Rights Watch.

opposition from the representatives in favour of the government's stand. The language will change slightly as we move to the second half of 2000.

IN-BETWEEN TWO EXPRESSIONS—
THE SECOND HALF OF 2000

In Chapter 5, I mentioned Prakash Ambedkar, the grandson of B.R. Ambedkar, and the symbolic significance of his invitation when the RPI was revived in Lucknow. From the beginning Prakash Ambedkar had a role to play also in the NCDHR. For example, he was one of the group of convenors who presented the Campaign Memorandum to K.R. Narayanan, the then President of India during a ceremony in New Delhi in connection with the inauguration of the campaign in December 1998.[5]

In August 2000, Prakash Ambedkar was among the group of Dalit activists, representing the NCDHR, who went to Geneva for a meeting of the UN Sub-Commission on the Promotion and Protection of Human Rights.[6] At this meeting two important resolutions were passed. First, a working paper on discrimination based on work and descent was to be written by Rajendra Kalidas Wimala Goonesekere, Expert Member of the Sub-Commission from Sri Lanka, to be presented one year later at the next session of the Sub-Commission in August 2001.[7] The second resolution was that descent-based discrimination should be included on

[5] For more on this occasion see 'National Campaign for Dalit Human Rights', in *Dalit International Newsletter*, vol 4, no.1, February 1999. Narayanan was the first SC ever elected as president in 1997, with 95 per cent of the votes, by the members of the national parliament and state legislatures. This could be interpreted as a sign that Indian politicians during the 1990s have come to realize the strength of the Dalit movement as well as that of the SC votes—and, at least, on a symbolic level want to show their goodwill.

[6] The Sub-Commission was set up by the Commission on Human Rights in 1947. It is made up of 26 independent experts representing countries from five regional groups. According to its mandate, it undertakes studies and makes recommendations to the Commission (UN document HR/4550, 27 July 2001).

[7] The working paper had three objectives: to (a) identify, (b) examine, and (c) make concrete recommendations and proposals.

the agenda at the World Conference on Racism. From now on the subject among the Dalit activists, in the official context, was 'discrimination based on work and descent'. Caste discrimination was mainly spoken of as a clarification in the reports emailed to the Dalit networks in India and the IDSN, when the activists wanted to explain that 'discrimination based on work and descent' was the same thing as 'caste discrimination'.

According to the NCDHR website, the Indian government was opposing the resolutions adopted by the UN Sub-Commission, reiterating its stand in the first Preparatory Committee in May that caste was not race and did not fall within the scope of the World Conference in Durban.[8] It is interesting to note that the same was said about caste and race in India's 14th periodic report to the Committee on the Elimination of Racial Discrimination (CERD) in 1996 (see Narula 1999). CERD, however, rejected the statement the same year, in the following words: '[...] the term "descent" mentioned in article 1 of the Convention does not solely refer to race. The Committee affirms that the situation of the scheduled castes and scheduled tribes falls within the scope of the Convention'. (CERD/C/304/Add.13. 17 September 1996. Concluding Observations. See also Narula 1999: 267, Appendix E). To clarify the position, CERD agreed with the Indian government on the argument that discrimination based on race is not synonymous with discrimination based on caste. 'Descent', however, does not refer solely to race, CERD stated. The point where they disagreed was mainly as to whether discrimination against 'SCs' was a matter for the UN or not. The Indian government in 1996, as well as in preparation for the Durban conference, found it to be an internal matter. CERD, on the other hand, found SCs to be covered by the term 'descent' in article 1 of the Convention, and consequently a matter for the UN.

One month later, in September 2000, a Dalit activist reported to the Dalit discussion group on the web from the (Asia-Pacific Experts Seminar in Bangkok) as follows:

Altogether, 19 NGOs supported by three other organizations submitted a statement that caste discrimination against Dalits was one of the vital themes that needed to be addressed by the WCAR.

[8] http: //www.dalits.org/UNInterventions.htm.

Again the Indian government opposed this, on the same ground as they did in the first Prep Com in May and in the Sub-Commission meeting in August, that is, caste is not race. The government was supported by the same Dalit delegation, from the International Institute for Non-Aligned Studies and the Indian Council of Education, which supported the stand of the government in the two previous meetings.

He comments further:

However, it was stated by a member of CERD that CERD had decided that the issue of caste is relevant on the basis of occupation and descent-based discrimination. ...The chairman of the seminar also stated that: 'CERD has put the matter to rest by holding that caste is discrimination on the basis of occupation and descent.' ...The outcome of the seminar was that the draft recommendations made references to caste in several places.

We, thus, see a repetition in 2000 of the communication between the Indian government and CERD in 1996 (Narula 2001).

During the second half of 2000 the Dalit activists mainly used the expression 'discrimination based on work and descent' already existing in the UN framework and interpreted within this framework to include discrimination against SCs. The Dalit activists representing NCDHR were well acquainted with the UN framework and knew that SCs among other categories was intended when talking about 'work and descent'.

It is important for what follows to understand that this first change in language for the NCDHR representatives, from 'caste discrimination' to 'discrimination based on work and descent' within the UN framework, during the first year of negotiations, was *already* a compromise on their part. In local/regional, translocal, and transnational contexts (within the counterpublic) the specific features of caste discrimination are pointed out; in these Dalit discourses, as we have seen, caste discrimination is closely related to the religious system of Hinduism. The change in language, in the international context, was made by the Dalit activists in order to have any chance at all to get their issue on to the agenda at the conference in Durban. It would turn out later that even 'work and descent', as an expression, was sensitive in the international context.

'THE LANGUAGE RELATING TO CASTE DISCRIMINATION'—THE FIRST HALF OF 2001 (SECOND PREPARATORY COMMITTEE)

The reports emailed to the Dalit networks and sympathizers from the negotiating meetings in preparation for the Durban conference all give an impression of an extremely hectic atmosphere. The activists are taking part in many meetings with different organizations and individuals and lobbying to get the issue of discrimination against SCs on to the agenda. But the representatives for the opposite stand are also lobbying *not* to include it in the agenda. Let me cite an activist's report from the meeting of the Intersessional Working Group in the middle of May 2001. He reported on the process of preparing a draft declaration, to be negotiated by the governments during the Second Preparatory Committee in Geneva (20 May–1 June 2001):

It was a tough process since we had to get the language relating to caste discrimination into this document and the draft that was presented to us did not have a word of it and this had been ensured by the Indian diplomats. It was after a lot of lobbying [joined by other organizations]... that we were successful in getting the support of two small countries, namely, Switzerland and Barbados, to support some of our clauses and get them introduced into the document. This brought a lot of opposition from India which is all out to ensure that this was out...

In this message we find the activist reporting about getting the language *relating* to caste discrimination into the document. When speaking about 'the language relating to caste discrimination' he actually means the expression 'discrimination based on work and descent'.

The Dalit activists who took part in the preparatory meetings upheld two arguments simultaneously. In the official language related to the UN they spoke about 'discrimination based on work and descent'. In reports emailed to their home audience whom they were representing, they talked about getting 'caste discrimination' or 'language related to caste discrimination' into the documents. The expressions 'discrimination based on work and descent' and 'caste discrimination' were also used interchangeably in their reports, to clarify and convince their home audience that caste discrimination was still on the agenda.

These reports were often written under pressing conditions, late in the evening, at night or in the early morning, after or before a full day's attendance at meetings. Still, the reports were often detailed and it seems that these activists did their best to give a clear picture of the meetings they had attended.

The risk was, however, in relation to the home audience—that there was some confusion regarding what the NCDHR representatives involved in the negotiations actually aimed to include on the agenda in Durban. The relationship between the expressions 'caste discrimination', 'racism', and 'discrimination based on work and descent' became obscure. The activists at the preparatory meetings, reporting home, may have been mistaken in arguing that 'caste discrimination' was the same as 'racism' and for that reason was within the scope of the conference in Durban. The argument may have been misunderstood as being that caste discrimination was also, like race, based on 'descent', and therefore the same. The arguments in the official context, however, looked quite different. The activists attending these meetings knew that not only racism but also other types of discrimination were included when talking about 'descent' within the UN framework.

The widespread, and incorrect, conclusion (mainly to be seen among some academics who were also following the course of events) was, however, that the Dalit activists negotiating as representatives of the NCDHR found caste discrimination to be synonymous with racism. Furthermore, many wrongly believed that the inclusion of discrimination against SCs in a UN framework was a new, first-time achievement. As already shown, the Dalit activists, on the contrary, wanted to include 'work and descent' in the documents at the Durban conference for the reason that 'descent' *already* referred to the SCs in the UN framework since 1996. The *new* achievement, on the other hand, was that discrimination against SCs—not as racism but as caste discrimination related to Hinduism—came to be reported in an official UN report (written by Goonesekere), which was publicly debated in a UN body. This should be compared to reports written earlier on this matter by NGOs and presented by NGOs to the UN (see, for example, Narula 2001).

The misunderstanding led to a debate in the Indian media in which some academics directed criticism against the Dalit activists as well as against the UN, as they were supposed to be equating caste with race, which had never been the case. The UN report of Goonesekere, quite contrary to what many in this debate supposed, made an even clearer distinction than before, and explicitly stated that 'discrimination based on work and descent' did *not* refer to racism, but specifically to discrimination against SCs. The report included the same kind of discrimination in other countries as well, but SCs in India was the main example.

'TAKE WORK AND DESCENT APART'—THE SECOND
HALF OF 2001 (THIRD PREPARATORY COMMITTEE)

In July 2001, between the Second and Third Preparatory Committees, the Committee of the NCDHR summarized, in an email to the Dalit networks, what had happened to the paragraphs supported by Barbados and Switzerland:[9]

In spite the fact that we had managed to get a small paragraph into the text...through an intervention by Barbados, you are all aware that this para was found missing in the text that was circulated around for the Second Preparatory Committee meeting

[9] The paragraph supported by Barbados read: 'The World conference affirms that discrimination on the basis of work and descent involves a complex and deeply entrenched obstacle to the realization of the civil, cultural, economic, political, and social rights of members of the affected communities, and that while most closely associated with caste systems in South Asia, this type of discrimination is encountered in other parts of the world as well. The World Conference therefore: (a) Calls upon the Office of the United Nations High Commissioner for Human Rights to undertake an indepth study of the question of discrimination on the basis of work and descent in cooperation with the Committee for the Elimination of Racial Discrimination; (b) Encourages Governments concerned to undertake public awareness raising and educational initiatives in order to promote positive changes in attitude towards and within communities discriminated against on the basis of work and descent.' (Barbados 11 May 2001). The paragraph supported by Switzerland read: 'To ensure that all necessary constitutional, legislative and administrative measures, including appropriate form of affirmative action, are in place to prohibit and redress discrimination on the basis of work and descent and that such measures are respected and implemented by all States authorities at all levels' (Switzerland 1 June 2001).

to the WCAR... Similarly, the small paragraph with reference to discrimination based on work and descent that was introduced by Switzerland and present throughout the Second Prep Com in the draft document has now disappeared in the draft prepared by the Group of 21 for consideration of the Third and Final Prep Com to the WCAR when the actual Negotiations would commence.

This was when the NCDHR committee circulated an appeal by email to get the missing paragraphs put back into the document. The struggle at this point was no longer a matter of linguistic nuances regarding 'caste discrimination' or 'discrimination based on work and descent', as it was before the First Preparatory Committee. It is important to note this change. The Dalit activists now had to devote all their energies to getting 'discrimination based on work and descent' back into the document. The email asked for help from the world community in getting as many signatures as possible from eminent persons to an enclosed memorandum,[10] to be presented at the Third Preparatory Committee, urging the Chair and Members of the Third Preparatory Committee to reinsert the paragraphs supported by Barbados and Switzerland into the Draft Declaration and Programme of Action.

An activist reports from the Third Preparatory Committee how the Dalit activists were lobbying to get the missing paragraph back into the document:

In the meantime we had also started discussions with Mr Pitso of South Africa, the Chair of the Group of 21, to find out how our Para 109 had been lost in the process. He was happy to inform us that this was only a mistake and that the fact is that Para 109 which was found missing was not the only Para and it was in the company of 6 other similar paras—one of which was also on Palestine! We were quite surprised that the missing Paras were such important Paras and were wondering who was the architect of this loss !! We still do not believe that this was just an error—we strongly feel that there had been something more to it and it is because of the opposition that was building on to this loss of Para 109 that there was a sudden volte face.

Later on the same activist reports that the European Union had decided to stand by the paragraph initiated by Switzerland,

---

[10] For the memorandum, see www.ahrchk.net/ua/caste.

regarding work and descent-based discrimination. However, he reports, there is opposition from the side of the Indian government and this has led to the idea of a compromise:

...we are lobbying for listing multiple factors of discrimination, which would also include sexual orientation so that we could then get work and descent there. There is also a proposal making the rounds informally in the EU that the compromise that may come out is listing work, then labor and then descent so that it is not seen as work and descent and at the same time both work and descent figure in the list. You can imagine now what it is to do all this and also keep watch with what is happening and at the same time meet people [and] write these updates etc.

What I want to point out with this quotation is that the Dalit activists, during the process preceding the Durban conference, were forced further and further away from their original expression 'caste discrimination'. They were obliged to change their language to get the necessary support also from the EU Member State representatives, if they wanted to have any chance of putting their issue on the agenda in Durban. They were now, in the Third Preparatory Committee meeting, at a point where even the expression 'work and descent' according to their reports, was sensitive to the extent that it could not be supported by Member State representatives at the UN.

According to the activists, it was informally suggested by representatives of the EU Member States that 'work and descent' should be taken apart, so as to not give the impression of referring to the caste system in India. Maybe then it could be supported. Work and descent would in that case both be included in a common list, but not put together as an expression. The idea was, as seen in the quotation, to insert labour between the two words, so as to list work, then labour, and then descent. Still, the Dalit activists argued, work and descent would at least be in the same list. The subsequent comment expressed something of despair: 'You can imagine now what it is to do all this...'

THE REPORT OF GOONESEKERE—'A GLORIOUS MOMENT'

In the meantime, between the second and third Preparatory Committees, the UN Sub-Commission met.

It was on 9 August 2001 that Rajendra Kalidas Wimala Goonesekere from Sri Lanka presented his working paper on 'discrimination based on work and descent' to the Sub-Commission. An activist reports from the meeting, which he regards as historic, as follows:

This was a very historic and memorable moment for all of us in the National Campaign on Dalit Human Rights and the International Dalit Solidarity Network for many reasons. This was the first time in the history of the United Nations that in one of its official meetings an official report (as opposed to reports from NGOs so far) was discussing an officially approved study on discrimination based on work and descent which is nothing short of caste discrimination....

He expresses how privileged he and his friends are at being in Geneva on this occasion:

...but we had all the members of the NCDHR, all members of IDSN and the numerous supporters that we have around the globe in our minds when we hugged each other with happiness on this occasion because it was a very significant moment in our own lives too and we have also each of us contributed our fair share to this glorious moment in the history of the struggle of our people and their sacrifice.

The occasion takes on historic dimensions for the Dalit activist, as it was the first time that caste discrimination was taken up in an official UN report and officially discussed in a UN forum. The language he uses also has seriousness to it, when he expresses it as a 'glorious moment in the history of the struggle of our people and their sacrifices'.

The report by Goonesekere[11] makes clear in the introduction that the International Convention on the Elimination of All Forms of Racial Discrimination (ICERD) specifically prohibits discrimination based on 'descent'. CERD has interpreted 'descent' to mean 'not solely race but tribal or caste distinctions

---

[11] Commission on Human Rights—Sub-Commission on the Promotion and Protection of Human Rights Fifty-third session, item 5 of the provisional agenda. Distr. GENERAL. E/CN.4/Sub.2/2001/16, 14 June 2001. Prevention of Discrimination and Protection of Indigenous Peoples and Minorities—Working paper by Rajendra Kalidas Wimala Goonesekere on the topic of discrimination based on work and descent, submitted pursuant to Sub-commission resolution 2000/4.

as well' (E/CN.4/Sub.2/2001/16: paragraph 4). CERD further stated in its General Recommendation XIV that 'in seeking to determine whether an action has effect contrary to the Convention, it will look to see whether that action has an unjustifiable disparate impact upon a group distinguished by race, colour, descent or national or ethnic origin' (ibid.).

Let me make a brief comment on this statement by CERD in relation to the SCs, to understand the stand taken by the UN in this regard for the further discussion regarding caste and race. CERD has interpreted 'descent' to mean—and this is important to note—*not solely* race but tribal or caste distinctions as well. It is clear from the two short words 'not solely' that race distinctions are not seen to be the same as caste distinctions. Nevertheless, though, discrimination based on caste distinctions falls under the ICERD.

Goonesekere makes a clearer distinction between discrimination against SCs, based on work and descent, and racism than had been the case earlier within the UN. He explains in his introduction: 'Victims of discrimination based on descent are singled out, not because of difference in physical appearance or race, but rather, by their membership in an endogamous social group that has been isolated socially and occupationally from other groups in society' (E/CN.4/Sub.2/2001/16: paragraph 7).

India is then taken as the main example, in the report, of countries where discrimination based on work and descent occurs.[12] The other countries, which are also stated in the report to be influenced by the tradition of caste, are Bangladesh, Nepal, Pakistan, and Sri Lanka. Japan is also taken as an example where the Burakumin (or Buraku) group is discriminated against (ibid.: paragraphs 40–2).[13] In the concluding remarks the

[12] Goonesekere differentiates between the SCs who suffer discrimination based on work and descent and the STs and OBCs, other underprivileged segments of Indian society, where the discrimination when it exists, cannot strictly be said to be based on work and descent (E/CN.4/sub-2/2001/16: paragraph 13).

[13] India is dealt with at length, in paragraphs 9–27, while the other countries are dealt with in paragraphs 28–44. Gender discrimination directed against Dalit women and girls in Asia, in addition to discrimination based on work and descent is dealt with separately in paragraphs 45–7.

author comments that he dealt only with countries in Asia in the report, but that the problem also exists in some other countries, mainly in Africa.

What is said in the report about 'discrimination based on work and descent' in India? Goonesekere first of all clarifies the stand of B.R. Ambedkar who, he says, 'traced the social injustice in contemporary Indian society, namely the caste system, to Hindu scriptures', and for this reason decided to renounce Hinduism. He compares Ambedkar's stand with that of Mahatma Gandhi, who was not prepared to blame Hinduism for the discrimination, and he quotes Gandhi as follows:

Caste has nothing to do with religion. It is a custom whose origin I do not know and do not need to know for the satisfaction of my spiritual hunger...The law of Varna teaches us that each one of us earns our bread by following the ancestral calling. It defines not our rights but our duties. It also follows that there is no calling too low and none too high. All are good, lawful and absolutely equal in status (E/CN.4/Sub.2/2001/16: paragraph 9).

However, Goonesekere does not take a stand in this debate, but asserts that 'whether caste is or is not derived from Hindu scriptures need not detain us because 85 per cent of India's 1 billion people remain Hindu' (ibid.: paragraph 11).

He states that the practice of untouchability has changed, but still persists:

Because of the social ostracism and economic deprivation they suffer, they often fall prey to the most serious forms of persecution in their society, including killings, mutilation, rape, arson, destruction of property and other forms of violence (sometimes regrettably by State agents) when they assert their rights (E/CN.4/Sub.2/2001/16: paragraph 18).

Next the report states that the government has recognized the problem of caste discrimination, and 'made determined efforts to deal with it'. The articles in the Constitution and the different laws dealing with SCs are taken up at length and the section ends with the following positive statement:

It is an impressive list of the actions that have been taken by the Government of India. That improvements have taken place cannot be doubted and credit should probably go to the National Human

Rights Commission, the National Commission for Women, the Scheduled Castes and Scheduled Tribes Commission and the National Commission for Safai Karamcharis [manual scavengers] (ibid.: paragraph 19).

Yet, acts of violence against SCs are not isolated events, but are sometimes performed by militia groups employed by the higher castes, according to the report. Goonesekere comments on the backlash when more systematic violence against SCs is not dealt with by the police and the courts: 'The inability of the police and courts to deal with crimes has had a backlash effect on young Dalits who also themselves have formed armed groups or Naxalites' (E/CN.4/Sub.2/2001/16: paragraph 26).

Goonesekere ends his report on India with a quotation taken from the National Scheduled Castes and Scheduled Tribes Commission. The strategy recommended here is to put the focus on the basic needs of the SCs and STs, so as to get 'social dignity and the economic capability to come at par with other sections of society'. This would lead to the SCs and STs becoming active partners in nation building, Goonesekere says, and would 'end the alienation, frustration and rising military and civil strife' on the part of these categories.

SUMMARY—NCDHR FROM THE FIRST PREPARATORY
COMMITTEE TO THE ABOLITION OF THE
UN SUB-COMMISSION

In this chapter I have shown the interplay between a Dalit discourse about caste discrimination and international cultural conceptions of human rights and racism. Nitza Berkovitch (1999: 101), talking about the international women's movement, has convincingly demonstrated how women's groups, on the one hand, were shaped by international cultural conceptions but simultaneously had a significant role to play in changing these conceptions of what could and should be done regarding women's issues. Dalit NGOs intersect with international cultural conceptions relevant at the moment. From the very beginning in 1998, caste discrimination was spoken about in the NCDHR within the internationally well-known discourse of human rights. Dalit activists have been acutely aware that they have to fit their discourse on caste discrimination into a broader prevailing framework in order to obtain recognition from the UN and the international community. In relation to the UN World Conference in Durban the discourse on 'racism, racial discrimination, xenophobia and related intolerance' was the broader framework into which to fit caste discrimination.[14]

This is not an exercise in discourse analysis in its narrower sense of language analysis or in terms of an in-depth study of nuances in language for its own sake. My point has been to show how the Dalit activists had to fit their ideas, created within an alternative counterpublic in India, into the framework of the UN and the World Conference that was to be held in Durban. The rules were clearly set by the existing cultural conceptions and the space extremely limited within the UN framework. To get their question on to the agenda in Durban they had to fit into this framework, which was a strictly guarded and limited space. Squeezing their message into this official international space made the NCDHR discourse partly incomprehensible in relation to the original discourse about caste discrimination, not only to those who were ignorant about the movement, but also to many Dalit activists and Indian intellectuals interested in the subject. Locally/regionally, translocally, and transnationally the Dalit discourse is to a great extent religious and political, as we have seen, but less so when directed at the Indian state. Finally, it is totally transformed and rendered devoid of all religious or political content or connotations in the official international context leading to the UN Durban conference.[15]

The situation of the Dalit activists, on their way to the Durban conference, was that their relatively newly created space that reached outside their own counterpublic and was directed at the Indian state, had to be created all over again in an international context. And this turned out to be a complicated task. Despite all the efforts on the part of the Dalit activists to modify the language of caste discrimination, no expressions in any way

[14] For a related discussion on the notion of 'indigenous people' in the context of India and in relation to the United Nations, see Norström (2003: 255ff).

[15] For an interesting related discussion about NCDHR's international work and BSP's regional work, see Lerche 2008.

associated with caste discrimination were to be found in the final document from the Durban Conference, when the negotiations were over.[16]

Since the report of Goonesekere, the Sub-Commission received a mandate from the former Commission on Human Rights (resolution 2005/109) to undertake a study on 'discrimination based on work and descent' and to develop guidelines for the elimination of it. The two experts who carried out the task over three years, Professor Yozo Yokota and Professor Chin-Sung Chung completed their report in 2007. But at this time the UN had undergone an organizational restructuring in which the Sub-Commission ceased to exist. As a result, it was unclear by which mechanisms the report could be transferred to the Human Rights Commission (HRC) or its Advisory Committee (HRCAC), which replaced the Sub-Commission. (See also p. 11).

Nevertheless, the discourse of the Dalit activists in relation to the UN contributed to the international cultural conceptions about what could and should be done (Berkovitch 1999: 101) regarding SCs' issues. The Dalit groups succeeded in getting the SCs on to the UN agenda, although the issue was not aired at the UN World Conference in Durban that was to come. Surprisingly the report of Goonesekere was in tune with the Dalit discourse and made references to the differences between Ambedkar and Gandhi, to the caste system and to Hinduism. With the Goonesekere report to that enormous apparatus which constitutes the UN, Dalit activists had finally carved out a small but important space for themselves in a formal international context. This was probably one of the reasons why the activist spoke of the day when the report was presented to the UN Sub-Commission as a 'glorious moment in the history of the struggle of our people'.

Framing women's issues within the UN cultural discourse of, first, human rights and then development achieved for the women's movement 'qualitative and quantitative changes on both national and international fronts', according to Berkovitch

---

[16] For the final document, that is, the Declaration and Programme of Action, see www.unhchr.ch/html/racism. For a discussion among Dalit activists, see, for example, Paul Divakar, Peter Prove, and James Massey (2002).

(1999: 119). When the Dalit activists similarly framed caste discrimination within the discourses of 'human rights', 'work and descent', and 'racism and related intolerance', it could be seen as a starting point in mutual interplay. Caste discrimination was at least, through the Goonesekere report, introduced into an international cultural discourse.[17]

[17] It should be recognized that I differentiate between the restricted influence of the Dalit discourse in relation to this international (intergovernmental) discourse, and the considerably larger influence of the Dalit discourse in relation to the global cultural discourse of other activists in, for example, the global justice movement. See Chapter 9.

8

Dalit Feminism in a Neoliberal World

There has been ambivalence towards feminism in India for different reasons. The main reason perhaps is that the concept has been associated with the dominant West and colonial rule. Thus, when talking about feminism in India one has to put it in the framework of an unequal global world.

It was not until the 1990s that the concept was really taken up by feminist scholars within the Indian academia.[1] One reaction against the 'westerness' of the concept has been an essentialization of 'Indian culture', pictured as synonymous with an 'indigenous Hindu culture' in contrast to the 'West'. Indian women have been seen as belonging to one and the same general category and have been put into this kind of Hindu framework (Chaudhuri 2004: xix). Feminism has accordingly often been used synonymously with a 'general feminism' within the framework of a 'Hindu culture'.

Rege (2006: 67) has discussed how Dalit feminists argue that this kind of feminism is not a general feminism, but a Hindu *brahmani* feminism and so challenge its all-inclusive demand. Dalit feminists do not see themselves as part of 'Hindu culture', nor do they identify with brahmani feminism, which is seen as a *different* kind of feminism. Dalit feminism thus becomes the normative defining point. Similarly as 'brahmani' feminists resisted the all-inclusive demands of 'western' feminists, the

---

[1] This does not mean that movement activists were not earlier informed by these kinds of ideas. Already during the nineteenth century, activists debated questions related to feminism. For a discussion see Chaudhuri (2004: xiii–xv).

Dalit feminists now resist the all-inclusive demands of brahmani feminists.

Gender is further, as John (2004a) reminds us, a relational term, taking not only women but also men into account. How, then, should one look at the gendered relations of power between men and women from the exploited sections of society, she asks.[2]

John (2004b) has commented that the stereotype of associating women with the inside private sphere and men as a general category with the outside world of economic and political power as done in, for example, the World Bank's *Gender and Poverty Report* (1991) is very misleading. She writes: 'Such power is in fact in the hands of very few men, who are upper caste and Hindu, and middle or upper class, and who may constitute no more than 10 per cent of the male population' (John 2004b: 253). Dalit men are not, with few exceptions, among the 10 per cent of men holding economic and political power in the Indian society.

Let me relate these observations by John to the argument of Randeria (2007) that the Indian state has come to redistribute its responsibilities to other actors in society. In 1991, India introduced a new economic policy and the country was ushered into a neoliberal global economy. What has happened in India since the so-called 'adjustment programmes' with extensive privatization was introduced in the beginning of the 1990s is that the state has reduced social expenditures and has withdrawn from its economic and social responsibilities towards its citizens.

This is thoroughly discussed and analysed by Randeria (ibid.) and although she is not specifically focusing on gender relations, her arguments are most relevant in this context. Randeria challenges a western-centrism, which makes a binary division of states into strong and weak. In this binary cliché India is regarded as a weak state in relation to international institutions like the World Bank, the International Monetary Fund (IMF), and the World Trade Organization (WTO). Randeria, however,

[2] Ruth Vanita (2004) further reflects on the categories of 'woman' and 'man'. These are 'illogical categories', she states, 'based on certain parts of the body which may or may not be used to certain predefined ends. We might as well divide all human beings into big-eared and small-eared people and hope to work out a sane society based on such a division' (ibid.: 73).

argues that the Indian state is neither a strong state, nor a weak state. India is a *cunning state*,[3] she suggests. This means that the Indian state is selectively strong in advancing the interests of the privileged, but strategically weak in fulfilling even its constitutional duties towards the poor.

The World Bank, the IMF, and the WTO have set the agenda for the Indian 'adjustment programmes' as we know, but there are possibilities for the Indian state to act independent of these institutions to a larger extent than is now the case. However, the state represents itself as a *weak* state in relation to these international institutions for the purpose of withdrawing from its responsibilities in relation to its citizens. Simultaneously they seek to redistribute these responsibilities to other actors in the Indian society (Randeria 2007).

I am not going further into Randeria's argument here, but just want to relate it to the discussion about Dalit feminism by John (2004b), who has pointed out how women in so-called 'empowering programmes' have been made individually responsible to react to 'structural adjustment'. She shows how the World Bank in its *Gender and Poverty Report* draws on previous feminist findings, but now interprets these findings in a new way.

Feminists have, for example, shown how poor women often contribute mostly to household income, *in spite of* lower wage earning and they even know how to handle scarce resources. It has been in the broader context of women's exploitation in the labour market. Now, in the World Bank's report these same facts are instead put forward as a proof of women's efficiency.

Let us reflect briefly about this new priority of focus. The broader context is put aside and the focus now becomes the

[3] The concept of 'cunning' is not meant to define a characteristic of the state structure or capacities, but rather 'the changing nature of the relationship of national elites (very often in concert with international institutions) to citizens,' according to Randeria. These elites 'deploy the rhetoric of sovereignty strategically,' she argues, 'to prevent international intervention in certain realms (human rights, rights of indigenous peoples), but are willing to implement policies prescribed by international institutions in others (economic policy, fiscal discipline, trade rules).' In this way these kinds of states have developed an art to stand unaccountable to international institutions as well as to the citizens, she comments (Randeria 2007: 3ff).

micro-relations within the household between the wife and husband. The World Bank's report concludes that 'poor women are clearly more efficient economic actors, with greater managerial and entrepreneurial skills than men' (1991: 248).

We could in this example clearly see how the focus has shifted away from the broader structural context. The World Bank itself, IMF, and WTO, as well as the Indian state and transnational corporations need to be taken into account and analysed to understand the situation of the women and men locally. Instead, there is a focus on the micro-level and an interpretation and agreement that the 'poor women' are the 'good subjects' with economical skills. The men in these analysis are consequently unruly and prone to violence, especially if they are Dalits or Muslims, and they thus become the 'bad subjects of modernity' (Chaudhuri 2004: xxxviii; John 2004b). It could be added that these men are thus also on an individual level deprived of their 'masculinity' in the traditional sense of being economically responsible in the household.

Due to privatization and a decreasing public sector, SC women and men have since the neoliberal economic policies and 'adjustment programmes' were introduced, experienced greater difficulty in finding jobs, getting bank loans, a competitive education, healthcare, etc. (Thorat 2004). These problems are thus seen by the World Bank and the Indian state alike as best solved by individual women if they move into entrepreneurship and micro-finances, for example, in an expanding private sector. The economic responsibilities are thus not only redistributed by the state to the individual women but in a society still imbued with traditional gender distinctions, associating male roles with economic responsibility, the men are simultaneously deprived of their so-called masculinity.

In a second interpretive move, the responsibilities are also channelled away from the state domain and public sector into the private sector. The problems faced by SC women are not seen to be the consequences of neoliberal policies, but rather the effect of irresponsible men (lacking 'masculinity') on a local level. Thus they are also seen to be best solved by individuals (read 'poor women' without economic and political positions) moving into an expanding private sector. In the package so to speak, together with the micro-finance programmes for women, a neoliberal economic ideology, politically coloured, is transferred to a local level by representatives of the Indian state, macro-institutions like the World Bank, and transnational corporations alike.[4]

What is the Dalit feminist stand in this context? Ruth Manorama, Dalit feminist and recipient of the 2006 Right Livelihood Award, while delivering a lecture in Stockholm University, was asked by a person in the audience whether micro-finance programmes for Dalit women should be seen as something positive or negative. Manorama replied: 'It is a complicated question and there are many different views, but most often feminists have said: "What is this?! Buying *small, small* things—a pig or a hen—while the big money goes somewhere else. Give us land!"'[5]

I will demonstrate how a Dalit woman may be pictured, when she actually achieves political and economic power, and the attempts to deprive her of a traditional 'femininity', associated with morality and privacy of the body. The example of this will be the Dalit politician Mayawati. But first, I will give an overview of Dalit women's relation to the Dalit movement and the women's movement.

DALIT WOMEN:
THE ROAD TO RECOGNITION

Dalit women have since the 1980s more explicitly formed their own networks separate from the Dalit men to be able to get their voices heard. They preceded the broader Dalit movement in building a nationwide network in the second half of the 1980s (separate from the Dalit men). In 1995 National Federation of Dalit Women (NFDW) was formed and the same year they also

[4] Poster and Zalime (2002: 198ff) have in their article 'The Limits of Micro-credit' shown how microcredit programmes are framed in a neoliberal paradigm. They have given an illustrative example of how a neoliberal discourse favouring micro-credit programmes is created by USAID and transmitted transnationally by NGOs to the grassroots level in Morocco.

[5] Lecture in the Department of Social Anthropology, Stockholm University, 20 November 2007.

took part in the Fourth UN International Women's Conference in Beijing, building transnational alliances.[6]

The Dalit women thus organized themselves on a national and also an international level at the same time as a broader national network among Dalit activists (women and men) took shape. This meant that when the NCDHR was formed in 1998, Dalit women had already been organized on a national scale for three years, since 1995. From the 1980s onwards they had carved their own space within the Dalit movement. It is important to note, however, that even if they have organized separately from Dalit men, they tried to work in collaboration with them in the NCDHR. When reflecting on the first years of the NCDHR, Manorama described the women's participation in the following way: 'We hurtled into the campaign with all our force.' The Dalit women and men went into the campaign on an equal footing and the NFDW came to play a crucial role in Durban three years later, in 2001. This meant that not only did the Dalit movement and questions related to SC become known internationally, but international focus, to a large extent, came to be placed on the situation of SC women.

DALIT SPACE IN THE WOMEN'S MOVEMENT

Dalit women have, as already mentioned, formed their own organizations and networks, separate from, but still closely connected to, both the Indian women's movement and the broader Dalit movement. The reason given for this is that they are discriminated against both within the Dalit movement and the women's movement. In the Dalit movement a patriarchal structure is prevalent in the same way as in the rest of society. Within the women's movement, the Dalit women feel discriminated against by the high-caste women and sense that their issues are not taken up seriously for debate.[7]

[6] For more about the 1995 UN Fourth World Women's Conference in Beijing and the parallel NGO forum, see Brown Thompson (2002: 96ff). For a more general overview of feminism, social movements and globalization see Eschle (2001). For economic globalization and feminism, see Sassen (1998, 2007).

[7] See Hester Betlem, http://www.dalitusa.org/ch2a.html.

The women's movement that took shape during the nineteenth century was closely connected with the Hindu caste reform movement, working for reform and betterment for women, but not interested in a restructuring of society. However, Dalit women have not been absent historically, although their history has been neglected until recently. From the 1920s the Dalit women were active in what I have called the autonomous anti-caste tradition, although they did not organize separately to the extent we have seen since the middle of the 1980s. With Ambedkar in the 1930s, women became even more aware and organized separate meetings and conferences:

The movement begun by Dr Ambedkar generated an even more enthusiastic participation. Dr Ambedkar organised several conferences of the Untouchables. He saw to it that women's conferences were held simultaneously with those for men. By 1930 women had become so conscious that they started conducting their own meetings and conferences independently (Moon and Pawar 2006).

Meenakshi Moon has interviewed 60 women in Maharashtra and in Delhi who were connected with the Ambedkarite movement in the 1930s. She shows how women took part in Ambedkar's movement and independently supported his claims in separate women's conferences and in direct action. When Ambedkar in Mahad in 1927 claimed the right of the 'untouchables' to take water from a public tank, women participated in the procession; equally important, they took part in the meetings when the resolutions were passed about demands for equal rights. They were also part of the movement in Nasik from 1930 when Ambedkar demanded temple entry for 'untouchables', up to 1935 when he declared that he had been born as a Hindu but would not die a Hindu. During this period the women conducted meetings and supported Ambedkar's claim for separate electorates (ibid.). In the earlier passage we can see how Dalit women began to organize separately from Dalit men early on, but my point in this context is that they supported the claims of Ambedkar and consequently organized separately from women within the Hindu caste reform tradition at the time.[8]

[8] For more about the women's movement connected to M.K. Gandhi in the Hindu caste reform tradition, see, for example, Forbes (1984: 365–81).

Also in Dalit Sahitya, from the 1950s onwards, Dalit women came to express their experiences as different from the Hindu women, as seen in Chapter 3.

The revival of the women's movement in India came with the 'new women's movement' in the 1970s. Dalit women activists, however, see this movement as a continuation of what I have called the Hindu caste reform tradition. The activists in the 'new women's movement' were said to focus in the same way as their predecessors on the problems of upper- or middle-caste women, and they were further said to be governed by Hindu values, without any understanding of the caste-based discrimination to which the Dalit women were exposed. Dalit women activists also accuse the broader women's movement of not having taken the SC women along in the betterment they experienced since the 1970s, in education and in the social sphere. Dalit women also find the problems of the SCs to be very specific, and not very well highlighted in the broader women's movement (see, for example, Dolas 1995; Jondhale 1995; Prabhavati 1995).

However, in the second half of the 1980s, Dalit women came to express a need for a separate platform within the broader women's movement. In 1987 the first Dalit women's national meeting, Dalit Women's Struggles and Aspirations, was held in Bangalore. About 200 women from the south of India, but also from Delhi, Maharashtra, Uttar Pradesh, and West Bengal are said to have attended. This was the beginning of a national network of Dalit women which on 11 August 1995 formed the NFDW (Guru 1995: 2548–9). One of the main initiators, Ruth Manorama, told me during a conversation: 'We were about to get Paswan in Dalit Sena to hold the inauguration, but then we thought: "why him?"[9] Instead, we chose a Devadasi woman.'[10]

[9] Ram Vilas Paswan was the top male Janata Dal politician, heading the national Dalit network called Dalit Sena.

[10] The practice of Devadasi is reported to still be in existence in parts of southern India. It means that a girl, usually before reaching puberty, is ceremonially dedicated or married to a deity or temple, that is, becomes a 'female servant of god'. These girls are often SCs from an economically poor background. Once dedicated to a temple they will later have problems getting married. Men, who can afford to pay the temple rituals, are reported to be the patrons of these girls. The

Three years later some women from NFDW took part in the formation of the NCDHR.

Also in 1994, in the fifth national women's conference, All India Women's Activists Conference in Tirupathi (Andhra Pradesh), Dalit women spontaneously arranged a separate session on Dalit women. (See poster below exhibited at the conference, quoted by Setalvad 2001: 9.)

'The Rights and Responsibilities of Dalit Women'

To own bodies—and be controlled by state,
'upper' castes and men
To be untouchable by day—and touchable by night
To be the cultivators—and starve unto death
To work, labour—and profit others
To cast our votes—and seat others

In September 1995, the UN Fourth World Conference on Women was held in Beijing, China. Among the hundreds of women who went to the conference from India, SC women were well represented, which was an achievement for the Dalit women activists. A seminar focused on Dalit women was held titled 'Dalit Women Transforming Pain into Power'.

Women's Space in the Dalit Movement

One of the initiators of the NFDW and one of the most visible members of the NCDHR in international contexts is Ruth Manorama from Bangalore. The first time I met her was in March 1994 when she participated in a Dalit women's conference in New Delhi, arranged by the Dalit Solidarity Programme (DSP).[11] The event was reported in the press as a unique gathering of Dalit women, under headings such as 'Dalit women share traumas' (*Patriot*, 8 March 1994) and 'The voiceless speak out' (*Hindustan Times*, 8 March 1994). In her speech

---

girls are also reported to be sexually exploited and often end up as sex workers in urban brothels (Narula 1999: 150ff).

[11] Some other women present at this conference were also among those who, one year later, led the initiative for the NFDW. They were also among the visible women in NCDHR when it was formed in 1998.

entitled 'Crimes against Dalits are Crimes against Humanity', Manorama stressed that Dalits 'in the wake of rising atrocities are now organizing themselves to change their situation'. A young girl at the conference expressed her worries about the state of affairs in Indian society:

There is something extremely rotten in our society where the little girl who should be the recipient of love and affection is being increasingly subjected to brutal assault. Sadly no steps are being taken to constrain the inhumane in our society. How can we forget that in free India, it is we who are being paraded naked [referring to an incident in Ghoorpur police station in Allahabad District, where a Dalit woman was paraded naked], raped and mercilessly murdered? (Nalanda Sampla speech held at the Women's Conference, Dalit Solidarity Programme, 3–6 March 1994).

She went on to express her fascination with the achievements of 'Madam Toni Morrison, a black woman writer and a Nobel laureate this year'. Finally, in a similar vein to Manorama, she urged the audience to take the destiny of the Dalit women in their own hands: 'A new generation of committed girls has arrived. I ask you, my sisters, how long shall we keep waiting for justice?' (ibid.).

Ruth Manorama often refers to Dalit women as 'the thrice discriminated', meaning that women are discriminated against on the bases of class, caste, and gender. Another expression she often uses about Dalit women is 'Dalits among the Dalits' or 'downtrodden among the downtrodden'. In an early article published in the context of Dalit theology (see Chapter 4, note 16), she describes Dalit women as the most exploited in Indian society but makes it clear, at the end of the article (citing Gail Omvedt), that women are not simply passive victims. The current mood seems to be not one of mute acceptance, she writes, but one of bitterness, anger, and sadness (Manorama 1988: 75). Manorama is of the opinion that women should have their own organizations and work out solutions through a dialogue with men, for the reason that women are never let into the organizations governed by men on equal terms.

What is, then, the attitude among Dalit men to the Dalit women leadership that is now arising? Durban was the occasion when 'casteism was taken to the world', in the words of Kancha

Ilaiah, professor and Dalit.[12] A few years earlier he gave voice to
his vision of a Dalit women's leadership in an interview in the
magazine *Ghadar*. In his concluding comments he expressed
his view that under Dalit women leaders, a Dalitist state and
society ought to be established. 'Then', he said 'we will see a very
bright future for the whole country' (*Ghadar*, (2), 26 November
1997). This may be seen as a Dalit vision remote from present-
day Indian social life, both regarding the vision that a Dalitist
state and society may be established in the near future and
regarding the hope of finding this society under the leadership
of women. However, in Durban in 2001, Dalit women played a
salient role.

Chandrabhan Prasad, a Dalit activist and journalist, has
commented on the role of Dalit women in Durban in the same
vein as Ilaiah:

From within India, iron lady Jyothi Raj of Karnataka made Dalits
proud in Durban. Her hunger strike in front of the ICC resulted in
huge support for Dalits. Above 500 people from all over the world
assigned our memorandum and wrote down their e-mail addresses
assuring support in any further convention. And who can forget
V. Vansanthi Devi, former VC from Tamil Nadu and another
majestic Dalit lady, a professor of management from Andhra
Pradesh, Shyamala of Anveshi, the articulate Ms Lalitha, or the
legendary Ruth Manorama, who all together gave a new dimension to the Dalit campaign in Durban?

Prasad goes on to list Dalit women activists from the north:

From north, Nasreen Faiyas, Pushpa Valmiki, Rajani Tilak, Vimal
Thorat left their deep imprint in the campaign against caste at
Durban. They are very much active in India as well.... In all, Dalits'
Durban experiment witnessed a great leap forward as a large num-
ber of women participated in the campaign (*Woman Power in Dalit
Movements*, Chandrabhan Prasad).[13]

This article is worth paying to attention for more than one
reason. First, the journalist focuses on the women within the
Dalit movement, expressing in a respectful manner pride in

[12] Interview with R. Umameshwari in *Seminar*, no. 508, December
2001.
[13] http: //www.ambedkar.org/chandrabhan/Womanpower.htm.

being a Dalit and seeing the activities of experienced Dalit women in Durban. Chandrabhan Prasad reflects further on the new dimension of this large-scale participation by women at the World Conference.

The presence and visibility of Dalit women in Durban should be seen in contrast to the dominance of men in leadership positions within the Dalit movement locally/regionally in India and also in the Dalit diaspora. Prasad's account may further be seen in contrast to a view prevalent among a large section of the older men within the movement, among whom the *ideal* leadership in society as well as within the movement is still regarded as male. However, within small circles of Dalit men, often in the younger generation, among Dalit students in colleges or universities, for example, it is at least an *ideal* which *may* be expressed and worked for to also have a Dalit women leadership. Hence, some changes could be discerned in the Dalit movement, otherwise imbued with a patriarchal structure.

When I met Ruth Manorama in the spring of 2002 she was satisfied with the role women had played in Durban and the media's exposition of the situation of SC women. She expressed the relationship between Dalit women and Dalit men in the following way: 'Dalit women have to challenge Dalit men to reach the leading posts also within their own movement'. The reason for this, she says, is that the Dalit men have been discriminated against for their entire lives, not only by high-caste men but also by high caste-women:

You see they [the Dalit men] are scared of us. They have been discriminated against their whole lives and think their own women are the same as the high-caste women. Now, when they have finally grasped the leadership posts they will not part from them. You have to understand them.

She tells me about her work among the women in the villages, and how she describes the relationship between women and men in Indian society to them. Manorama picks up a pen and quickly sketches on a piece of paper four earthenware pots on top of each other to illustrate it. Laughingly she says that she will now explain this to me, as a teacher would:

This is how I describe it to the women in the villages and they understand very well. Ambedkar also told it in this way. You see, in each hut in the villages you have the rice stored in the corner in earthen pots. Naturally you have to put the large pot at the bottom and smaller and smaller, up to the top. It will look like a pyramid, broad at the base and small at the top. At the bottom you have the large pot of the Shudras, on the top of that a smaller one, that is the Vaishyas. Next, on top of that the Kshatriyas. Finally, at the very top you will find the small pot of the Brahmins. In each and every one of these pots you will find the dust or powder of the rice that has fallen to the bottom. That is the women. But below and outside the four pots is the earth, the dust, the crushed, the nothing, devadasis, scavengers.... That is the women and men of the untouchables.[14]

The illustration, according to Manorama, shows that women are being discriminated against in relation to men at all levels. This is combined with the dimension of caste discrimination, according to which Dalit women and Dalit men have been discriminated against by those, women as well as men, higher up in the hierarchy.

TWO WELL KNOWN DALIT WOMEN: MAYAWATI AND PHOOLAN DEVI

Regarding Dalit women's visibility in the public sphere I will give two examples to show how they have been presented in media. There are two famous Indians through whom the situation of so-called untouchables has become better known during the past decade. The first I have in mind is Uttar Pradesh Chief Minister and BSP President, Mayawati. The other is Phoolan Devi, 'the Bandit Queen'. Mayawati is known as the first Dalit woman ever to reach the top of Indian politics, holding the post of Chief Minister in Uttar Pradesh. She has been praised and regarded as a role model for Indian SC women, and it is often claimed that she alone has raised their level of political awareness. However, she is also severely criticized in many quarters and not only on political grounds. The criticism is often put in moral terms. In the 1990s she was condemned for 'living with a man [Kanshi Ram] without being married' and for the reason that 'she carried out an abortion'. In 1996 a

[14] For a similar description, see also Manorama (1995: 165–76).

politician stated that she had an unknown 12-year-old daughter, secretly hidden in New Delhi, in spite of being unmarried. This comment was referred to by a journalist in a newspaper and resulted in a heated debate about the ethics of journalism in India.[15] These same comments, on moral grounds, are often heard against Mayawati from men within the Dalit movement. A Dalit woman activist, otherwise not sympathizing with the BSP, commented on this moral slandering of Mayawati as follows: 'All the men at the top slept with women without being married to them. Everybody knows about it. How come they single out the first Dalit woman who reached the top and criticize her? Did they not recognize this behaviour before? It is very gender-biased.'

The other woman, Phoolan Devi, was the woman through whom caste and gender discrimination in India became known internationally through widespread media attention, specifically through the book about her life, *India's Bandit Queen* by Mala Sen (1991), and later on also through the film *Bandit Queen*. The movie was a 'Bollywood' production made also with a 'Western' audience in mind by Shekhar Kapur.[16] Phoolan Devi belonged to the Mallah community.[17] She became known as the low-caste woman who was raped, first by the man whom she was married to, at the age of 11, later by a gang of high-caste Thakurs in her village of origin, and finally also by the policemen in jail. In between she had also been 'paraded naked'. When she was released on bail she was carried away by a gang of dacoits. It was said that, in revenge for the rapes and the killing of her lover Vikram Mallah, she led the murder of 22 high caste Hindu men, a crime performed by the gang she belonged to. In 1983 Phoolan Devi surrendered to the police under ceremonial forms. In 1994, after 11 years in jail without

[15] For an interesting discussion about how the media covered Mayawati in relation to the statement from the politician that she had an illegitimate daughter, see Ståhlberg (2002a, 2002b).

[16] Bollywood is a popular expression for the Hindi film industry in Mumbai (Bombay).

[17] Mallah (also known as Kewat or Nishad) belong to OBCs in Uttar Pradesh. But in Delhi and West Bengal, Mallahs have been included among the SCs. I am thankful to Umakant in New Delhi for this clarification regarding Mallahs.

trial, she was released. This was during the time when the Chief Minister of Uttar Pradesh was Mulayam Singh Yadav of the Samajwadi Party. Two years later, in 1996, Phoolan Devi became a Member of Parliament for this party. Her life ended in July 2001 when she was shot dead at the age of 38.

The movie about Phoolan Devi became a success for the men who produced it. Phoolan Devi, on the other hand, expressed her dislike for the movie about her life. She said in an interview that she regarded Shekhar Kapur (director) and Bobby Bedi (producer of the film) to be no better than the men who had raped her.[18] A Dalit woman activist commented once to me about Phoolan Devi: 'She was exploited in all senses. First, because of gender and caste, later also by the media.' Arundhati Roy, in an article about the movie, states that Shekhar Kapur had not met Phoolan Devi even once during the making of the film. He neither invited her to comment on the film during its production, nor to see it in any of the private screenings before it was released. Many months after the premièr in Cannes and weeks after it had been released in Bombay and Delhi, when Roy met her, Phoolan Devi had still not seen it. 'She was not invited', Roy comments, 'but was supposed to be safely in jail.'[19]

Roy in her article points to the terrifying fact that, while still in jail and being treated for an ovarian cyst, Phoolan Devi's uterus was removed—without her knowledge and inspite of it not being necessary. The prison doctor laughed and told Mala Sen (1991) when asked about it: 'We don't want her breeding any more Phoolan Devi's'. Roy comments that this was not even *mentioned* in the movie: 'When it comes to getting bums on seats, hysterectomy just doesn't measure up to rape', she concludes in the article.[20]

Let me reflect on Mayawati and Phoolan Devi, these two Dalit women who drew recognition in different but also similar ways. Kumud Pawde (1995: 145) comments that SC women are raped

---

[18] *Pioneer*, 15 August 1994, cited in Roy, http: //www.umiacs.umd. edu/users/sawweb/sawnet/roy_bql.html. The article 'The Great Indian Rape-Trick' (1994) by Arundhati Roy, is found on the website of South Asian Women's Network (Sawnet).

[19] http: //www.umiacs.umd.edu/users/sawweb/sawnet/roy_bql.html.

[20] Ibid.

more often than women in other categories and '[t]he Dalit women are being raped because in the opinion of the high caste society, they have no morals and they deserve it'. Phoolan Devi is just the best known among these women raped each year in India.[21] It seems that one reason why SC women are raped and paraded naked is *to make them experience* and *to make visible* to their families and others the already assumed fact that that they lack morality, just by being born into the category of SCs. If you reach a position of political power as an SC woman, like Mayawati, which is highly unusual, there are yet other ways to expose your immorality. When exposed in the media, whether it is the purpose of publication or not, Mayawati's asserted immorality is made visible in public.

An SC woman lacks morality just by being born into this category, and again, this should be 'proved' or shown to her and to the world. This may be done either by rape, by 'parading her naked' or by exposing her private life (in the case of Mayawati) or the sexual aggressions against her (Phoolan Devi) in the media. In this sense the lives of Phoolan Devi and Mayawati resemble each other, inspite of their otherwise different experiences. The privacy of their bodies is made public—in the movie *Bandit Queen* and also by politicians and journalists, as regards Mayawati.

Neither Phoolan Devi nor Mayawati were asked to give comments before bits and pieces of the imagined private life (of Mayawati) and the assumed acts of sexual violence (against Phoolan Devi) were released for public consumption. Mayawati and Phoolan Devi, two Dalit women, were both exposed in the media—by men.

My argument has been that Dalit women historically have struggled to get some space not only in the Indian women's movement but also within the Dalit movement. When they were

[21] Women born into the category of SCs, whether they are seen as lacking morals or not, are more exposed to crimes like rape than other women, due to their working circumstances, etc. For references to articles on SC women and rape, see, for example, Leslie Calman (1992: 141, note 8). For case studies regarding rape of SC women and laws regarding sexual abuses and rape, see, for example, Narula (1999: 166–78).

silenced they formed their own separate Dalit women networks–
a counterpublic within the Dalit counterpublic. Turning to Dalit
women's space in the public sphere I have given two examples
to show how they, when portrayed by others, have been exposed
by journalists imbued by patriarchal values.

DALIT FEMINISM BEYOND GENDER

Let me now return to my introductory discussion in this chapter.
During the twentieth century activists in the Dalit movement
have, within the anti-caste tradition of Ambedkar, deconstructed
an identity as untouchable and ritually impure. Gender
distinctions, on the other hand, were less important and subordinated to the religious worldview that the material bodies of
untouchable women and untouchable men were ritually unclean
in relation to others.

Dalit activists could be understood in line with Butler (1999),
to insist upon the legitimacy of their own human bodies. The
bodies of Dalit women and Dalit men have not only been
regarded as 'false, unreal, and unintelligible' (ibid.: xxiii), but
ritually impure. The ritual impurity of untouchables has been
a true, intelligible reality for others as well as SCs themselves.
In performativity, simply meaning in repetitive practices and
rituals, untouchability was created and recreated over
generations. Untouchability has further been effective through
its naturalization in the context of the body, understood as 'a
culturally sustained temporal duration' (Butler) or embodied
habitus, in line with Bordieu.

At the deepest level Butler understands women's liberation
as liberation *from* identity, since she views identity as inher-
ently oppressive, writes Fraser in a criticism. But, according to
Fraser, 'Feminists need both deconstruction and reconstruction,
destabilization of meaning and projection of utopian hope'
(Fraser 1997: 219, also quoted in John 2004a).[22]

What happens at a point in history when Dalit activists are
about to deconstruct an image of the material bodies of Dalit
women and Dalit men as impure and reconstruct it as human?

[22] For a related debate between Fraser and Butler, see Benhabib
et al. (1995).

In this chapter I have tried to point out how Dalit women, when reaching a political and economic position, may be accused of being immoral and thus deprived of constructing a so-called 'femininity'. Dalit men, on the other hand, are accused of economic irresponsibility in relation to their family, and thus deprived of creating a so-called 'masculinity'. To Dalit women and Dalit men, oppression becomes thus not a question about ascribed gender identities in a heteronormative society, in line with Butler. Let me suggest that the way Dalit women and Dalit men are not *ascribed* gender identities, but on the opposite *prevented from constructing* gender identities is related to a neoliberal economic order in the Indian society, where traditional gender roles are clearly defined. Cultural recognition becomes in this way entangled with economic position and at one and the same time undermined.[23]

Let me clarify. The World Bank, the Indian state, and international corporations agree that one solution to the economic problems for SCs in the Indian society is that 'poor women' enter the private sphere as entrepreneurs. Why 'poor women' and not 'poor men'? We have seen the implicit assumption to be that Dalit men are economically irresponsible in relation to their families. They are deprived of their economic, so-called male responsibility, and as a result they are devoid of constructing their masculinity associated with respect. Women are supported to enter the economic sphere, but when they on the other hand reach an economic and political position, like Mayawati, they are pictured as immoral and deprived of constructing a so-called femininity, valued and respected in the Indian society.

[23] For a related discussion about Dalit women domestic workers in Karnataka, analysed within Fraser's framework of recognition and redistributive claims for justice, see Chigateri (2007).

9

Dynamics of Diversity

INTERNALLY—WITHIN THE MOVEMENT

INTERNAL TENSIONS

We have seen different attempts to silence and distort the message of the Dalit activists when they try to direct it to an audience outside their own counterpublic, contesting the values of the 'most other', that is, 'the Hindu'. These interpublic conflicts may have the effect of distancing them even further from their opponents. I have argued that intrapublic tensions, on the other hand, among networks *within* the movement, may strengthen the Dalit identity, given the circumstances that there are already some formulated ideas and tacit knowledge (always in the process of being created anew and reformulated) about the 'most other'.

The reason is that communication between activists with different movement perspectives, arguing and debating among themselves, activates the networks of the Dalit counterpublic. This at the same time opens up the renewed possibility of repeating their common points of references. At the same time as the Dalit activists disagree on some points, it will be shown how their common points of references are agreed upon. Another way of expressing the same thing is to say that the discourses and tensions between different movement perspectives take place within the framework of the tacit knowledge regarding the 'most other', 'the Hindu'. Communication continues to take place between Dalit activists, daily in face-to-face interactions, more sporadically at meetings and conferences, in common festivals such as Ambedkar's birthday and death anniversary, via letters, in phone calls, over the Internet, in movement publications, etc. The internal tensions and conflicts between Dalit activists will thus be shown to have a part in upholding social relations within the counterpublic. When the dissociation from 'Hindu values' is constantly repeated and agreed upon over days, weeks, months, years, and decades, as has been the case within the Dalit movement, the tacit knowledge, I have demonstrated, will undoubtedly be strengthened. Their common points of references are further elaborated upon (parallel to the internal tensions), clarified, and developed into more refined ideas about the common Dalit identity and culture. The intrapublic tensions thus indirectly seem to strengthen a common Dalit identity.[1]

Internal tensions within the Dalit movement should, thus, be understood against the background of their historical tacit agreement. They agree, independent of movement perspective, on the point that they take a common stand in a principal conflict with the Hindus and with Hindu values. Perspectives are perspectives towards perspectives (Hannerz 1992a: 67), and 'some others are more other than others.'[2] That is to say that Dalit activists relate differently to the perspective of others. They agree that the 'Hindus' are 'more other' than any of those Dalit activists within the counterpublic who hold movement perspectives different from their own. We have found that the intrapublic tensions are, moreover, often related to the interpublic conflict, in the sense of being disputes about how best to be dissociated from an ascribed Hindu identity, the Hindu community, and Hindu values.

My argument has been that it is not *only* through the expressed main conflict in relation to 'the Hindus' that a Dalit identity is formulated. Tensions within the Dalit counterpublic, between activists with diverse movement perspectives, have been shown to contribute indirectly to the confirmation and refinement of the Dalit identity, which has been in the process of taking shape since the 1920s at least.[3] Regardless of the topics under discussion

---

[1] I do not mean to say that all intrapublic tensions and conflicts within social movements strengthen a common identity. My point is, rather, to repeat that the tacit knowledge among the activists must be taken into account in order to understand whether tensions in a movement will weaken or strengthen an identity.

[2] The expression was used by Appadurai (1986: 357) in a critical discussion of how anthropologists have related to the field.

[3] Cf. Fuchs (2000a: 17), who discusses identity formation as follows: '"Difference" does not mean something to be overcome, or something

between contemporary Dalit activists, the communicative occasions per se activate the networks in the movement, and simultaneously make it possible to repeat and confirm their common identity. This book has been an attempt to show how a broad-based and heterogeneous Dalit counterpublic is reproduced and kept alive.[4]

RELIGIOUS AND POLITICAL MESSAGES WITHIN

Having focused on the heterogeneity regarding movement perspectives, let me point out some of the similarities and shared points of references among Dalit activists, which form the common movement framework within which intrapublic tensions or debates take place. First of all, compared with the Hindu caste reform tradition, in which many activists are drawn from caste groups higher up in the status hierarchy, the activists within the Dalit movement come, almost exclusively, from among SCs. Furthermore, it is a movement led by these activists with the explicit aim of fundamentally transforming society and changing the circumstances for SCs. Caste and class membership often coincide among SCs, and a large proportion of SCs are urban workers or agricultural labourers and belong within the working class.[5]

Among the Dalit activists, though, many have experienced a 'class-journey' during their lifetime, in the sense of moving from the class membership of their parents and grandparents to an economic position better described as (educated) urban middle class (Saberwal 1990 [1976]). Their economic situations have,

---

that could in principle be overcome without destroying one or the other. Difference is aimed at mediation (at least it opens that possibility)— and yet it is in constant danger of being overemphasized through rigorous demarcation.'

[4] The aim of this study has neither been to trace the original formulation of a non-Hindu identity among the SCs (although I gave a historical context in Chapter 3), nor to discover the origin of an alternative counterpublic. My concern has rather been with the processes within the contemporary Dalit movement, in which some common understanding and tacit knowledge were already at work.

[5] For discussions about the relation between caste and class and the interrelation between social and economic processes see, for example, Omvedt 1994a; Sharma 1994; Molund 1988; Cederlöf 1997.

in many regards, changed for the better due to education and affirmative action, but they still feel discriminated against in more subtle ways. Endogamy is still, for example, a strong feature of Indian society, strictly followed by the majority of people. This means that, even though Dalit activists may have risen economically, endogamy—prescribing whom you may or may not marry—still excludes SCs in an important matter from the rest of society.

Looking at the content of the Dalit messages, we have seen how these, when expressed within the Dalit counterpublic, on local/regional, translocal, and transnational levels, have strong religious and political connotations and are explicitly directed against caste discrimination. The global discourses in cyberspace, such as those in the Dalit discussion groups on the Internet, are related to the religious/political discourses as well.

Taking a closer look at the content of the discourses within the counterpublic, some common elements are to be found across the spectra of movement perspectives. With regard to religion, the Dalit activists aim to be dissociated from Hindu religious values. I have examined some of the discourses among Ambedkarite Buddhists and also their relation to Ravidasis and Sikhism. The Ambedkarite Buddhists deplore the fact that the Ravidasis do not break completely with Hinduism to complete a commenced 'Sikhization', to use the concept introduced by Juergensmeyer. Further, I investigated the Dalit Christian theology and also gave some examples of how Dalit activists have emphasized their close relations with Muslims. Dalit activists have been shown, in their activities as well as in their rhetoric, to be favourably disposed towards all the main religions in India, namely Buddhism, Sikhism, Christianity, and Islam. The exception is of course Hinduism, from which they dissociate regardless of religious or political choice. It should be noted that the Dalit activists aim to be dissociated from Hinduism and the Hindu community, not from the wider Indian civil society, in which they want to be integrated on equal terms (see also Juergensmeyer 1982: 269ff).

Religious and political perspectives in the movement are closely fused together. At the same time as the activists dissociate themselves from Hindu values and a view that defines them as Hindu, they aim to change political and economic power relations. Activists with different movement perspectives jointly demand a political system in which the SCs are able to choose their own representatives, as supported by Ambedkar in relation to the Poona Pact. The right to land is a recurrent theme and, independent of movement perspective, Dalit activists have been involved in actions of forcibly seizing land and putting up statues of Ambedkar to mark plots of land to which they regard themselves as entitled.

Within the counterpublic Dalit activists are combining religious and political/economic messages—locally/regionally, translocally as well as transnationally and globally (on the Internet)—in an endeavour to transform Indian society. A comparison with liberation theology is close at hand, and has also been made by some researchers as well as by Dalit activists themselves. Dalit Buddhism has been compared with liberation theology (Omvedt 2001), and the same kind of comparison was made between Dalit (Christian) theology and liberation theology (Azariah 1989; Webster 1994; Clarke 1998).

This study has reinforced an analysis in this direction, first, by showing how Ambedkarite Buddhism, as well as Dalit (Christian) theology, are influenced as worldviews by socialist and Marxist ideals. Second, I have shown that local/regional and translocal Dalit Buddhist networks in northern India are organizationally fused with political Dalit networks related to the RPI, BSP, and also Janata Dal.[6] The Dalit activists in these networks condemn the Indian Marxist political parties, CPI and CPI(M), for being led by 'upper castes'.[7] The reason for their criticism, though, is not mainly ideological but is directed against the leadership in these political parties. I have demonstrated how the Dalit activists in the fused religious/political networks I dealt with in northern India, in different ways and contexts, expressed how they were influenced by socialist and often Marxist ideals, and also a vision to transform Indian society

[6] The transnational Dalit networks between northern India and Britain revealed a similar pattern.

[7] On the question as to why Ad Dharm did not support the Marxists in Punjab, Juergensmeyer received from a senior Chamar the answer: 'They are our class enemies'. Some contemporary Dalit activists explained their discontent with the political parties CPI and CPI(M) to me in the same vein.

totally. The Ambedkarite Buddhists dealt with in Britain were shown to be part transnationally of the same Dalit counterpublic. They belonged to the same organizational networks and took part in the same Dalit discourses. In their movement activities the Ambedkarite Buddhists in Britain to a large degree focused on the question of changing the circumstances of the SCs in India—transforming their country of origin.[8]

This is part of the story. To equate entirely the Dalit movement and liberation theology movements in Latin America would certainly not be correct. Networks within the Dalit movement fuse and divide, and there are Dalit activists who are not willing to subscribe to any kind of religion. They regard themselves as atheists or rationalists with no connection whatsoever with any religious ideals. The former BSP party leader Kanshi Ram was an example of this. Dalit activists with a religious interest may, for their part, show a minimum of interest in party-politics. This question is further complicated by the fact that the Dalit activists do not regard Ambedkarite Buddhism as a religion or theology. Buddhism is seen to be in consonance with a rationalist worldview, without belief in gods or any supernatural beings. In summary, what has been striking about the Dalit movement is, first of all, its diversity and second, the strong socialist and Marxist influence and also the explicit anti-Hindu, anti-Gandhi, and anti-Congress stand that permeates all the Dalit networks among which I carried out my fieldwork.

NATIONALLY AND INTERNATIONALLY—
RELATED TO THE INDIAN STATE AND THE UN

The discourses among Dalit activist were thus, in spite of their diversity, permeated by a surprisingly similar message, the reason being, as I have tried to show, that among themselves these discourses—locally/regionally, translocally (within India) as well as transnationally (between India and Britain) or globally

---

[8] Parallel local activities were also going on in Britain, as we have seen, which had more the character of congregational work, such as the building of a community centre, celebrating common holidays, etc. To be engaged in the betterment of others, transnationally, may involve different considerations regarding one's own status, etc.

(on the Internet)—take place within one and the same common counterpublic sphere. When directed to recipients outside the Dalit counterpublic, on the other hand, the message was changed. It was redesigned when transmitted between the different contexts. Depending on who the recipients (in actual interaction or imagined contact) were, different aspects of the message were emphasized. When the activists aimed to circulate their message and expand their networks and their field of activity outside their own counterpublic, it was sometimes deliberately redesigned, at other times forcibly changed or muted.[9]

When we move to the state-related context, the message of the NCDHR was expressed more in terms of a prevalent international cultural discourse of 'human rights' and less in political and religious terms. The Indian constitution was influenced by the human rights discourse to be seen in the UN Universal Declaration of Human Rights of 1948, and the NCDHR attached its own discourse to this broader international discourse and consequently also to the Indian constitution. The discourse was also to a large degree dissociated from the debate between Gandhi and Ambedkar, constantly referred to within the counterpublic. In relation to the state, the Dalit discourse was widened geographically so as to deal with human rights among Dalits, not only in India but also in other parts of Asia (and even in other parts of the world). Nevertheless, there were some remnants of the discourse within the counterpublic. Caste discrimination and Ambedkar were explicitly mentioned, but the debate between Ambedkar and Gandhi, or references to Dalit Panthers, were implicit and mainly to be read between the lines. The emotion talk, though, was still present, and the folders produced by the

[9] It should be noted that since the 1960s the counterpublic has been interlinked transnationally between India and Britain. When I talk here about an expansion of the field of activity, it has no geographical connotations, but refers to a field outside their own counterpublic, regardless of geographic locality. I also want to point out in this context that I differ from those who have dealt with transnational movements as part of a transnational public sphere (see, for example, Guidry, Kennedy, and Zald 2000). Instead, I consider the activities within the Dalit movement across state borders to be taking place mainly between private spheres transnationally or in a transnational counterpublic sphere (with webs to sympathizers in the public sphere).

campaign were explained as being 'our language of anger simmering in our hearts' (NCDHR 1999).

In the state-related and the international contexts Dalit women appear to hold a status position equal to that of Dalit men within the movement. But it should be remembered, as was shown in Chapter 8, that the movement is strongly imbued with patriarchal values.

Belausteguigoitia (2005) comments that the demands of the revolutionary women within the Zapatista movement in Mexico are silenced not only in the broader civil society, but also by a patriarchal structure within their own movement, which does not allow them to represent themselves. This feature is thus similarly to be found in the Dalit movement in India. Since the middle of the 1980s a counterpublic among Dalit women has grown from within the movement, as the women find themselves excluded by a patriarchal structure, not only on a local level but also on a national and international level.

In the beginning of the 2000s, Dalit women were taking a forefront position in, for example, the UN conference in Durban. In the long run, however, it seems that Dalit women, who want to collaborate with Dalit men, have failed in their attempts to represent themselves internationally. International conferences may include the problems of Dalit women, who participate in the role of testifying emotionally about their experiences of violence, prostitution etc. However, when it is not exclusively women's international conferences, Dalit women seldom represent themselves outside these roles internationally. They fail to get included, in the sense of putting the agenda or being elected or chosen to boards, committees, etc., in these contexts. When Dalit men turn international, they collaborate with men *and* women from 'the North'. But still Dalit women are often excluded from decision-making processes—not least from financial decisions.

GLOBALLY—IN THE GLOBAL JUSTICE MOVEMENT

DALITS IN THE WSF PROCESS

The annually held WSF, which offers an alternative to the World Economic Forum in Davos (Switzerland), has since its inception in 2001 drawn movement activists, intellectuals, musicians, artists, and others together under the slogan: 'Another world is possible.' Hundred thousands of people have attended the occasion every year and the number of participants has constantly increased. The international media and journalists have been attentive and curious.

However, in the WSF in Nairobi 2007, the number of participants decreased for the first time since in 2001. The WSF also seems to have lost some of its initial news-value to the journalists and media. Could these facts be interpreted as a sign that activists within the global justice movement have become passive lately? Immanuel Wallerstein (2007) notes, on the contrary, that participants in the WSF have moved from a loud but defensive stance, to a more active role. In 2001 they were loudly denouncing the World Bank, the WTO, and the IMF. Six years later, during WSF in Nairobi 2007 they were much more actively and explicitly 'creating a web of networks whose political clout will emerge in the next five to ten years'. The WSF process is not a once-in-a-year happening, but has become an ongoing process throughout the year among activists, keeping up communication across the globe.

Wallerstein has taken examples, in which one category of people with the same main focus is creating a web of networks transnationally. Feminists collaborate transnationally with a main focus on gender issues and agricultural labourers collaborate transnationally on the issue of land-rights, for example. Interestingly, however, activists with different main focuses have also begun to collaborate. Movements, with their specific and unique histories are now being related to each other by activists, within the broader context of what Hannerz (2007) has called 'the neoliberal culture complex'.

During my fieldwork in WSFs and during conferences, I have found that Dalit activists are now relating to other movement activists transnationally, in spite of varied focuses and in spite of involving diverse categories of people. One example are the networks between Dalit activists based in South Asia collaborating with activists in three other quite different movements: the agricultural labourers movement originating in Latin America represented by Via Campesina; the movement among urban homeless with a strong base in France represented by

No-Vox; and the Burakumin movement focused on indigenous people with its base in Japan represented by Buraku Liberation League.

Simultaneously with these collaborations, Dalit women now relate to broader alliances of women activists transnationally. We find two parallel processes going on among the Dalit networks: fusion and fission. On the one hand, the Dalit networks connect and fuse with other movement networks to create global networks. At the same time we find fission from within the movement, with Dalit women breaking away to form there own counterpublic in alliances with women globally.

By participating in WSFs and collaborating with women in other parts of the world, Dalit feminists have thus found a way to become more independent of the brahmani women's movement and also the patriarchal Dalit movement. They have begun to relate to the Dalit movement and the brahmani women's movement when needed and on their own premises.

WHY ARE DALITS SUDDENLY EVERYWHERE?

It may not be obvious what made Dalit activists, who are focused on such a unique and regionally specific question as caste discrimination in India, interested in or even able to relate to activists in other parts of the world. But they have rather easily found their way, often in a leading role, into the networks of the global justice movement.[10] The reasons are related to their historical experiences in India during the twentieth century, which I have dealt with throughout this volume and also elsewhere (Hardtmann 2005).

What circumstances have made Dalit activists extraordinary prepared to be active in these new alternative networks? Or, in other words, why are Indian Dalits suddenly everywhere? There may of course be many different answers to why they are well prepared to take an active part in the global justice movement, but let me for the sake of clarity conclude by briefly dwelling on

[10] Parts of the discussion in this section was published in a similar form in the article 'Les Dalits Indiens sont Soudainment Partout!— La création de nouveaux réseaux internationaux alternatifs' in *Anthropologie et Sociétés*, 29 (fn. 3), 2005: 97–122. The theme for the issue was Alterglobalization, edited by Manon Boulianne. For a related discussion see Peter (Jay) Smith 2008.

and summarizing five of the reasons, which should have become obvious through my earlier historical overview of the Dalit movement. Dalit activists have earlier experiences of (a) inter-relating and forming a counterpublic over vast geographical areas; (b) differentiating between interpublic and intrapublic conflicts; (c) using negative symbols internally and externally to their own benefits; (d) redesigning and contextualizing messages, from the local to the global levels; and (e) flexibly organizing and reorganizing movement networks.

First, Dalit activists have a historical experience of forming an alternative counterpublic over vast geographical areas: since the 1920s across India and since the 1950s and 1960s transnationally. To interrelate and keep up social relations in spite of geographical distances are certainly not something new to the Dalit activists. In their interrelations across India with all its different local languages, the leadership was forced to use English as their common language, which is now also one of the factors to facilitate their communication with other movement activists across the world. The Internet has certainly activated already existing Dalit networks and extended the Dalit counterpublic to cyberspace since the middle of the 1990s, but also more recently facilitated the process of creating new relations. Activists in social movements, geographically far away from each other, seem easily to find references for communication. In their interrelations the activists construct new shared understandings on the basis of shared circumstances (Hannerz 1992a: 153). The Internet becomes then an effective medium to share experiences and also the means to an extended transnational counterpublic in its making. The Internet brings new opportunities to everyone, but at the moment global activists seems to benefit more than their opponents (Van Aelst and Walgrave 2004: 121).

Second, the Dalit activists know how to debate and keep tensions going among heterogeneous networks regarding content and strategies, and to note, they know how to simultaneously keep a broader context in mind. They argue with a common horizon, sharing a tacit knowledge about their common exclusion from 'the others'. 'The other' has been those others related to the 'Hindu world', as I have shown. Among scholars the Indian caste system has often been regarded as culturally specific to the extent of not being able to be compared to any other phenomenon in the world. When the Dalit activists now put their experiences of the caste system in terms of social and ritual exclusion and economic exploitation and not in terms of ritual interdependence and occupational harmonious exchange (Dumont 1980[1966]), it becomes more obvious how and why they relate to other movement activists outside of India.

In 1991 India implemented far-reaching reforms in the direction of market liberalization and privatization of the Indian public sector. The Dalit activists have more recently put the development of the Indian economy in the light of their broader understanding of the roles played by the World Bank, WTO, and IMF for the countries' internal economic policies. They now put caste discrimination and economic inequalities in the context of economic globalization. In the local Indian context 'the other' may be associated with the 'Hindu world', but in an international context 'the other' is now also institutions associated with 'economic globalization'. The Dalit activists know how to differentiate in an Indian context between interpublic and intrapublic conflicts. They now bring these experiences into new global arenas in which the heterogeneity among movement activists in, for example, the WSFs is huge, including landless labourers, environmentalists, sexual minorities, and ethnically discriminated minorities from across the world.

Third, the Dalit activists have the experiences of making use of negative symbols. Anti-Gandhism could never attract the world audience, among whom Gandhi is rather positively associated with non-violence and resistance against colonialism. In an Indian religious and political context, however, Gandhi as a negative symbol has been a reference for discussions and also a bridge between differences internally. On the other hand, negative symbols may also be used to highlight frontiers in relation to 'the others'—it may be Gandhians or propagators of the World Bank, IMF, and WTO—who threaten to blur boundaries by putting their discourses in similar frameworks about human rights, democracy, and economic equality as the movement activists, without sharing their basic values.

Fourth, it seems that Dalit activists have become experts in flexibility over the years and know how to put the elasticity of networks into practical use. They are rather experienced in contextualizing their messages when organizing on different levels, depending on real or imagined recipients, from the local level to regional level, and further to the national level in relation to the Indian government. Outside their own counter-public, they have always restricted their use of Gandhi as an anti-symbol in the Indian context. In an international context they have chosen to put their demands in the international language of, for example, human rights. The concept of 'caste discrimination', with its specific Indian connotations, has in relation to the UN been translated in terms of 'discrimination based on work and descent', which is applicable to many different categories of people, not only in India, but all over the world. The activities in the movement are also carried out simultaneously on different levels.

Finally, the organizational structure of the Dalit movement is flexible and constantly changing, which makes the movement difficult to suppress. It is a movement guided by innumerable leaders, where none could claim to be the one and sole leader. Fissions and fusions in the networks are constantly taking place and activists cross back and forth between networks, often taking part in more than one group or organization. The organizational structure also allows for mobilization within a broad spectrum of political, religious, and cultural groups and organizations. The Dalit activists, as Escobar has commented in another context, further '[...] rely on an ongoing tacking back and forth between cyberpolitics and place politics—that is, between political activism in the internet [...] and activism in the physical location in which the networkers sit and live' (Escobar 2001: 167).[11] It seems that transnational social movements are more able than ever before to challenge the process of neoliberal economic globalization with the help of new ICTs[12] and in particular the Internet (Ribeiro 1998; Smith and Smythe 1999: 84, Smythe and Smith 2002: 50, Smith 2004, Van Aelst and Walgrave 2004).

[11] Anthropologists have shown that communication in cyberspace is best understood not in contrast to but rather as embedded in other social spaces. It is possible to transform these mundane social structures and relations, but not to escape them (Miller and Slater 2000: 5, also quoted in Wilson and Peterson 2002: 453; Uimonen 2001).

[12] Information and communications technologies.

The organizational aspects of the Dalit movement seems to fit well with the overarching alter-globalization networks, which is similarly impossible to overview: heterogeneous, directed by uncountable numbers of leaders, fission and fusion constantly taking place, activists crossing back and forth between different networks or even being active in many networks simultaneously (cf. Escobar 2004: 352ff; Waterman 2004: 55ff; Smith *et al.* 2008).

Out of new interrelations between activists in various movements, heterogeneous and dynamic network of networks seems to emerge, or meshworks, which 'grow in unplanned directions, following the real-life situations they encounter' (Escobar 2004: 352). This may be one of the reasons to why the challenge now looks different. We witness the many-headed hydra, in the words of Gerlach and Hine (1970a), on a global scale.

Dalit activists are part of these global processes. An identity as 'untouchable' and 'impure' has not only been deconstructed during the twentieth century, but an identity has through performativity also been reconstructed—now as Dalit—with a 'projection of utopian hope', in terms of Fraser.[13] When Dalit activists relate to others within the diverse global justice movement, economic problems and traditional gender roles are not only discussed as individual problems or problems within the household. It is understood within a broader context of international power relations.

Differences among activists are discussed and tensions may arise and be reflected upon. Transnational collaborations within the global justice movement seem to be more a matter of frictions, mutual respect and situational support than an all-inclusive harmonious merging of networks. Dalit activists uphold their unique identities and contribute to the global justice movement with their own specific historical experiences. At the same time they support and take the support of others in similar situations. When silenced, however, activists may do as the Dalit feminists did, make a crack from within to form a new counterpublic. This is the dynamics of diversity.

[13] It should be remembered that we have throughout this volume been talking more specifically about Dalit activists and not about the broader general category of SCs.

Bibliography

Ahir, D.C. 1992. *Dr Ambedkar and Punjab*. Delhi: B.R. Publishing Corporation.

Alvarez, Sonia E. 1997. 'Reweaving the Fabric of Collective Action: Social Movements and Challenges to Actually Existing Democracy in Brazil'. In Richard Fox and Orin Starn (eds), *Between Resistance and Revolution—Cultural Politics and Social Protest*. New Brunswick, NJ and London: Rutgers University Press.

———. 1998a. 'Latin American Feminisms "Go Global": Trends of the 1990s and Challenges for the New Millenium'. In Sonia E. Alvarez, Eveliva Dagnino, and Arturo Escobar (eds), *Cultures of Politics, Politics of Cultures: Revisioning Latin American Social Movements*. Boulder, Co. and Oxford: Westview Press.

———. 2000. 'Translating the Global: Effects of Transnational Organizing on Local Feminist Discourses and Practices in Latin America'. *Global Solidarity Dialogue*. http://www.antenna.nl/~waterman/alvarez.html.

Alvarez, Sonia. E., Evelina Dagnino, and Arturo Escobar (eds). 1998. *Cultures of Politics, Politics of Cultures: Revisioning Latin American Social Movements*. Boulder, CO and Oxford: Westview Press.

———. 1998b. 'Introduction: The Cultural and the Political in Latin American Social Movements'. In Sonia E. Alvarez, Evelina Dagnino, and Arturo Escobar (eds). *Cultures of Politics, Politics of Cultures: Re-visioning Latin American Social Movements*. Boulder, CO and Oxford: Westview Press.

Ambedkar, B.R. 1979 [1936]. *Dr Babasaheb Ambedkar, Writings and Speeches*, Vol. 1: *The Annihilation of Caste*. (Compiled by Vasant Moon). Bombay: Education Department, Government of Maharashtra.

———. 1987a. *Babasaheb Ambedkar, Writings and Speeches*, Vol. 3. (Unpublished writings, compiled by Vasant Moon). Bombay: Education Department, Government of Maharashtra.

———. 1987b. *Dr Babasaheb Ambedkar, Writings and Speeches*, Vol. 4: *Riddles in Hinduism* (Unpublished writings, compiled by Vasant Moon). Bombay: Education Department, Government of Maharashtra.

———. 1990 [1947]. *Dr Babasaheb Ambedkar, Writings and Speeches,* Vol. 7 (Compiled by Vasant Moon). Bombay: Education Department, Government of Maharashtra.

———. 1991a [1945]. *Dr Babasaheb Ambedkar, Writings and Speeches,* Vol. 9: *What Congress and Gandhi have done to the Untouchables.* (Compiled by Vasant Moon). Bombay: Education Department, Government of Maharashtra.

———. 1991b [1957]. *The Buddha and His Dhamma.* Bombay: Siddharth Publication.

———. 1994. *Dr Babasaheb Ambedkar, Writings and Speeches,* Vol. 13. (Compiled by Vasant Moon). Bombay: Education Department, Government of Maharashtra.

Amin, Shahid and Dipesh Chakrabarty (eds). 1996. *Subaltern Studies IX—Writings on South Asian History and Society.* Oxford: Oxford University Press.

Anand, Mulk Raj and Eleanor Zelliot (eds). 1992. *An Anthology of Dalit Literature (Poems).* New Delhi: Gyan Publishing House.

Appadurai, Arjun. 1986. 'Theory in Anthropology: Center and Periphery', *Comparative Studies in Society and History,* 28: 356–61.

———. 1990. 'Topographies of the Self: Praise and Emotions in Hindu India'. In Catherine Lutz and Lila Abu-Lughod (eds). 1990. *Language and the Politics of Emotion.* Cambridge: Cambridge University Press.

———. 2002. 'Deep Democracy: Urban Governmentality and the Horizon of Politics'. *Public Culture,* 14(1): 21–47.

Arnold, David and David Hardiman (eds). 1994. *Subaltern Studies VIII, Essays in Honour of Ranajit Guha.* Oxford: Oxford University Press.

Ayrookuzhiel, A.M. Abraham. 1988. 'Dalit Theology: A Movement of Counter-Culture'. In M.E. Prabhakar (ed.), *Towards a Dalit Theology.* Delhi: ISPCK.

Azariah, Masilamani. 1988. 'The Church's Healing Ministry to Dalits'. In M.E. Prabhakar (ed.), *Towards a Dalit Theology.* Delhi: ISPCK.

———. 1989. *Mission in Christ's Way in India Today.* Madras: The Christian Literature Society.

Ballard, Roger (ed.). 1994. *Desh Pardesh—The South Asian Presence in Britain.* London: Hurst & Company.

Balley, L.R. 1990. 'Introductory Note'. In B.R. Ambedkar, *State Socialism.* Jalandhar: Bheem Patrika Publicaions.

Barker, Colin, Alan Johnson, and Michael Lavalette (eds). 2001. *Leadership and Social Movements.* Manchester and New York: Manchester University Press.

Barnes. 1954. 'Class and Committees in a Norwegian Island Parish'. *Human Relations,* 7: 39–58.

Barth, Fredrik. 1992. 'Towards Greater Naturalism in Conceptualizing Society'. In Adam Kuper (ed.), *Conceptualising Societies*. London and New York: Routledge.

Bartholomew, Amy and Margit Mayer. 1992. 'Nomads of the Present: Melucci's Contribution to "New Social Movement" Theory' [review article]. *Theory, Culture and Society*, 9: 141–59.

Bateson, Gregory. 1972. *Steps to an Ecology of Mind*. New York: Ballantine Books. Rpt with a forward by Mary Catherine Bateson. 2000. Chicago: Chicago University Press.

Bayly, Susan. 1999. *Caste, Society and Politics in India from the Eighteenth Century to the Modern Age*. Cambridge: Cambridge University Press.

Belausteguigoitia Rius. 2005. 'Zapatista Women: Place-based Struggles and the Search for Autonomy'. In Wendy Harcourt and Arturo Escobar (eds), *Women and the Politics of Place*. Bloomfield: Kumarian Press.

Benhabib, Seyla, Judith Butler, Drucilla Cornell, and Nancy Fraser (eds). 1995. *Feminist Contentions: A Philosophical Exchange (Thinking Gender)*. New York: Routledge.

Berg, Dag Erik. 2007. 'Sovereignties, the World Conference against Racism 2001 and the Formation of a Dalit Human Rights Campaign.' In *Questions de Recherche/Research in Question*, No. 20, April.

Berkovitch, Nitza. 1999. 'The Emergence and Transformation of the International Women's Movement'. In John Boli and George H. Thomas (eds), *Constructing World Culture: International Nongovernmental Organizations since 1875*. Stanford, California: Stanford University Press.

Betlem, Hester. 'Between Two Movements: The Emergence of a Dalit Women's Liberation Movement'. http://www.dalitusa.org.

Béteille, André. 2001. 'Race and Caste', *The Hindu*, 10 March.

Bob, Clifford. 2007. '"Dalit Rights are Human Rights": Caste Discrimination, International Activism, and the Construction of a new Human Rights Issue'. *Human Rights Quarterly*, 29: 169–93.

Boli, John and George M. Thomas (eds). 1999. *Constructing World Culture: International Nongovernmental Organizations since 1875*. Stanford, California: Stanford University Press.

Bourdieu, Pierre. 1977. *Outline of Theory of Practice*. Cambridge: Cambridge University Press.

Briggs, Georg W. 1995 [1920]. *The Chamars*. Calcutta: Association Press.

Brockington. 1985. *The Sacred Thread: Hinduism in its Continuity and Diversity*. Edinburgh: Edinburgh University Press.

Brown Thompson, Karen. 2002. 'Women's Rights Are Human Rights'. In Sanjeev Khagram James V. Riker, and Kathryn Sikkink (eds), *Restructuring World Politics: Transnational Social Movements,*

Networks and Norms. Minneapolis and London: University of Minnesota Press.

Buhler, G. (ed.). 2004. *The Laws of Manu*. New Delhi: Cosmo Publications.

Butler, Judith. 1999. *Gender Trouble: Feminism and the Subversion of Identity*. New York and London: Routledge.

Calhoun, Craig (ed.). 1992. *Habermas and the Public Sphere*. Cambridge, MA and London: MIT Press.

Calman, Leslie J. 1992. *Toward Empowerment: Women and Movement Politics in India*. San Fransisco: Westview Press.

Carroll, Lucy. 1975. 'Caste, Social Change, and the Social Scientist: A Note on the Ahistorical Approach to Indian Social History', *Journal of Asian Studies*, 35: 63–84.

————. 1978. 'Colonial Perceptions of Indian Society and the Emergence of Caste(s) Associations', *Journal of Asian Studies*, 37: 233–50.

Castells, Manuel. 1996. *The Information Age. Economy, Society and Culture*. Vol. 1: *The Rise of the Network Society*. Oxford: Blackwell Publishers.

Cederlöf, Gunnel. 1997. *Bonds Lost. Subordination, Conflict and Mobil-isation in Rural South India c.1900–1979*. New Delhi: Manohar.

Charsley, Simon R. and G.K. Karanth. 1998. *Challenging Untouchability: Dalit Initiative and Experience from Karnataka*. New Delhi, Thousand Oaks, and London: Sage Publications.

Chatterjee, Partha and Gyanendra Pandey (eds). 1992. *Subaltern Studies VII, Writings on South Asian History and Society*. Oxford: Oxford University Press.

Chatterji, Saral K. 1988. 'Why Dalit Theology'. In M.E. Prabhakar (ed.), *Towards a Dalit Theology*. Delhi: ISPCK.

Chaudhuri, Maitrayee (ed.). 2004. *Feminism in India*. New Delhi: Kali for Women.

Chigateri, S. 2007. 'Articulations of Injustice and the Recognition-Redistribution Debate: Locating Caste, Class and Gender in Paid Domestic Work in India'. *Law, Social Justice and Global Development Journal* (LGD), 1.

Christopher, Rowland (ed.). 2007. *The Cambridge Companion to Liberation Theology*. Cambridge: Cambridge University Press.

Clarke, Jocelyn. 1988. 'Caste, Untouchability and the Indian Nationalist Movement'. Paper presented at the 15th European Conference on Modern South Asian Studies, 8–12 September, Charles University, Prague.

Clifford, James. 1997. *Routes: Travel and Translation in the Late Twentieth Century*. Cambridge, MA and London: Harvard University Press.

Cohen, Jean L. 1985. 'Strategy or Identity: New Theoretical Paradigms and Contemporary Social Movements', *Social Research*, 52(4) (winter).

Cone, James H. 1970. *A Black Theology of Liberation*. Philadelphia and New York: J.B. Lippincott Company.

Crossley, Nick. 2002. *Making Sense of Social Movements*. Philadelphia: Open University Press.

Dagnino, Evelina. 1998. 'Culture, Citizenship and Democracy: Changing Discourses and Practices of the Latin American Left'. In Sonia E. Alvarez, Evelina Dagnino and Arturo Escobar (eds), *Cultures of Politics, Politics of Cultures: Re-visioning Latin American Social Movements*. Boulder, CO and Oxford: Westview Press.

Dangle, Arjun (ed.). 1992a. *No Entry for the New Sun: Translations from Modern Marathi Dalit Poetry*. Bombay: Orient Longman.

———. (ed.) 1992b. *Poisoned Bread—Translations from Modern Marathi Literature*. Bombay: Orient Longman.

Das, Bhagwan and James Massey (eds). 1995. *Dalit Solidarity*. Delhi: ISPCK.

Davis, Joseph E. (ed.). 2002. *Stories of Change—Narrative and Social Movements*. New York: State University of New York Press.

Delanty, Gerard. 1997. *Social Science: Beyond Constructivism and Realism*. Minneapolis: University of Minnesota Press.

DeLillo, D. 1984. *White Noise*. New York: Penguin.

della Porta, Donatella, and Kriese, Hanspeter (eds). 1999. *Social Movements in a Globalizing World*. London: Macmillan Press.

della Porta, Donatella, Massimiliano Andretta, Lorenzo Mosca, and Herbert Reiter (eds). 2006. *Globalization from Below: Transnational Activists and Protest Networks*. Minneapolis and London: University of Minnesota Press.

Divakar, Paul, Peter Prove and James Massey. 2002. 'Post Durban Reflections I–III', *Dalit International Newsletter*, 7(1), February.

Dhanagare, D.N and J. John. 1988. 'Cyclical Movements Toward the "Eternal"'. *Economic and Political Weekly*, 21 May.

Dhawan, S.K. 1991. *Dr B.R. Ambedkar: A Select Profile*. Delhi: Wave Publications.

Dolas, Avinash. 1995. 'Dalit Women and the Women's Movement in India'. In P.G. Jogdand (ed.), *Dalit Women in India: Issues and Perspectives*. New Delhi: Gyan Publishing House.

Doniger, Wendy and Brian K. Smith (trans.). 1991. *The Laws of Manu*. New York: Penguin.

Dumont, L. *Homo Hierarchicus*. 1980 [1966]. Chicago and London: University of Chicago Press.

Eschle, Catherine. 2001. *Global Democracy, Social Movements, and Feminism*. Boulder and Oxford: Westview Press.

Escobar, Arturo and Sonia E. Alvarez (eds). 1992. *The Making of Social Movements in Latin America—Identity, Strategy and Democracy*. San Francisco: Westview Press.

Escobar, Arturo. 1992. 'Culture, Practice and Politics—Anthropology and the Study of Social Movements'. *Critique of Anthropology*. 12(4): 395–432. London, Newbury Park and New Delhi: Sage Publications.

————. 2001. 'Culture Sits in Places: Reflections on Globalism and Subaltern Strategies of Localization', *Political Geography*, 20: 139–74.

————. 2004. 'Other Worlds are (Already) Possible: Self-organisation, Complexity, and Post-Capitalist Cultures'. In Jai Sen, Anita Anand, Arturo Escobar and Peter Waterman (eds), *Challenging Empires*. New Delhi: Viveka Foundation.

Eyerman, Ron and Andrew Jamison. 1991. *Social Movements. A Cognitive Approach*. Cambridge: Polity Press.

Felski, Rita. 1989. *Beyond Feminist Aesthetics*. Cambridge: Harvard University Press.

Forbes, Geraldine H. 1984 [1979]. 'The Women's Movement in India: Traditional Symbols and New Roles'. In M.S.A. Rao (ed.), *Social Movements in India: Studies in Peasant, Backward Classes. Sectarian, Tribal and Women's Movements*. New Delhi: Manohar.

Foucault. 1972. *The Archaeology of Knowledge and the Discourse of Language*. New York: Pantheon.

Fox, Richard G. 1967. 'Resiliency and Change in the Indian Caste System: The Umar of U.P.', *Journal of Asian Studies*, 26: 575–87.

————. 1970. 'Avatars of Indian Research', *Comparative Studies in Society and History*, 12: 59–72.

Fox, Richard G. and Orin Starn. 1997. *Between Resistance and Revolution: Cultural Politics and Social Protest*. New Brunswick, NJ and London: Rutgers University Press.

Fraser, Nancy. 1992. 'Rethinking the Public Sphere: A Contribution to the Critique of Actually Existing Democracy'. In Craig Calhoun (ed.), *Habermas and the Public Sphere*. Cambridge, MA and London: MIT Press.

————. 1997. *Justice Interruptus: Critical Reflections on the Postsocialist Condition*. New York: Routledge.

Fuchs, Martin. 1999. *Kamp um Differenz. Repräsentation, Subjektivität and soziale Bewegungen—Das Beispiel Indien*. Frankfurt: Suhrkamp.

————. 2000a. 'The Universality of Culture: Reflection, Interaction and the Logic of Identity.' *Thesis Eleven*, 60: 11–22, February.

————. 2000b. 'Articulating the World: Social Movements, the Self-Transcendence of Society and the Question of Culture.' *Thesis Eleven*, 61: 65–85.

————. 2001. 'A Religion for Civil Society? Ambedkar's Buddhism, the Dalit Issue and the Imagination of Emergent Possibilities'. In Vasudha Dalmia, Angelika Malinar, and Martin Christof (eds), *Charisma and Canon: Essays on the Religious History of the Indian Subcontinent*. New Delhi: Oxford University Press.

Fuchs, Martin. 2004. 'Buddhism and Dalitness: Dilemmas of Religious Emancipation'. In Surendra Jondhale and Johannes Beltz (eds), *Reconstructing the World: B.R. Ambedkar and Buddhism in India*. New Delhi: Oxford University Press, pp. 283–300.

Galanter, Marc. 1991 [1984]. *Competing Equalities—Law and Backward Classes in India*. Delhi: Oxford University Press.

Gandhi, M.K. 1969a. 'Extract from S.D. Nadkarni's letter 17/11 1927', *The Collected Works of Mahatma Gandhi*. New Delhi: The Publication Division, Ministry of Information and Broadcasting, Government of India.

————. 1969b [1927]. 'Young India 17/11 1927'. *The Collected Works of Mahatma Gandhi*. New Delhi: The Publication Division, Ministry of Information and Broadcasting, Government of India.

————. 1972 [1932]. 'Letter to Ramsay MacDonald, 9 September 1932', *The Collected Works of Mahatma Gandhi*. New Delhi: The Publication Division, Ministry of Information and Broadcasting, Government of India.

————. 1976a [1936]. 'Dr Ambedkar's Indictment I', *The Collected Works of Mahatma Gandhi*. New Delhi: The Publication Division, Ministry of Information and Broadcasting, Government of India.

————. 1976b [1936]. 'Dr Ambedkar's Indictment II', *The Collected Works of Mahatma Gandhi*. New Delhi: The Publication Division, Ministry of Information and Broadcasting, Government of India.

————. 1976 [1936–7]. 'Harijan', *The Collected Works of Mahatma Gandhi*. New Delhi: The Publication Discussion, Ministry of Information and Broadcasting, Government of India, 64 (3 November 1936–14 March 1937).

Garsten, Christina. 1994. *Apple World: Core and Periphery in a Transnational Organizational Culture*. Stockholm Studies in Social Anthropology, 33. Stockholm: Almqvist & Wiksell International.

Genberg, Daniel. 2002. 'Public Space Inside Out: Beirut's Private and Public Spaces Under Reconstruction'. In Eva Poluha and Mona Rosendahl (eds), *Contesting 'Good' Governance: Crosscultural perspectives on Representation, Accountibility and Public Space*. London and New York: Routledge Curzon.

Gerlach, Luther P. and Virginia H. Hine. 1970a. *People, Power and Change—Movements of Social Transformation*. Indianapolis and New York: Bobbs-Merrill Company.

————. 1970b. 'The Social Organization of a Movement of Revolutionary Change: Case Study, Black Power'. In Norman E., Whitten Jr and John F. Szwed (eds), *Afro-American Anthropology*. New York: Free Press.

Gingrich, Andre and Richard G. Fox. (eds). 2002. *Anthropology, by Comparison*. London and New York: Routledge.

Gladstone, J.W. 1988. 'Christian Missionaries and Caste in Kerala.' In M.E. Prabhakar (ed.), *Towards a Dalit Theology*. Delhi: ISPCK.

Gopinath, M. and Pramod K. Kureel (eds). 1999. *Rulers Alone Can Create Casteless Society*. Bangalore: BSP.

Gore, M.S. 1993. *The Social Context of an Ideology: Ambedkar's Political and Social Thought*. New Delhi, Thousand Oaks, and London: Sage Publications.

Government of India. 1980. 'Police and the Weaker Sections of Society', Chapter XIX, in *Third Report of the National Police Commission*. New Delhi.

Graham, Mark and Shahram Khosravi. 2002. 'Reordering Public and Private in Iranian Cyberspace: Identity, Politics, and Mobilization', *Identities: Global Studies in Culture and Power*, 9: 219–46.

Gramsci, Antonio. 1971. *Selections from the Prison Notebooks*. Quentin Hoare and Geoffrey Noel Smith (eds and trans). New York: International Publishers.

Guha, Ranajit (ed.). 1982–9. *Subaltern Studies I–VI, Writings on South Asian History and Society*. Oxford: Oxford University Press.

Guidry, John A, Michael D. Kennedy, and Mayer N. Zald (eds). 2000. *Globalizations and Social Movements: Culture, Power and the Transnational Public Sphere*. Ann Arbor: University of Michigan Press.

Gupta, Akhil and James Ferguson (eds). 1997. 'Discipline and practice: "the field" as site, method and location in anthropology' *Anthropological Locations: Boundaries and Grounds of a Field Science*. Berkeley and Los Angeles: University of California Press.

————. (eds). 2001 [1997]. *Culture, Power, Place: Explorations in Critical Anthropology*. Durham, NC and London: Duke University Press.

Gupta, Dipankar. 2000. *Interrogating Caste–Understanding Hierarchy and Difference in Indian Society*. New Delhi: Penguin Books.

————. 2001. 'Caste, Race, Politics'. In *Seminar*, 'Exclusion–A Symposium on Caste, Race and the Dalit Question', 508, December.

Gupta, P.K. 1991. *The Scheduled Caste and Scheduled Tribes (Prevention of Atrocities Act, 1989)*. Lucknow: Eastern Book Company.

Guru, Gopal. 1991. 'Hinduisation of Ambedkar in Maharashtra', *Economic and Political Weekly*, 26(7), 16 February, pp. 339–41.

————. 1992. 'Review of Dalit-Panther Movement in Maharashtra by Lata Murugkar', *Contribution to Indian Sociology*, 26(2).

————. 1995. 'Dalit Women Talk Differently'. *Economic and Political Weekly*. October, pp. 2548–2630.

Gusterson, Hugh. 1996. *Nuclear Rites: A Weapons Laboratory at the End of the Cold War.* Berkeley/Los Angeles/London: University of California Press.

————. 1997. 'Studying up Revisited', *Political and Legal Anthropology Review*, 20(1):114–19.

Gutiérrez, Gustavo. 1973. *A Theology of Liberation*. Maryknoll, NY: Orbis Books.

Habermas, Jürgen. 1981. 'New Social Movements', *Telos*, vol. 49 (Fall): 33–7.

————. 1989 [1981]. *The Theory of Communicative Action*, vol. 2. Boston, MA: Beacon Press.

————. 1992. 'Further Reflections on the Public Sphere'. In Craig Calhoun (ed.), *Habermas and the Public Sphere*. Cambridge, MA and London: MIT Press.

————. 1994. 'Three Normative Models of Democracy', *Constellations*, 1(1): 1–10.

Hannerz, Ulf. 1980. *Exploring the City*. New York: Columbia University Press.

————. 1989. 'Notes on the Global Ecumene', *Public Culture*, 1(2): 66–75.

————. 1992a. *Cultural Complexity: Studies in the Social Organization of Meaning*. New York: Columbia University Press.

————. 1992b. 'The Global Ecumene as a Network of Networks'. In Adam Kuper (ed.), *Conceptualising Societies*. London: Routledge.

————. 1998. 'Transnational Research'. In H. Russell Bernard (ed.), *Handbook of Methods in Cultural Anthropology*. London: Altamira Press.

————. (ed.). 2001. *Flera Fält i Ett—Socialantropologer om Translokala Fältstudier*. Stockholm: Carlsson bokförlag.

————. 2003. 'Being there…and there…and there!—Reflections on multi-site ethnography', *Ethnography*, 4(2): 229–44.

————. 2007. 'The Neo-liberal Culture Complex and Universities: A case for Urgent Anthropology?' *Anthropology Today*, 23(5).

Harcourt, Wendy (ed.). 2000. *Women@Internet: Creating New Cultures in Cyberspace*. London and New York: Zed Books.

Harcourt, Wendy and Arturo Escobar (eds). 2005. *Women and the Politics of Place*. Bloomfield: Kumarian Press.

Hardt, Michael and Antonio Negri. 2004. *Multitude: War and Democracy in the Age of Empire*. New York: The Penguin Press.

Hardtmann, Eva-Maria. 2005. 'Les Dalits Indiens sont Soudainement Partout! La création de nouveaux réseaux internationaux alternatifs', *Anthropologie et Sociétés*, 29(3): 97–122.

Hasan, Zoya. 1998. *Quest for Power—Oppositional Movements and Post-Congress Politics in Uttar Pradesh*. Delhi: Oxford University Press.

Hastrup, Kirsten and Karen Fog Olwig. 1997. 'Introduction'. In Karen Fog Olwig and Kirsten Hastrup (eds), *Siting Culture*. London: Routledge.

Heimsath, Charles H. 1978. 'The Function of Hindu Social Reformers—With Special References to Kerala'. *The Indian Economic and Social History Review*, 15(1): 21–39.

Hellman, Eva. 1993. *Political Hinduism: The Challenge of the Visva Hindu Parisad*. Uppsala: Department of Religion, Uppsala University.

Ilaiah, Kancha. 1996a. *Why I am not a Hindu*. Calcutta: Samya.

———. 1996b. 'Productive Labour, Consciousness and History: The Dalitbahujan Alternative'. In Shahid Amin and Dipesh Chakrabarty (eds), *Subaltern Studies IX—Writings on South Asian History and Society*. Oxford: Oxford University Press.

———. 1997. 'The God of Little Men'. (Review of *Worshipping False Gods* by Arun Shourie) *Biblio,* November.

Inkinen. Magdalena. 2003. *Mobilising the Lower Castes: The Rise of the Bahujan Samaj Party in India*. Uppsala: Department of Government, Uppsala University.

Jaffrelot Christophe. 2003. *India's Silent Revolution: The Rise of the Low Castes in North Indian Politics*. Delhi: Permanent Black.

———. 2004. *Dr Ambedkar and Untouchability—analyzing and Fighting Caste*. New Delhi: Permanent Black.

Jeffery, Roger and Jens Lerche (eds). 2003. *Social and Political Change in Uttar Pradesh: European Perspectives*. New Delhi: Manohar.

Jeffrey, Robin. 2000. *India's Newspaper Revolution: Capitalism, Politics and the Indian-Language Press 1977–99*. Delhi: Oxford University Press.

Jogdand. P.G. (ed.). 1995. *Dalit Women in India: Issues and Perspectives*. New Delhi: Gyan Publishing House.

John, Mary E. 2004a. 'Feminism in India and the West: Recasting a Relationship'. In Maitrayee Chaudhuri (ed.), *Feminism in India*. New Delhi: Kali for Women.

———. 2004b. 'Gender and Development in India, 1970–90s: some reflections on the constitutive role of contexts'. In Maitrayee Chaudhuri (ed.), *Feminism in India*. New Delhi: Kali for Women.

Jondhale, Surendra. 1995. 'Theoretical Underpinning of Emancipation of Dalit Women'. In P.G. Jogdand (ed.), *Dalit Women in India: Issues and Perspectives*. New Delhi: Gyan Publishing House.

Juergensmeyer, Mark. 1982. *Religion as Social Vision: The Movement against Untouchability in the 20th Century Punjab*. Berkeley/Los Angeles/London: University of California Press.

Kappen, S. 1986. *Liberation Theology and Marxism*. Ahmedanagar District: Ajit Muricken, p. 126.

Karlsson, B.G. 1997. *Contested Belonging: An Indigenous People's Struggle for Forest and Identity in Sub-Himalayan Bengal*, Lund Monographs in Social Anthropology. Lund: Department of Sociology, Lund University.

Keane, John (ed.). 1988. *Civil Society and the State*. London: Verso.

Keck, Margaret. E. and Kathryn Sikkink. 1998. 'Transnational Advocacy Networks in the Movement Society'. In David S. Meyer and Sidney Tarrow (eds), *The Social Movement Society: Contentious Politics for a New Century*. Lanham, MD, Boulder, CO, New York and Oxford: Rowman & Littlefield Publishers.

Keer, Dhananjay. 1990 [1954]. *Dr Ambedkar, Life and Mission*. Bombay: Popular Prakashan.

Khagram, Sanjeev, James V. Riker, and Kathryn Sikkink (eds). 2002. *Restructuring World Politics: Transnational Social Movements, Networks and Norms*. Minneapolis and London: University of Minnesota Press.

Khare, R.S. 1984. *The Untouchable as Himself: Ideology, Identity, and Pragmatism among the Lucknow Chamars*. Cambridge: Cambridge University Press.

Kothari, Rajni. 1970. 'Introduction'. In Rajni Kothari (ed.), *Caste in Indian Politics*. New Delhi: Orient Longman.

Kothari, Rajni and Rushikesh Maru. 1970. 'Federating for Political Interests: The Kshatriyas of Gujarat'. In Rajni Kothari (ed.), *Caste in Indian Politics*. New Delhi: Orient Longman.

Kuklick, Henrika. 1997. 'After Ishmael: The Fieldwork Tradition and Its Future'. In Akhil Gupta and James Ferguson (eds), *Anthropological Locations: Boundaries and Grounds of a Field Science*. Berkeley and Los Angeles: University of California Press.

Larsson, Marie. 2006. '*When Women Unite!'—The Making of the Anti-Liquor Movement in Andhra Pradesh*. Stockholm: Stockholm Studies in Social Anthropology, no. 60.

Latour, Bruno. 1996. 'The trouble with Actor-Network Theory', *Philosophia*, 25(3–4): 47–64.

Lerche, Jens. 2008. 'Transnational Advocacy Networks and Affirmative Action for Dalits in India. In *Development and Change*, 39 (2), pp. 239–61.

Lorenzen, D.N. (ed.). 1995. *Bhakti religion in North India: Community Identity and Political Action*. New York: State University of New York Press.

Lutz, Catherine L. and Lila Abu-Lughod (eds). 1990. *Language and the Politics of Emotion*. Cambridge: Cambridge University Press.

Lynch, Owen M. 1969. *The Politics of Untouchability: Social Mobility and Social Change in a City of India*. New York and London: Columbia University Press.

————. 1972. 'Dr B.R. Ambedkar—Myth and Charisma'. In J. Michael Mahar (ed.), *The Untouchables in Contemporary India*. Tucson, AR: University of Arizona Press.

————. 1998. 'Dalit Buddhism: The Liberate Bodh Gaya Movement', *Dalit International Newsletter*, 3(1).

Madsen, Stig Toft. 1996. *State, Society and Human Rights in South Asia*. New Delhi: Manohar.

Mahler. Sarah J. 1999. 'Theoretical and Empirical Contributions Toward a Research Agenda for Transnationalism'. In Michael Peter Smith and Luis Eduardo Guarnizo (eds), *Transnationalism from Below*. New Brunswick, NJ: Transaction Publishers.

Malinowski, Bronislaw. 1987 [1922]. *Argonauts of the Western Pacific*. London and New York: Routledge & Kegan Paul.

Manohar, Yeshwant. 1992. I'm Ready for Revolt', translated by S.K. Thorat in Mulk Raj Anand and Eleanor Zelliot (eds), *An Anthology of Dalit Literature (poems)*. New Delhi: Gyan Publishig House.

Manorama, Ruth. 1988. 'Dalit Women: the Thrice Alienated'. In M.E. Prabhakar (ed.), *Towards a Dalit Theology*. Delhi: ISPCK.

————. 1995. 'Dalit Women: Downtrodden among the Downtrodden'. In Bhagwan Das and James Massey (eds), *Dalit Solidarity*. Delhi: ISPCK.

Marcus, Georg E. 1995. 'Ethnography in/of the World System: The Emergence of Multi-Sited Ethnography', *Annual Review Anthropology*, 24: 95–117.

————. 2002. 'Beyond Malinowski and After *Writing Culture*: On the Future of Cultural Anthropology and the Predicament of Ethnography', *The Australian Journal of Anthropology*, 13 (2): 191–9.

Marcus, G.E. and M. Fischer. 1999 [1986]. *Anthropology as Cultural Critique: An Experimental Moment in the Human Sciences*. Chicago: University of Chicago Press.

Marriott, McKim (ed.). 1955. *Village India*. Chicago: University of Chicago Press.

Martin. Emily. 1994. *Flexible Bodies: Tracking Immunity in America from the Days of Polio to the Age of AIDS*. Boston, MA: Beacon Press.

McDonald, Kevin. 2006. *Global Movements: Action and Culture*. Oxford: Blackwell Publishing.

Melucci, Alberto. 1985. 'The Symbolic Challenge of Contemporary Movements', *Social Research*, 52 (4) (winter).

————. 1988. 'Social Movements and the Democratization of Everyday Life'. In John Keane (ed.), *Civil Society and the State*. London: Verso.

————. 1989. *Nomads of the Present*. Philadelphia: Temple University Press.

————. 1992. 'Challenging Codes: Framing and Ambivalence in the Ideology of Social Movements', *Thesis Eleven*, 31: 131–42.

————. 1998. 'Third World or Planetary Conflicts?'. In Sonia E. Alvarez, Evelina Dagnino, and Arturo Escobar (eds), *Cultures of Politics, Politics of Cultures: Re-visioning Latin American Social Movements*. Boulder, CO and Oxford: Westview Press.

Merton, Robert, K. 1961 [1949]. *Social Theory and Social Structure*. New York: Free Press.

Miller, Daniel and Don Slater. 2000. *The Internet: An Ethnographic Approach*. Oxford: Berg.

Mitchell. J.C. 1969. 'The Concept and Use of Social Networks'. In J.C. Mitchell (ed.), *Social Networks in Urban Situations*. Manchester: Manchester University Press.

————. 1973. 'Networks, norms and institutions'. In J. Boissevain and J.C. Mitchell (eds), *Network Analysis*. The Hague: Mouton.

————. 1974. 'Social networks', *Annual Review of Anthropology*, 3: 279–99.

Molund, Stefan. 1988. *First we are People...: The Koris of Kanpur between Caste and Class*, Stockholm Studies in Social Anthropology, no. 20. Stockholm: Department of Social Anthropology, Stockholm University.

Moon, Meenakshi and Urmila Pawar. 2006. *We also made History*. New Delhi: Zubaan Books, an imprint of Kali for Women.

Murugkar, Lata. 1991. *Dalit Panther Movement in Maharashtra*. London: Sangam Books.

Nandy, Ashis. 1994. 'The Fear of Gandhi: Nathuram Godse and His Successors', *The Times of India*, 27 April.

Naples, Nancy A. and Manisha Desai (eds). 2002. *Women's Activism and Globalization: Linking Local Struggles and Transnational Politics*. New York and London: Routledge.

Narula, Smita. 1999. *Broken People: Caste Violence against India's 'Untouchables'*. New York: Human Rights Watch.

————. 2001. 'Caste Discrimination'. *Seminar*, no. 508, December.

National Campaign on Dalit Human Rights. 1999. *Black Paper, Broken Promises and Dalits Betrayed. Secunderabad*: NCDHR.

National Campaign Manifesto—Dalit Human Rights. 1998. *Secunderabad*: NCDHR.

Nesbitt, Eleanor. 1991. '"My Dad's a Hindu, my Mum's side are Sikhs": Issues in Religious Identity'. Warwick: NFAE and University of Warvick.

————. 1997. '"We are all equal": Young British Punjabis' and Gujaratis' Perception of Caste', *International Journal of Punjab Studies* 4(2).

Nirmal, Arvind P. 1988. 'A Dialogue with Dalit Literature.' In M.E. Prabhakar (ed.), *Towards a Dalit Theology*. Delhi: ISPCK.

Norström, Christer. 2003. *'They Call for Us'. Strategies for Securing Autonomy Among the Paliyans, Hunter-Gatherers of the Palni Hills, South India*, Stockholm Studies in Social Anthropology 53. Stockholm: Almqvist and Wiksell International.

Ochs, Elinor and Lisa Capps. 1996. 'Narrating the Self', *Annual Review of Anthropology*, 25: 19–43.

Olwig, Karen Fog and Kirsten Hastrup (eds). 1997. *Siting Culture*. London: Routledge.

Omvedt, Gail. 1993. *Reinventing Revolution—New Social Movements and the Socialist Tradition in India*. New York: M.E. Sharpe.

———. 1994a. *Dalits and the Democratic Revolution—Dr Ambedkar and the Dalit Movement in Colonial India*. New Delhi, Thousand Oaks, and London: Sage Publications.

———. 1994b. 'Peasants, Dalits and Women: Democracy and India's New Social Movements', *Journal of Contemporary Asia*, 24: 35–48.

———. 1998 [1994]. 'Kanshi Ram and the Bahujan Samaj Party'. In K.L. Sharma (ed.), *Caste and Class in India*. Jaipur: Rawat Publications.

———. 1999. 'Ambdedkar's New Buddhism', *The Hindu*, 25 February.

———. 2001. 'Ambedkar and After: The Dalit Movement in India'. In Ghanshyam Shah (ed.), *Dalit Identity and Politics*. New Delhi, Thousand Oaks, and London: Sage Publications.

Ortner. S. 1997. 'Fieldwork in the Postcommunity', *Anthropology and Humanism*, 22(1): 61–80.

Pai, Sudha. 1998. 'New Political Trends in Uttar Pradesh—The BJP and the Lok Sabha Election, 1998', *Economic and Political Weekly*, XXXIII (28), 11 July.

———. 2000. *State Politics—New Dimensions (Party System, Liberalisation and Politics of Identity)*. New Delhi: Shipra.

———. 2001. 'From Harijans to Dalits: Identity Formation, Political Consciousness and Electoral Mobilisation of the Scheduled Castes in Uttar Pradesh'. In Ghanshyam Shah (ed.), *Dalit Identity and Politics*. New Delhi, Thousand Oaks, and London: Sage Publications.

———. 2002. *Dalit Assertion and the Unfinished Democratic Revolution: The Bahujan Samaj Party in Uttar Pradesh*. New Delhi, Thousand Oaks, and London: Sage Publications.

Parry, Jonathan. 1974. 'Egalitarian Values in a Hierarchical Society', *South Asian Review*, 7(2): 95–121.

Pawde, Kumud. 1995. 'The Position of Dalit Women in Indian Society'. In Bhagwan Das and James Massey (eds), *Dalit Solidarity*. Delhi: ISPCK.

Polakow-Suransky, Sasha. 2002. 'A Politics of Denial', *The American Prospect*, 13(1), 1–14 January.

Poluha, Eva and Mona Rosendahl (eds). 2002. *Contesting 'Good' Governance: Crosscultural perspectives on Representation, Accountibility and Public Space*. London and New York: Routledge Curzon.

Poster, Winifred and Zakia Salime. 2002. 'The Limits of Microcredit: Transnational Feminism and USAID Activities in the United States and Morocco'. In Nancy A. Naples and Manisha Desai (eds), *Women's Activism and Globalization: Linking Local Struggles and Transnational Politics*. New York and London: Routledge.

Prabhakar, M.E. (ed.). 1988. *Towards a Dalit Theology*. Delhi: ISPCK.

Prabhavati. M. 1995. 'Dalit Women in Contemporary Indian Situation'. In P.G. Jogdand (ed.), *Dalit Women in India: Issues and Perspectives*. New Delhi: Gyan Publishing House.

Queen, Christopher, S. 1994. 'Ambedkar, Modernity, and the Hermeneutics of Buddhist Liberation'. In A.K. Narain and D.C. Ahir (eds), *Dr Ambedkar, Buddhism and Social Change*. Delhi: B.R. Publishing Corporation.

Radcliffe-Brown, A.R. 1952 [1940]. 'On Social Structure', *Journal of the Royal Anthropological Institute*, 70: 1–12.

Raj, M.C. 2001. *Dalitology: The Book of the Dalit People*. Tumkur: Rural Education for Development Society.

Rajshekar, V.T. 1987. *Dalit: The Black Untouchables of India*. Atlanta GA: Clarity Press.

———. 1989. *Mahatma Gandhi and Babasaheb Ambedkar—Clash of Two Values*. Bangalore: Dalit Sahitya Akademy.

Ram, Kanshi. 1982. *The Chamcha Age—An Era of the Stooges*. New Delhi: Kanshi Ram.

Randeria, Shalini. 2007. 'The State of Globalization'. *Theory, Culture and Society*, 24(1): 1–33.

Rao. M.S.A. (ed.). 1984 [1979]. *Social Movements in India: Studies in Peasant, Backward Classes. Sectarian, Tribal and Women's Movements*. New Delhi: Manohar.

Redfield, R. and Singer, M. 1954. 'The Cultural Role of Cities', *Economic Development and Cultural Change*, 3: 53–73.

Rege, Sharmila. 2006. *Writing Caste / Writing Gender—Narrating Dalit Women's Testimonies*. New Delhi: Zubaan.

Ribeiro, Gustavo Lins. 1998. 'Cybercultural Politics: Political Activism at a Distance in a Transnational World'. In Sonia E. Alvarez, Evelina Dagnino and Arturo Escobar (eds), *Cultures of Politics, Politics of Cultures: Re-visioning Latin American Social Movements*. Boulder, CO and Oxford: Westview Press.

Rodrigues, Valerian. 1993. 'Buddhism, Marxism and the Conception of Emancipation in Ambedkar'. In Peter Robb (ed.), *Dalit Movements and the Meanings of Labour in India.* Oxford: Oxford University Press.

Rowe, William L. 1968. 'The New Cauhans: A Caste Mobility Movement in North India'. In James Silverberg (ed.), *Social Mobility in the Caste System in India.* The Hague: Mouton.

Rudolph, Lloyd I. and Susanne H. Rudolph. 1967. *The Modernity of Tradition.* Chicago: University of Chicago Press.

Saberwal, Satish. 1990. [1976]. *Mobile Men: Limits to Social Change in Urban Punjab.* Shimla and New Delhi: Indian Institute of Advanced Studies and Manohar.

Sampla, Nalanda. 1994. 'How Long Shall We Wait for Justice?', Paper presented at the Women's Conference, Dalit Solidarity Programme, Jamia Milia, New Delhi. 3–6 March.

Sassen, Saskia. 1998. *Globalization and Its Discontents.* New York: The New Press.

————. 2007. *A Sociology of Globalization.* New York: W.W. Norton and Company.

Schaller, Joseph. 1995. 'Sanskritization, Caste Uplift and Social Dissidence in the Sant Ravidas Panth.' In D.N. Lorenzen (ed.), *Bhakti religion in North India: Community Identity and Political Action.* New York: State University of New York Press.

Sen, Jai, Anita Anand, Arturo Escobar, Peter Waterman (eds). 2004. *Challenging Empires.* New Delhi: Viveka Foundation.

Sen, Mala. 1991. *India's Bandit Queen: The True Story of Phoolan Devi.* New Delhi: HarperCollins Publishers.

Setalvad, Teesta. 2007. 'Thrice Oppressed', *Communalism Combat,* May.

Shah, Ghanshyam. 1990. *Social Movements in India: A Review of the Literature.* New Delhi, Newbury Park and London: Sage Publications.

————. (ed.). 2001. *Dalit Identity and Politics.* New Delhi, Thousand Oaks, and London: Sage Publications.

————. (ed.). 2002. *Dalits and the State.* New Delhi: Concept Publishing Company.

Sharma, K.L. (ed.). 1994. *Caste and Class in India.* Jaipur: Rawat Publications.

Shourie, Arun. 1997. *Worshipping False Gods, Ambedkar and the Facts Which Have Been Erased.* New Delhi: ASA Publication.

Simmons, Ruth Schäfer. 1971. *The Berwas of Delhi: Social and Political Mobility in a Caste of Ex-Untouchables.* Doctoral thesis, University of California, Berkeley.

Singer, Milton and Bernard S. Cohn (eds). 1996 [1968]. *Structure and Change in Indian Society.* Jaipur: Rawat Publications.

Slater, David. 1998. 'Rethinking the Spatialities of Social Movements: Questions of (B)orders, Culture, and Politics in Global Times'. In

Sonia E. Alvarez, Evelina Dagnino, and Arturo Escobar (eds), *Cultures of Politics, Politics of Cultures: Re-visioning Latin American Social Movements*. Boulder, CO and Oxford: Westview Press.

Smith, Jackie, Marina Karides, Marc Becker, Dorval Brunelle, Christopher Chase—Dunn, Donatella della Porta, Rosalba Icaza Garza, Jeffrey S. Juris, Lorenzo Mosca, Ellen Reese, Peter (Jay) Smith, Rolando Vázquez (eds). 2008. *Global Democracy and the World Social Forums*. Boulder and London: Paradigm Publishers.

Smith, Michael Peter and Luis Eduardo Guarnizo (eds). 1999. *Transnationalism from Below*. New Brunswick, NJ: Transaction Publishers.

Smith, Peter J. 2004. 'New Information Technologies and Empowerment: The Implications for Politics and Governance'. In E. Lynn Oliver and Larry Sanders (eds), *E-Government Reconsidered: Renewal of Governance for the Knowledge Age*. Regina: University of Regina.

—————. 2008. 'Going Global: The Transnational Politics of the Dalit Movement'. *Globalization*, 5(1), 1 March, pp. 13–33.

Smith, Peter J. and Elisabeth Smythe. 1999. 'Globalization, Citizenship and Technology: The MAI Meets the Internet'. *Canadian Foreign Policy*, 7(2): 83–105.

Smythe, Elisabeth and Peter J. Smith. 2002. 'New Technologies and Networks of Resistance'. In Evan H. Potter (ed.), *Cyber-Diplomacy*. Montreal and Kingston, London and Ithaca: McGill-Queen's University Press.

Spivak, Gayatri. 1988. 'Can the subaltern speak?' In Cary Nelson and Larry Grossberg (eds), *Marxism and the Interpretation of Culture*. Chicago: University of Illinois Press.

Srinivas, M.N. 1952. *Religion and Society among the Coorgs of South India*. Oxford: Clarendon Press.

—————. 1962. *Caste in Modern India and Other Essays*. Bombay: Asia Publishing House.

Srinivas, M.N. and Béteille, A. 1964. 'Networks in Indian social structure', *Man*, 64: 165–8.

Stocking Georg W. 1992. *The Ethnographer's Magic and Other Essays in the History of Anthropology*. Madison, WI: University of Wisconsin Press.

Ståhlberg, Per. 2002a. *Lucknow Daily: How a Hindi Newspaper Constructs Society*, Stockholm Studies in Social Anthropology 51. Stockholm: Almqvist & Wiksell International.

—————. 2002b. 'The Illicit Daughter: Hindi-Language Newspapers and the Regionalisation of the Public Sphere in India'. In Eva Poluha and Mona Rosendahl (eds), *Contesting 'Good' Governance: Cross-*

cultural perspectives on Representation, Accountibility and Public Space. London and New York: Routledge Curzon.

Tarrow, Sidney. 2005. *The New Transnational Activism.* Cambridge: Cambridge University Press.

Tartakov, Gary Michael. 1998. 'Ambedkar's Statues.' *Dalit International Newsletter,* 3(2).

Thorat. S.K. 1979. 'Passage to Adulthood: Perceptions from Below'. In Sudhir Kakar (ed.), *Identity and Adulthood.* Oxford: Oxford University Press.

―――. 1996. 'Dalits and the New Economic Policy'. *Dalit International Newsletter,* 1(2).

―――. 1998. *Ambedkar's Role in Economic Planning and Water Policy.* Delhi: Khama.

―――. 2000. 'Dr Babasaheb Ambedkar: Film as a Lost Opportunity', *Economic and Political Weekly,* 8–14 April.

Thorat, S.K. and E-M Hardtmann. 2003. 'Religious Duties of Economic Ostracism: The Difficulties of Implementing Indian Law'. In B. Karlsson (ed.), *The Universe of Rights: Anthropology and the Discourse on Human Rights.* Chennai: Earthworm.

Thorat, S.K. and Umakant (eds) 2004. *Caste, Race and Discrimination— Discourses in International Context.* Jaipur and New Delhi: Rawat Publications.

Thorat, Vimal. 2001. 'Dalit women have been left behind by the Dalit movement and the women's movement'. *Communalism Combat,* 69, May.

―――. 2003. *The Silent Volcano: English Translation of Dalit Women's Poetry.* Bangalore: National Federation of Dalit Women.

Touraine, Alan. 1985. 'An Introduction to the Study of Social Movements', *Social Research,* 52(4) (winter).

Uimonen, Paula. 2001. *Transnational.Dynamics@Development.Net: Internet, Modernization and Globalization.* Stockholm Studies in Social Anthropology, 49. Stockholm: Almqvist and Wiksell International.

United Nations. 1996. Committee on the Elimination of Racial Discrimination (CERD). Concluding Observations of the CERD: India 17 September. CERD/C/304/Add. 13.

―――. 2001. *Acknowledgement of Past, Compensation Urged by many Leaders in Continuing Debate at Racism Conference.* UNRD 1942, 4 September.

Upadhyaya, Prakash Chandra. 1992. 'The Politics of Indian Secularism', *Modern Asian Studies* 26(4): 815–53.

Van Aelst, Peter and Stefaan Walgrave. 2004. 'New media, new movements? The role of Internet in shaping the anti-globalization movement'. In van de Donk *et al.* (eds), *Cyberprotest: New*

Media, Citizens and Social Movements. London and New York: Routledge.

van de Donk, Wim, Brian D. Loader, Paul G. Nixon, and Dieter Rucht (eds). 2004. *Cyberprotest: New Media, Citizens and Social Movements*. London and New York: Routledge.

Vanita, Ruth. 2004. 'Thinking Beyond Gender in India'. In Maitrayee Chaudhuri (ed.), *Feminism in India*. New Delhi: Kali for Women.

Vincent, Joan. 1990. *Anthropology and Politics: Visions Traditions and Trends*. Tucson, AR: University of Arizona Press.

Wallerstein, Immanuel. 2007. 'The 'alter-globalists' hit their stride.' *International Herald Tribune*, 3–4 February.

Washbrook, David. 1975. 'The Development of Caste Organisation in South India 1880 to 1925'. In C.J. Baker and D.A. Washbrook (eds), *South India: Political Institutions and Political Change 1880–1940*. Delhi: The Macmillan Co.

Waterman, Peter. 2004. 'The Global Justice and Solidarity Movement and the World Social Forum: A Backgrounder'. In Jai Sen, Anita Anand, Arturo Escobar, and Peter Waterman (eds), *Challenging Empires*. New Delhi: Viveka Foundation.

Webster, John C.B. 1994. *The Dalit Christians—A History*. Delhi: ISPCK.

Wilson, S.M. and L.C. Peterson (2002). 'The Anthropology of Online Communities.' *Annual Review of Anthropology*, 31(1): 449–67.

Wittgenstein, Ludwig. 1981. *Zettel*, in Gertrude E.M. Anscombe and George Henrik Von Wright. Oxford: Blackwell.

World Bank. 1991. *Gender and Poverty in India*. Washington DC: The World Bank.

Wyatt, Andrew. 2000. 'The Bahujan Samaj Party and the Changing Nature of Party Politics in North India'. In V. Gathy and E. Komarov, *Towards a New Polity*. New Delhi: Manohar. (http://mail.bris.ac.uk/~poakjw/AWBSP.htm).

Zaehner, R.C. 1984 [1962]. *Hinduism*. Oxford: Oxford University Press.

Zelliot, Eleanor. 1992. *From Untouchable to Dalit—Essays on Ambedkar Movement*. New Delhi: Manohar.

———. 2002. 'Dalit Web Sites', *Dalit International Newsletter*, 7(1), February.

Index